Toussaint Louverture and the American Civil War

The Promise and Peril of a Second Haitian Revolution

Matthew J. Clavin

PENN

UNIVERSITY OF PENNSYLVANIA PRESS

PHILADELPHIA

Published by University of Pennsylvania Press
Philadelphia, Pennsylvania 19104-4112

Printed in the United States of America on acid-free paper

10 9 8 7 6 5 4 3 2 1

A Cataloging-in-Publication Record is available from the Library of Congress
ISBN 978-0-8122-4205-8

For the loves of my life, Gladys, Madeline, Joseph, and Joshua

CONTENTS

Introduction

"The role which the great Negro Toussaint, called L'Ouverture, played in the history of the United States has seldom been fully appreciated."
—W. E. B. Du Bois, *The Suppression of the African Slave Trade to the United States of America, 1638–1870*

ON 18 MARCH 1862, as the first year of the American Civil War drew to a close, New England abolitionist Wendell Phillips entered the lecture hall of the Smithsonian Institution, the largest auditorium in Washington, D.C., and before a capacity crowd of some two thousand spectators delivered an oration entitled, "Toussaint L'Ouverture." In the lengthy address, Phillips recounted the incredible story of one of the central figures of the Haitian Revolution, a massive slave insurrection that began at the close of the eighteenth century when bondpeople in the French Caribbean colony of Saint-Domingue revolted and embarked on a war of attrition with their former white masters as well as the armies of France, England, and Spain.[1] It was "a chapter of bloody history," Phillips began, "a war of races and a war of nations." Louverture was a fifty-year-old slave of African descent, a literate coachman and "village doctor" who at the start of the insurrection secured the safe passage of his master and mistress to the United States. But he soon joined the rebellion and promptly rose to command a massive army of rebel slaves that for nearly a decade defeated all its rivals.[2] French officials ultimately arrested the "General-in-Chief" and sent him to die in a cold French prison before he could see the results of his hard-fought military victories—the permanent abolition of slavery throughout the colony and the establishment of the independent republic of Haiti. His legacy, nevertheless, was secure. On his departure from the colony, Louverture remarked to his captors, "You think you have rooted up the tree of liberty, but I am only a branch; I have planted the tree of liberty so deep that all France can never root it up."[3]

According to Phillips, Louverture's extraordinary life offered important lessons for the American people at a time when their nation was like Saint-Domingue before it, ripped apart by a bloody confrontation over slavery. Phillips reminded his audience "There never was a slave rebellion successful but once, and that was in St. Domingo"; still, he warned that the repetition of such a catastrophic event was now likely in the United States, given the chaos and confusion of war. Phillips sought divine intervention to prevent such a catastrophe from taking place, and he prayed to God "that the wise vigor of our government may avert that necessity from our land,—may raise into peaceful liberty the four million committed to our care, and show under democratic institutions a statesmanship . . . as brave as the negro of Hayti!" The panegyric concluded with a memorable passage, which takes on added significance when we consider that Phillips was speaking in the federal city that carried the name of the eminent founding father and first president of the United States. "I would call him Napoleon, but Napoleon made his way to empire over broken oaths and a sea of blood. . . . I would call him Cromwell, but Cromwell was only a soldier, and the state he founded went down with him into his grave. I would call him Washington, but the great general had slaves." Finally, Phillips intoned: "You think me a fanatic to-night, for you read history not with your eyes, but with your prejudices. But fifty years hence, when Truth gets a hearing, the Muse of History will put Phocion for the Greek, and Brutus for the Roman, Hampden for England, Fayette for France, choose Washington as the bright, consummate flower of our earlier civilization, and John Brown the ripe fruit or our noon-day [thunders of applause], then, dipping her pen in the sunlight, will write in the clear blue, above them all, the name of the soldier, the statesman, the martyr, TOUSSAINT L'OUVERTURE. [Long-continued Applause]."[4]

Abolitionists hailed the oration as a watershed. One observer in the *New York Tribune* remarked, "the effect of this lecture was indescribable. It was a biography of the warrior statesman as well as an argument in favor of the equality of the black race and its capacity for self-government." The audience responded enthusiastically and pronounced the oration "one of the greatest

efforts of his life." The paper noted the "wonderful change in public sentiment," asserting, "Only fifteen months since, Mr. Phillips could speak in
Boston only at the peril of his life; now his most radical views are enthusiastically applauded, night after night, by audiences filling the largest lecture
hall at the slaveholding Capital." Such an incident was trifling in itself, "but
when the long proscribed champion of an unpopular but righteous cause suddenly becomes the recipient of such attentions, they are worthy of mention as
indication that the cause is approaching its triumph."[5] A black writer found
the acceptance of Phillips's radical address in the southern city "evidence of
the radical change which has occurred in public opinion on the subject of
slavery, and an indication of the future triumph of the principles of common
justice and humanity."[6] The *Boston Journal* reported that the lecture took "the
town by storm." Phillips's reception was a triumph. "A year ago, I doubt if
his friends would have been able to have obtained a hall for him to lecture
in whereas now the portals of the Smithsonian swing invitingly open."[7] William Lloyd Garrison, the brash and bespectacled New England journalist
who published the nation's premier anti-slavery paper, upon learning of the
lecture summed up the prevailing optimism among abolitionists, "The times
are changing."[8]

Most Americans were not so sanguine. Throughout the war, critics in
both the United States and the Confederacy excoriated Phillips for exalting
a revolutionary black soldier. One northern writer condemned abolitionists
for causing the war and pushing the aims of the federal government beyond
the bounds of "civilized warfare." Among their many crimes, abolitionists
had, in the columns of their newspapers, "chuckled in fiendish glee at the
prospect of a servile insurrection in the South, and consequent repetition
of the horrors of St. Domingo." But it was Phillips—the group's "most able
champion and original thinker"—who committed the most unforgivable sin
of all. He "blasphemes the name of Washington in polished phrase and places
above him on the roll of fame, a midnight assassin and robber, a carrier of
the brand into peaceful homes at night, a butcherer of babes and violator of
women, a negro slave—Toussaint L'Ouverture."[9] A southern writer avowed
the "wild excesses of the American Jacobins are fast rivaling those of the
French Jacobins of the last century." Quoting the finale of Phillips's oration,
he intended to set the record straight on the rebel slave whom Phillips lion-
ized. "The bloody wretch who is thus, apotheosized, whose name is placed
'high above' that of Washington, massacred with fiendish cruelty about three
thousands of the white race. The scenes of horror which were witnessed in

St. Domingo under the leadership of the ghoul Toussaint long since became by-words for everything that is cruel and infamous." In colonial Haiti, "No age or sex was spared. The helpless infant was murdered in cold blood before the face of its screaming mother, whose cries were drowned by the yells of the infuriated demons in the form of human beings. The *flag* of Toussaint or of his coadjutors was a *white baby*, stuck upon the end of a pole and borne aloft amid the bloody orgies then and there perpetrated." Haiti had since become a wasteland of indolence, vice, and violence. "Wendell Phillips would doubtless consider this the sure evidence of a splendid civilization, to which this country should aspire!"[10]

The deeply divisive reaction to Phillips's popular Civil War oration illuminates the long-contested battle in the United States over the memory of Toussaint Louverture and the Haitian Revolution. For decades, Americans pondered the revolution's significance. They furiously debated whether the revolution was a nightmare to dread or a singular triumph worthy of admiration—and perhaps even emulation; whether Louverture was a bloodthirsty savage determined to avenge centuries of racial oppression or a brave and determined soldier and statesman who rivaled history's greatest men. Public memory of Louverture and the Haitian Revolution had a profound impact on the United States throughout the first half of the nineteenth century: it inspired bondpeople to strike for freedom and those who claimed ownership of them to take extraordinary measures to keep them enslaved; it helped widen the sectional gulf that was developing between the North and South at the same time it provided symbols that drew various constituencies in each of these sections closer together. As more than a half-century of reliable scholarship on slavery and slave resistance attests, it is no longer possible to understand the long and winding path the United States traveled to both the Civil War and emancipation without acknowledging its powerful influence.[11]

The Haitian Revolution is at the center of the recent explosion in Atlantic history, and historians are today considering its impact on early America and the revolutionary Atlantic world.[12] Yet no historian has considered its effects on the United States during the Civil War. This oversight is extraordinary. For at no other time in the history of the republic were the issues of black freedom and revolutionary black violence so widely discussed and debated. Extending the focus of this scholarship to the middle of the nineteenth century, this study asserts that the Haitian Revolution had a much greater impact on slavery and abolition than has been suggested.[13] Indeed, an examination of the struggle over the history and memory of Louverture and the Haitian Revolution in America on the eve of and during the Civil War reveals that at the height of the longstanding conflict between North and South, Louverture and the Haitian Revolution were resonant, polarizing, and ultimately subversive symbols, which antislavery and proslavery groups exploited to both provoke a violent confrontation and determine the fate of slavery in the United States. In public orations and printed texts, African Americans and their white allies insisted that the Civil War was a second Haitian Revolution, a bloody conflict in which tens of thousands of armed bondmen, "American Toussaints," would redeem the republic by securing the abolition of slavery and proving the equality of the black race. Southern secessionists and northern Unionists, who shared a commitment to slavery and white supremacy, responded by launching a cultural counterrevolution to prevent a second Haitian Revolution from taking place. To appreciate the symbolic power that Louverture and the Haitian Revolution embodied for both sides of the conflict, we must first revisit the dramatic events of 1791 and their immediate aftermath.

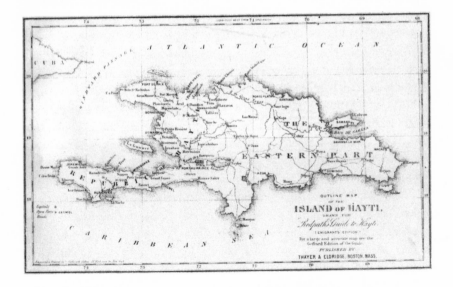

Figure 1. Map of nineteenth-century "Hayti" from James Redpath's emigration pamphlet *A Guide to Hayti* (1861). Courtesy of the Collections of the Library of Congress.

Saint-Domingue was at the end of the eighteenth century the most profitable European colony in the Americas. Known for its expansive sugar and coffee plantations, the French Caribbean territory was home to more than thirty thousand white settlers, nearly an equal number of free people of color, or *gens de couleur libres*, and as many as five hundred thousand enslaved Africans.[14] The outbreak of the French Revolution in 1791 and the adoption of the popular slogan, "liberté, égalité, fraternité," portended much for this outpost of European civilization, a colonial cauldron of racial, social, and economic contradictions. Still, it is wrong to find in the French Revolution the cause of the slave rebellion that we refer to today as the Haitian Revolution. The colony alone contained all the ingredients necessary for the production of an unimaginable social upheaval. The brutal enslavement of half a million men and women was enough to anticipate such an outcome.

A local spark ignited the international fire of the Haitian Revolution. In August 1791, enslaved Saint-Domingans responding to the words of a commanding Vodou priest named Boukman burned some of the wealthiest plantations in the colony's northern plain and began destroying both the property and lives of white colonists. The plan, according to one rebel leader, was simple: "All the drivers, coachmen, domestics, and confidential negroes, of the neighboring plantation and adjacent districts, had formed a plot to set fire to the plantations and to murder all the whites."[15] The insurrectionists did not discriminate, killing planters, overseers, and their families. Many whites fled the island. Those who stayed resisted with great ferocity. The rebellion spread, and soon blood flowed throughout the colony as colonists fought for survival and bondmen and -women both sought and achieved vengeance. Witnesses were unable to describe the horrors that unraveled before their eyes as white and black combatants maimed and murdered each other with impunity. The world watched in awe as the "Pearl of the Antilles" descended into anarchy and race war.

The French government responded quickly to the extraordinary challenge. Commissioners from the revolutionary administration arrived in Saint-Domingue with promises of freedom, equality, and land for rebels who rallied behind the flag of the French Republic. Most enslaved Saint Domingans trusted neither these diplomats nor the government that sponsored them. Among those lacking faith was François-Dominique Toussaint Brèda, a former enslaved coach driver of the Brèda plantation who later took the name Louverture, or "the Opener."[16] Though he spent much of his life in bondage, Louverture was by the time of the revolution a wealthy free man who rented both land and laborers and for a time owned at least one slave himself.[17] He was an exceptional horseman and healer, who possessed a mastery of West African medicines. Able to speak French, Haitian Creole, and his father's African dialect, Louverture was a bibliophile who preferred the classic works of political and military history. He esteemed the work of the eminent French abolitionist Abbé Raynal, who before the revolution predicted the time was approaching when a courageous leader would deliver the slaves of the Americas out of bondage and asked, "Where is he, this great man?"[18] Louverture stood on the sidelines in the early moments of the revolt.[19] Refusing to join the insurrection, he instead secured the safety of his former master. Only after witnessing the early successes of the rebels did he join them, eventually taking refuge in the Spanish army on the eastern side of the island in the colony of Santo Domingo. This was accomplished after the Spanish government offered rebel slaves freedom in addition to weapons. Louverture's reputation as a soldier grew quickly as he led former slaves into battle against both the French army and white colonists in behalf of the Spanish king, never losing sight of what would emerge as his primary objective: the abolition of slavery throughout the entire island.

Louverture's military conquests on the periphery of the French empire had a profound impact on both the thoughts and actions of political leaders at its core. There is no greater example of enslaved people affecting abolition than in Paris in February 1794, when the French National Convention eliminated slavery throughout its territories. It is hard to say whether the legislative body took this drastic measure primarily to extend the Rights of Man to all of the empire's subjects or simply to bring about an end to the bloodshed on Saint-Domingue. Nevertheless, this first emancipation proclamation must, as historian Laurent Dubois points out, be considered the most radical of all measures adopted during the exceptionally radical French Revolution.[20] The official abolition of slavery had the immediate effect of turning the military tide in favor of the French republican army in Saint-Domingue. For Louverture abandoned the Spanish and declared for the French Republic after being convinced of the legitimacy of the policy of emancipation. Donning the red, white, and blue cockade of republican France, he quickly rose to the command of France's colonial army. The colony's black insurgents rallied behind the charismatic leader who announced his return to the French cause fearlessly: "I am Toussaint Louverture. My name is perhaps known to you. I have undertaken vengeance. I want Liberty and Equality to reign in Saint-Domingue."[21] Louverture's forces, which consisted primarily of tens of thousands of ex-slaves, but also whites and free men of color, simultaneously waged a bold and brutal guerrilla war against Spain in the East, a substantial British invading force in the West and South, as well as the colony's remaining white Loyalists wherever they resided. By the end of the century, after defeating the Spanish, repelling a British invasion force of some 25,000 troops, and brutally crushing Royalist resistance as well as all other internal dissent, Louverture enforced a draconian labor system that, while alienating many former bondpeople, breathed new life into the embattled colony's economy.[22] Observers remarked that under Louverture's leadership Saint-Domingue began to resemble its former glory.

As a new century opened, Louverture vowed to destroy the revitalized colony rather than allow the return of slavery. Toward that end, he adopted a Constitution that in addition to appointing him president for life and permanently abolishing the institution of slavery, promised a colorblind society in which the government recognized the equality of all men under the law. Napoleon Bonaparte, the new French ruler and political rival of Louverture, interpreted the document as a declaration of independence and countered by sending a massive armada of some forty thousand men and fifty ships. He planned to seize Louverture, the de facto ruler of the colony, and return slavery to the island. All told more than eighty thousand French men arrived in Saint-Domingue as part of the invading force.[23] No ordinary undertaking, it was the largest French military expedition that ever departed from the continent.[24]

Bonaparte succeeded in achieving his first objective, arresting Louverture and sending him to die in a frigid European jail. But he failed to secure his second. Bonaparte predicted that without Louverture the will of the colony's former slaves to resist would dissipate. He was wrong. Instead of submitting to the invading army, black Saint-Domingans launched a suicidal campaign for freedom, which benefitted greatly from a devastating yellow fever outbreak that wrecked havoc on French troops. Among the many casualties was the leader of the expedition, Bonaparte's brother-in-law General Charles Victor Emmanuel Leclerc. French soldiers were helpless as they waged a futile two-sided war against a devastating tropical disease and an army of black men and women who reputedly laughed in the face of death.[25] The French mission suffered additionally as numbers of disillusioned troops abandoned their posts and took up the cause of the former slaves. Defeated, Bonaparte called his army home, exclaiming, "Damn sugar, damn coffee, damn colonies."[26]

Having lost confidence in his ability to reinvigorate the French empire in the Americas, he then sold the Louisiana Territory to the United States for $15 million. Neither the former French colony nor the United States was ever the same again. The U.S. acquisition of the expansive region, which stretched across central North America from the Gulf Coast to the Canadian border and effectively doubled the size of the republic, represents one of the great ironies in American history: though becoming a principle catalyst of the explosion of slavery across the continent, it owed its existence primarily to the determined efforts of the unconquerable black slaves of Saint-Domingue.[27]

The second independent nation in the Americas emerged from the smoke and ashes of this unprecedented slave rebellion and civil war when Jean-Jacques Dessalines, Louverture's chief lieutenant, tore the white stripe from the tri-colored French flag and declared independence on 1 January 1804. In honor of the indigenous people of Saint-Domingue who had resisted European imperialism for centuries, he assigned to the new nation the appellation used formerly by the island's original Taíno inhabitants, Haïti. Dessalines trusted no one, and just months after securing independence ordered the extermination of nearly the entire remaining white population. The dreadful massacres that followed would for generations serve as a reminder to Europeans and their descendants throughout the slave societies of the Atlantic world of the potential costs of slavery. The Haitian Revolution proved that wherever slavery existed it was not just black lives that were in jeopardy. After more than a decade, the bloodiest and most successful slave revolt in history had finally come to an end. But its impact and that of the great black general Louverture on the Atlantic world had only begun.

It is only in recent years with the rise of Atlantic history that scholars have begun to understand this impact. Producing a tidal wave of history, biography, and fiction, they have dramatically revised our understanding of both the event and its legacy.[28] Still, in spite of this surge in the historical literature, much work remains before the significance of the revolution resonates beyond the academy. In the words of a recent biographer, "Louverture can fairly be called the highest-achieving African-American hero of all time. And yet, two hundred years after his death in prison and the declaration of independence of Haiti, the nation whose birth he made possible, he remains one of the least known and most poorly understood among those heroes." Neither Louverture's life nor the history of Haiti's birth "figures very prominently in standard textbooks—despite, or perhaps because of, their critical importance from the time they began in the late nineteenth century to the time of our own Civil War."[29] This study offers a corrective, bearing fruit from a tree with deep historiographical roots.

Alfred Hunt in *Haiti's Influence on Antebellum America: Slumbering Volcano in the Caribbean* set the standard for the study of the impact of the Haitian Revolution on the United States. In addition to exploring the social, political, and cultural influences of tens of thousands of Haitian refugees along Louisiana's Gulf Coast, Hunt documented the deeply divisive sectional response in the United States to the revolution in newspapers, magazines, and literature. Asserting that the antebellum South comprised the northern-most region of the Caribbean, he interpreted U.S. southern slave society in an Atlantic context before most historians would have acknowledged such a framework of analysis existed. Hunt concluded of the impact of the revolution on antebellum America, "The mere mention of Haiti became one of the primary shibboleths of the South, for it validated their cherished notion of white supremacy and was a major factor in the development of racism as a doctrine. The southern interpretation of the Haitian Revolution and the way it was used strongly suggest one of the reasons why it took a civil war to emancipate the slaves."[30] Scholars have built extensively on Hunt's work. Underscoring both the survival of black Haitians' revolutionary ideology among free and enslaved African Americans and the transatlantic patterns of migration and communication between Haiti and the United States, they have illuminated the centrality of the Haitian Revolution in the construction of black nationalism from the early national period through the twentieth century.[31] A small library also now exists on both the political ramifications of the Haitian Revolution in the United States and the social and cultural impact of the refugees who after fleeing the revolution arrived at major North Americans seaports like Philadelphia, Baltimore, and New Orleans.[32]

While the literature on the influence of Haitian Revolution on the Atlantic world is expansive, to comprehend its international impact fully we must examine its continued resonance almost 70 years later during the American Civil War. It was, like the revolution in Haiti, a terrible war over slavery that culminated in the permanent abolition of the institution throughout an entire nation. Peter Linebaugh and Marcus Rediker in their survey of the revolutionary Atlantic world describe a series of radical and subversive "connections" that historians have, over time, "denied, ignored, or simply not seen."[33] *Toussaint Louverture and the Civil War* restores one of those connections.

"The Insurrection of the Blacks in St. Domingo": Remembering Toussaint Louverture and the Haitian Revolution

THE HAITIAN REVOLUTION cast a long, dark shadow over the Atlantic world long after its conclusion. Europeans, Africans, and Americans remembered the extraordinary upheaval in conversations in homes, taverns, and shops, on rural plantations, city streets, and ocean-going vessels. They remembered it in newspapers and pamphlets, portraits, engravings, histories, biographies, and fiction, which writers published, sellers traded, and consumers shared on both sides of the Atlantic. These memories were both numerous and contradictory. They were, like the revolution itself, fiercely contested. The result was the emergence of two competing narratives that promised to tell the true story of the events that took place in Haiti.

There was first the horrific Haitian Revolution. It told of vengeful African slaves committing unspeakable acts of violence against innocent and defenseless white men, women, and children. Among its most influential architects was Bryan Edwards, the Jamaican slaveowner and author who first published his widely read account of the revolution, *An Historical Survey of the French Colony in the Island of St. Domingo*, in 1794. The proslavery polemic catalogued the "horrors of St. Domingo" at great length: "Upwards of one hundred thousand savage people, habituated to the barbarities of Africa, avail themselves of the silence and obscurity of the night, and fall on the peaceful and unsuspicious planter, like so many famished tigers thirsting for human

Figure 2. This early rendering of "The Burning of Le Cap," tries to capture the horror of slave revolt. The caption reads, "General Revolt of the Negroes. The massacre of the whites." *Saint-Domingue, ou Histoire de Ses Révolutions. ca. 1815* (Paris: Chez Tiger, 1815). Courtesy of the Library Company of Philadelphia.

blood. Revolt, conflagration, and massacre, everywhere mark their progress; and death, in all its horrors, or cruelties and outrages, compared to which immediate death is mercy, await alike the old and the young, the matron, the virgin, and the helpless infant." There was no precedent for what took place in Haiti. "All the shocking and shameful enormities, with which the fierce and unbridled passions of savage man have ever conducted a war, prevailed uncontrolled. The rage of fire consumes what the sword is unable to destroy, and, in a few dismal hours, the most fertile and beautiful plains in the world are converted into one vast field of carnage;—a wilderness of desolation!" Though Edwards wrote for a British audience, he provided the text for images of the revolution that would haunt generations of American slaveowners.[1]

Second, there was the heroic Haitian Revolution. It was the story of an enslaved people who under the leadership of an extraordinary black man, a Great Man, vanquished their violent oppressors in an effort to secure both liberty and equality. This narrative was epitomized in the histories of Marcus Rainsford, which the British army captain printed multiple times in book and periodical form beginning in 1802. The soldier and author wrote that, while some acknowledged the "talents and virtues" of the African race, "it remained for the close of the eighteenth century to realize the scene, from a state of abject degeneracy:—to exhibit, a horde of negroes emancipating themselves from the vilest slavery, and at once filling the relations of society, enacting laws, and commanding armies, in the colonies of Europe." Rainsford anticipated "the wonderful revolution" that produced the second independent nation in the Americas would "powerfully affect the condition of the human race." Rainsford had met Louverture personally and venerated him. He considered him a "truly great man," whose character and principles, "when becoming an actor in the revolution of his country, were as pure and legitimate, as those which actuated the great founders of liberty in any former age of clime."[2]

These conflicting versions of the same event are difficult to reconcile. As anyone studying the Haitian Revolution is aware, the line separating fact from fiction is often indistinguishable. This is something that did not escape the contemporaries of Edwards and Rainsford. One critic writing from London abandoned his quest for the truth after negotiating some of the early print culture on the revolution, asserting, "The cruelties said to be daily perpetrated by the French and the Blacks of this island are, for the most part, fabricated." Writers were "very prodigal in their use of fire and sword, hanging and drowning." They would "occasionally, to furnish out a gloomy paper, massacre an army, or scalp a province." There was consequently no reason to "believe one half of the cruelties which are reported."[3] An American who shared these suspicions warned readers, "The late intelligence from the West-Indies rests principally on verbal accounts, and on rumor, which frequently is the echo of falsehood and always of exaggeration:—It must therefore be received with distrust, and credited with caution."[4]

We will never know the real history of the Haitian Revolution. There is no way to prove Edwards's claims based on hearsay evidence that rebel slaves committed such grisly acts as sewing the severed heads of white planters into the bellies of their pregnant wives. Nor is there evidence to confirm Rainsford's assertion that he provided the only true and authentic account of Louverture and the "black republic" in spite of the fact that he owed his life to the general, who saved him from the gallows.[5] What concerns us here is that as a symbol of both the horror and the heroism of slave rebellion, the Haitian Revolution resonated in both American and Atlantic public culture throughout the first half of the nineteenth century.

While the real story of what took place in Haiti between 1791 and 1804 is enigmatic, among historians one thing is axiomatic: the horrific narrative of the Haitian Revolution triumphed in early American memory. White southerners' fears of slave insurrection among an exploding black population explain why this is the case. These fears, which according to David Brion Davis were "like a weapon of mass destruction in the minds of slaveholders," are well documented.[6] One need take only a cursory glance at Herbert Aptheker's *American Negro Slave Revolts* to glimpse into white southerners' panicked and paranoid world.[7] In the equally groundbreaking *White over Black*, Winthrop Jordan writes that the specter of slave rebellion presented "an appalling world turned upside down, a crazy nonsense world of black over white, an anti-community which was the direct negation of the community as white men knew it."[8] It was because of this constant fear of having their world overturned that American slaveowners seized on the Haitian Revolution as a symbol of the horrors of a multiracial society without bondage.

The response to what many acknowledge as the bloodiest slave revolt in the history of the United States provides an example. In August 1831, Nat Turner, a plantation laborer and mystic, spurred dozens of bondmen to murder nearly sixty white men, women, and children under the cover of darkness in Southampton County, Virginia. Armed white bands apprehended Turner and his accomplices, and in their zeal to exact vengeance murdered countless African Americans who had no connection to Turner or his revolt. White officials eventually tried and executed Turner, leaving his body mutilated and dismembered.[9] The rebellion shocked the nation, leading to public debate over the future of slavery. While the Virginia legislature debated a plan of gradual emancipation, Assemblyman Thomas Jefferson Randolph warned, "The hour of the eradication of the evil is advancing, it must come. Whether it is affected by the energy of our minds or by the bloody scenes of Southampton and San Domingo is a tale for future history."[10] As the remark by Thomas Jefferson's grandson and namesake attests, memory of the Haitian Revolution infused the public response to the revolt.

Although there is no definitive link between Turner's revolt and the Haitian Revolution, and Turner made no mention of it in interviews conducted in the days leading up to his execution, one man insisted on the connection in a pamphlet published in the immediate aftermath of the revolt. Samuel Warner opened his sensational account of the insurrection with the titular exclamation "HORRID MASSACRE" and then began:

In consequence of the alarming increase of the Black population at the South, fears have long been entertained, that it might one day be the unhappy lot of the whites, in that section, to witness scenes similar to those which but a few years since, nearly depopulated the once flourishing island of St. Domingo of its white inhabitants—but, these fears have never been realized even in a small degree, until the fatal morning of the 22d of August last, when it fell to the lot of the inhabitants of a thinly settled township of Southampton county (Virginia) to witness a scene horrid in the extreme!—when FIFTY FIVE innocent persons (mostly women and children) fell victims to the most inhuman barbarity.[11]

Though the veracity of Warner's "Authentic and Impartial Narrative" is doubtful, he nevertheless claimed to have gathered information from face-to-face conversations with Turner's accomplices.[12] In these exchanges, they recorded that Turner spoke to them of "the happy effects which had attended the united efforts of their brethren in St. Domingo, and elsewhere, and encouraged them with the assurance that a similar effort on their part, could not fail to produce a similar effect." Like Haitian slaves, Turner "was for the total extermination of the whites, without regard to age or sex!" He promised "That by so doing, they should soon be able (in imitation of the example set them by their brethren at St. Domingo) to establish a government of their own." Warner concluded with a brief narrative of the revolution and a comment on the likelihood of its repetition in the United States: "Such were the horrors that attended the insurrection of the Blacks in St. Domingo; and similar scenes of bloodshed and murder might our brethren at the South expect to witness, were the disaffected Slaves of that section of the country but once to gain the ascendancy."[13]

A letter forwarded to the governor of Virginia from a man claiming to be a runaway slave offers additional evidence of the depth of the shadow the Haitian Revolution cast over the South in the aftermath of the Turner revolt. The author, who signed the letter "Nero," warned of a revolutionary conspiracy to destroy slavery in the United States. Nero described the formation of an abolitionist army under the direction of a Louverture-like figure who after escaping from slavery in the United States had fled to Haiti, where he joined a group that took "lessons from the venerable survivors of the Haytian Revolution." Describing the intentions of this "Chief" and his fellow insurgents, Nero taunted the Virginia governor: "They will know how to use the knife, bludgeon, and the torch with effect—may the genius of Toussaint stimulate them to unremitting exertion. It is not my intention to boast, nor to threaten beyond a certainty of performing. We have no expectation of conquering the whites of the South States—our object is to seek revenge for indignities and abuses received—and to sell our live[s] at as high a price as possible." The letter is revealing on a number of levels. First, while evidence suggests that Turner only needed to swallow the bitter pill of slavery to inspire him to sacrifice his life for freedom, his allies understood his actions in the framework of the transatlantic struggle for black freedom begun in Haiti four decades earlier. Second, apocryphal though the letter may be, it reinforced the widespread belief in the likelihood of a second Haitian Revolution in the antebellum South.[14]

The reaction to the Turner revolt demonstrates how, throughout the antebellum period, public memory of the Haitian Revolution endured through oral and printed accounts of southern slave revolts and conspiracies. These accounts served as "lieux de mémoires" or "metaphoric sites of collective memory," which recurrently implanted the revolution into American memory.[15] Conversations among participants, witnesses, and writers before, during, and after both real and imagined slave revolts activated collective remembering of the Haitian Revolution. The examples are numerous. Following the failed attempt of an enslaved blacksmith named Gabriel to launch a slave insurrection in Richmond, Virginia, in 1800, speakers and writers drew comparisons between local events and those taking place simultaneously in Saint-Domingue. Slave testimony added fuel to the conspiratorial fire, as bondmen revealed that Gabriel's army not only included a number of French immigrants, but planned to spare the lives of the members of several trusted groups, including Quakers and the "French people."[16]

Just over a decade later in Louisiana, after white locals and federal soldiers crushed an uprising of more than one hundred slaves, reports surfaced that the leader of the rebellion, a mulatto named Charles Deslondes, was in Saint-Domingue during the revolution; this is despite the fact that, Adam Rothman points out, no surviving primary evidence supports this claim.[17] Regardless of the leader's origins, one eyewitness described the relief of having averted "a miniature representation of the horrors of St. Domingo."[18] Last, in the wake of Denmark Vesey's failed attempt at revolt in Charleston, South Carolina, in 1822, variations of the words Haiti and St. Domingo appeared nearly twenty times in one account of the official investigation, which officials published and distributed freely.[19] The reaction to these failed stratagems suggests that, in the Old South, invocations of the Haitian Revolution were not meaningless tropes, but rather a sine qua non of any legitimate insurrectionary plot.

The pervasiveness of whites' fears of a second Haitian Revolution presents us with a paradox. In the antebellum South demographics, geography, and other factors resulted in bondpeople revolting less frequently than enslaved people in other times and locations—there was only one Nat Turner. This fact led one leading historian of the period to conclude, "The wonder, then, is not that the United States had fewer and smaller slave revolts than some other countries did, but that they had any at all."[20] More frequently, however, the dearth of antebellum slave rebellions encouraged scholars in the century after emancipation to insist that white slaveowners treated their slaves benevolently, and that in rare cases of whites' cruel treatment of their human property slaves passively accepted their fate.[21] In response to these findings, historians shifted their focus. Some turned their attention from the antebellum South to the colonial period, when violent slave resistance occurred more consistently. Others explored alternative, nonviolent forms of resistance, offering them as proof of the pervasiveness of slave subversion.[22] From breaking tools and burning buildings, to running away or threatening to do so in order to influence potential transactions between those who bought and sold people, slaves' actions give the lie to owners' paternalistic claims. Though recent works on antebellum slave markets and the contested public space of southern plantations are invaluable for bringing about a more realistic and nuanced understanding of American slavery, the focus on nonviolent forms of resistance has unfortunately shifted attention away from violent slave resistance and the impact of slave rebellion on the United States.[23]

To understand the widespread fear of slave insurrection requires an examination of the antebellum South in a transatlantic framework. After all, the Haitian Revolution gave southern slaveowners good reason to fear the men and women they enslaved. White southerners feared a second Haitian Revolution in particular for a number of reasons. First, there were obvious similarities between the American South and colonial Saint-Domingue. South Carolina governor Charles Pinckney made this sentiment clear in an address to the white colonists of Saint-Domingue during the revolution: "When we recollect how nearly similar the situation of the southern States and St. Domingo are in the profusion of slaves—that a day may arrive when they may be exposed to the same insurrections—we cannot but sensibly feel for your situation."[24] Geographic proximity was another reason for white southerners to fear a second Haitian Revolution. In 1799, reports surfaced that the French government sought Louverture's aid in launching a military invasion of the southern United States.[25] Louverture opposed the invasion; he was unwilling to alienate the powerful nation to the North, which aided his effort to rid the French from the island.[26] Still, his aspirations for black freedom threatened slavery wherever it existed.[27] Louverture never participated in a slave rebellion outside Haiti, but numbers of black and colored veterans of his army went on to wage revolutionary wars throughout the Atlantic world.[28] Last, the black revolutionary ideology that Haiti birthed had a profound effect on bondpeople throughout the slave societies of the Atlantic world, including the United States.[29]

African American sailors visited Haiti and encountered black Haitians throughout their journeys. World travelers, they served as the eyes and ears of local black communities.[30] The transatlantic communications network these mariners exploited was a cause of great concern for American slaveowners.[31] In 1804, more than one hundred Louisianans signed a petition begging military protection, which underscores the existing trepidation regarding this network: "The news of the revolution of St. Domingo and other places has become common amongst our blacks—and some here who relate the tragical history of the revolution of that island with the general disposition of the most of our slaves has become very serious—a spirit of revolt and mutiny has crept amongst them. A few days since we happily discovered a plan for our destruction."[32]

For more than a half-century, white southerners articulated their fears of a second Haitian Revolution. These fears were, like heirlooms, passed down from generation to generation. French Baron Joseph Pontalba of New Orleans remembered in a letter to his wife, "when we used to go to bed only if armed to the teeth. Often then, I would go to sleep with the most sinister thoughts creeping into mind, taking heed of the dreadful calamities of Saint-Domingue, and of the germs of insurrection only too widespread among our own slaves. I often thought, when going to bed, of the means I would use to save you and my son, and of the tactics I would pursuer if we were attacked."[33] Years later, plantation mistress and renowned Civil War diarist Mary Boykin Chesnut described a relative who was and had "always been afraid of negroes," because "In her youth, the San Domingo stories were indelibly printed on her mind."[34] Influential publisher James D. B. De Bow described the Haitian Revolution as a "narrative which frightened our childhood, and still curdles the blood to read." He recalled, "We have often listened to the terrible relations of the massacre of St. Domingo, made to us by Judge Grivot, of New-Orleans, whose father also was shot before his eyes, and who escaped himself the same fate by passing for a medical student, for such they needed."[35]

As De Bow's comments suggest, fears of slave revolt were for the descendants of the thousands of white refugees of the revolution particularly distressing. The internationally renowned American pianist Louis Moreau Gottschalk recalled, as his musical troupe sailed passed Haiti during a Caribbean tour in 1857, "Everything, and more especially the name of Santo Domingo, seemed to speak to my imagination by recalling to me the bloody episodes of the insurrection, so closely associated with my childhood memories. When very young, I never tired of hearing my grandmother relate the terrible strife that our family, like all the rest of the colonists, had to sustain at this epoch."[36] Gilbert Moxley Sorrel, a Georgia bank clerk who would go on to serve in the Army of the Confederacy with great distinction, wrote of his grandfather Antoine Sorrel des Revieres, who "was on his estates in the island of St. Domingo when the bloody insurrection of the blacks broke out at the opening of the century. His property was destroyed, and his life barely saved by concealment and flight to Cuba, thence to Louisiana, where a refuge was found among friendly kindred." Sorrel's father Francis was also fortunate. He "was saved from the rage of bloodthirsty blacks by the faithful devotion of the household slaves, and some years later succeeded in reaching Maryland."[37] In spite of his good fortune, Francis, according to his son, rarely spoke of his experience. "It was difficult to induce my father to speak of the awful tragedies of those days. . . . Recalling them even in his old age appeared to afflict him with shuddering excitement and we had to restrain our questions."[38]

The "horrors of St. Domingo" survived in American memory as a symbol of all that was wrong with abolition and right both about slavery and the white supremacist ideology that helped embed the institution deeply in the republic's foundation. Yet a counter-narrative existed that likewise had faithful adherents. The heroic narrative of the Haitian Revolution found a captive American audience from the late eighteenth through the second half of the nineteenth century. African Americans eagerly embraced the unique example of black military triumph. Prince Hall, the well-known abolitionist, founder of the black Masons, and veteran of the American Revolution, in 1797 predicted a brighter day for enslaved Americans based on the events in Haiti. Just years before in this free nation, "Nothing but the snap of the whip was heard from morning to evening; hanging, broken on the wheel, burning, and all manner of tortures inflicted on those unhappy people, for nothing else but to gratify their masters pride, wantonness and cruelty: but blessed be God, the scene is changed; they now confess that God hath no respect of persons, and therefore receive them as their friends, and treat them as brothers." In

Haiti the sons and daughters of Africa were emerging from "sink of slavery to freedom and equality." Hall considered the abolition of slavery a contagion sure to spread to the United States.[39]

One of the first African American college graduates chose the Haitian Revolution as the subject of his commencement address. John Brown Russwurm, who would go on to edit the first African American newspaper in the United States, *Freedom's Journal*, spoke of the effect of liberty on enslaved Haitians, who "stepped forth as men, and showed to the world, that though Slavery may benumb, it cannot entirely destroy our faculties." Invoking the founding fathers of the black republic, "Touissant L'Overture, Desalines and Christophe," Russwurm hoped and predicted that the freedom earned by these men had "laid the foundation of an Empire that will take a rank with the nations of the earth."[40] Nearly four decades after Haitian independence, the African American medical doctor and scholar James McCune Smith lectured in New York City on both Louverture and the revolution. Refuting those who claimed the insurrection was the result of French emancipation, Smith avowed, "Be it remembered that this insurrection was the legitimate fruit of slavery, against which it was a spontaneous rebellion. It was not, therefore, the fruit of emancipation, but the consequence of withholding from men their liberty." Far from providing "scenes of indiscriminate massacre from which we should turn our eyes," Smith argued that the revolution was instead, "an epoch worthy of the anxious study of every American citizen."[41]

Less anticipated is the enthusiastic response of European Americans to the Haitian Revolution. As was the case throughout the Atlantic world, there were those who sympathized with African Americans held in bondage and defended their tactics when they struck for freedom. Among them was an early antislavery radical who called on the American people to extend the inherent liberties described by Thomas Paine in his revolutionary tract *Rights of Man* to all men, regardless of color. Abraham Bishop reached an expansive audience when he first published "Rights of Black Men" in a local newspaper and then in Matthew Carey's widely read national magazine *American Museum*, one of the first successful periodicals in the United States. Bishop wrote of the events unfolding in Saint-Domingue, "I believe firmly, that the cause of the blacks is just. They are asserting those rights by the sword, which it was impossible to secure by mild measures." Comparing the plight of the Haitian rebels to America's founding fathers, Bishop entreated, "Let us be consistent, Americans, and if we justify our own conduct in the late glorious revolution, let us justify those, who, in a cause like ours, fight with equal bravery."[42]

Bishop was not alone in defending slave insurrection. Theodore Dwight delivered an antislavery speech in New England in which he commended bondmen in Saint-Domingue who were offering their lives in exchange for liberty. "Who then can charge the negroes with injustice, or cruelty, when 'they rise in all the vigor of insulted nature,' and avenge their wrongs?" Dwight asked defiantly. "What American will not admire their exertions, to accomplish their own deliverance? Every friend to justice and freedom, while his heart bleeds at the recital of the devastation and slaughter, which necessarily attend such convulsions of liberty, must thank his God for the emancipation of every individual from the miseries of slavery. This is the language of freedom; but it is also the language of truth—a language which ever grates on the ears of tyrants, whether placed at the head of a plantation, or the head of an empire."[43] Garry Wills illuminates the degree to which white Americans' support of the Haitian Revolution could reach the highest levels of government and consequently move beyond the realm of rhetoric. In his study of slavery in the Jeffersonian era, Wills describes how Timothy Pickering used the office of secretary of state to encourage American support for Louverture and his army. It was because of Pickering's colorblind foreign policy, Wills concludes, that the United States, "the first revolutionary regime in the New World," came "to the aid of the second one."[44]

The views of white men such as Bishop, Dwight, and Pickering were undoubtedly in the minority. However, there is no denying that in the new republic support for Haiti's revolutionary black army transcended race. There is also no denying as this study and a growing literature on radical abolitionism attests, that endorsement of revolutionary black violence existed and perhaps even grew among a cadre of black and white militants throughout the antebellum era as well.[45]

Those in the United States who recognized the heroic narrative of the Haitian Revolution advanced a subversive ideology that undermined the white supremacy that buttressed both the institution of slavery as well as the republic itself. Its subversiveness derived from two sources. First was the great faith that Americans placed in violent sacrifice. The United States was a nation born in blood, thus its citizens held the violent tactics patriots employed to secure independence in high regard.[46] Americans' respect for violence did more than explain the success of the republic: it rationalized the enslavement of African Americans at the same time that liberty and equality spread among whites. François Furstenberg surmises that the lack of any sustained or prolonged violent slave revolt in the United States justified bondage. Free Americans felt that, until bondpeople seized liberty from their masters in their own bloody hands, they were unworthy of enjoying its benefits. Though compelling, what is missing from this line of reasoning is that in early America the public knew that hundreds of thousands of enslaved Haitians had secured both freedom and national independence through violent means. While for most Americans the Haitian Revolution represented a nightmare of slave rebellion and race war, African Americans and their white allies revered it as a revolutionary symbol that shattered notions of white supremacy and black inferiority.[47]

The second source of subversiveness of the heroic narrative of the revolution was the ascendancy of the memory of Louverture, for his greatness affirmed the masculinity of black men. Repudiation of the manhood of African Americans attended the spread of plantation slavery across the continent. That white men held economic and political power reinforced the idea of white male supremacy. However, Louverture remained an undeniable symbol of black manhood. Indeed, in early American and Atlantic oral and print culture abolitionists constructed Louverture in the classical mold of a republican citizen soldier, a Great Man who sacrificed much to lead a desperate people to freedom. That the Louverture these speakers and writers manufactured only partly resembled the one in the historical record was immaterial. Louverture was an ambitious, deceptive, and at times vengeful leader who was wary of national independence. He often treated former slave owners with compassion and former slaves with disdain. He was, moreover, at the time of the revolution, a wealthy free landowner who employed at least one slave on his own plantation. There was more myth than reality in the perception that Louverture was a rebel slave who garnered the unanimous support of an entire population of bondpeople in the process of making Haiti.[48] Nevertheless, for African Americans and their white allies, Louverture and the bondmen who followed him into battle affirmed the redemptive quality of violence to prove black manhood. They moreover undermined one of the fundamental justifications of slavery. As one southern Governor famously announced, "Whenever we establish the fact that they [bondpeople] are a military race, we destroy our whole theory that they are unfit to be free."[49]

It is in evaluating white southerners' fears of the Haitian Revolution that this subversiveness is best illuminated. In spite of white southerners' professions of a peaceful society filled with friendly masters and submissive slaves—claims that still resonate today—references to the Haitian Revolution undermined their paternalistic defense of slavery.[50] In Haiti, black slaves used

violence to strike for freedom and in the end emerged victorious. White supremacy could rationalize the success of rebellious slaves over white colonists
whom they vastly outnumbered. It could justify the defeat of large European
armies thousands of miles from home in a tropical climate. But it could not
explain away the emergence of a figure like Louverture. In the antebellum
South, for example, there was no room for stories of a conquering black hero
and a triumphant black army in a region that was, according to Aptheker,
founded on the "colossal myth of the sub-humanity of the Negro."[51] There
is perhaps no greater evidence of the ability of the heroic narrative of the
Haitian Revolution to subvert white supremacy than when in one of the most
important defenses of slavery ever published in the Old South, leading white
southern intellectual Edmund Ruffin referred to Louverture as a "truly great
man."[52] Ruffin considered Louverture's greatness an anomaly—he acknowledged it nonetheless.[53]

The significance of Louverture's iconicism in transatlantic abolitionist
print culture cannot be overstated. For it was from this reservoir of public memory that American abolitionists continually borrowed and sampled.
In foreign newspapers, periodicals, and books, the memory of Louverture
survived. In 1802, England's *Annual Register*, a widely read chronicle of the
world's salient events, labeled Louverture its "man of the year."[54] Devoting its
pages to a biography of Louverture, the periodical detailed his great character
and accomplishments. It compared him favorably to both Washington and
Bonaparte, concluding he was "undoubtedly the most interesting of all the
public characters which appeared on the great stage of political events for the
present year."[55] The renowned British abolitionist and author James Stephen
referred to Louverture as a "great man" in numerous published accounts. He
insisted that Louverture "deserved the exalted names of Christian, Patriot,
and Hero. He was a devout worshipper of his God, and a successful defender
of his invaded country. He was the victorious enemy, at once, and the contrast of Napoleon Buonaparte, whose arms he repelled, and whose pride he
humbled."[56] Louverture's mythical stature ascended to new heights when the
French publisher Joseph François Michaud included an entry on Louverture
in the acclaimed *Universal Biography*, a mammoth, multivolume tome that
catalogued the lives of history's great men. Popular historian Alphonse Beauchamp wrote the sketch on Louverture, declaring he was "One of the most
extraordinary men of a time when so many extraordinary men appeared."[57]
The sentence would resound throughout the print culture of the Atlantic
world for generations.

Figure 3. Marcus Rainsford, *An Historical Account of the Black Empire of Hayti* (1805). Courtesy of the Collections of the Library of Congress.

Abolitionists were not alone in manufacturing the legend of Louverture. In 1828, a lengthy and sycophantic sketch of Louverture's life appeared in the *Oriental Herald*, a short-lived international journal published in London by free-spirited writer and reformer James Silk Buckingham. The introduction to the article highlighted the novelty of a Great Man of African descent. "The eventful history of Toussaint L'Ouverture is not that of a wild, sanguinary, untractable savage; the ferocious chieftain of a barbarous horde, whose prevailing virtues, heroic though they be, are nevertheless sullied with manifold brutalities; but that of the virtuous, even-minded, high-souled patriot, whose consummate abilities, in the combined and multifarious business of war and government, were only surpassed by his extreme humanity and innate goodness of heart." Louverture was both "a negro and a *slave*, but he was also a warrior and a hero—in every sense of the word—a hero! This we shall prove by presenting our readers with a plain unvarnished account of his extraordinary and eventful life." As a symbol of enlightened republican rule, Louverture's greatness required no qualification. "His life was one tissue of useful virtues, untarnished by a single crime, unstained by tyranny, and unmarked by any of those licentious evils which too often characterize the possessor of uninherited power."[58]

Each of these celebratory accounts of Louverture was derivative of Rainsford's histories. Indeed, both the name and publications of this soldier-historian were familiar to generations of readers on both sides of the Atlantic. While it is difficult to pinpoint what separated Rainsford's work from the other hagiographies of Louverture, one important distinction was that the third and final edition of his book included numerous illustrations—maps, drawings, and even a facsimile of a letter penned by Louverture. Rainsford alerted readers in the introduction to the importance of images explaining, "Mere description conveys not with so much force as when accompanied by graphic illustration."[59] Among the large engravings included in the book was a full-length portrait of Louverture, drawn by Rainsford, which extended the image of Louverture as a Great Man from print to visual culture (Figure 3). The portrait would become the most recognized visual representation of the Haitian founding father in the nineteenth century. In the illustration, Louverture stands erect with his eyes focused directly on the viewer. He is strong and undaunted. His figure dominates the landscape as well as the anonymous foot soldiers relegated to the background. Here is a Great Man, the embodiment of both a land and the nameless and faceless foot soldiers behind him.

The image proved resilient. Three decades after first appearing, a repro-

Monthly Supplement of

THE PENNY MAGAZINE

OF THE

Society for the Diffusion of Useful Knowledge.

385.]   February 28 to March 31, 1838.

ACCOUNT OF TOUSSAINT L'OUVERTURE.

[Toussaint L'Ouverture, in the costume of Commander of the Black Army of Hayti.—Copied from Rainsford.]

Figure 4. Harriet Martineau, "Account of Toussaint L'Ouverture," *Penny Magazine* (1838). Author's collection.

duction of the engraving appeared on the front page of the world's most popular periodical. Published simultaneously in London and New York, the *Penny Magazine* attracted a tremendous following. Its editor claimed an annual readership of one million in Britain alone.[60] Booksellers below the Mason-Dixon line also traded the publication. This was a fact that excited abolitionist Charles Wheeler Denison, who after seeing the illustration prominently displayed in a Delaware bookshop referred to it as "inflammatory and insurrectionary in the highest degree!"[61] In the text accompanying the illustration, British writer and reformer Harriet Martineau, who also authored *The Hour and the Man: An Historical Romance*, perhaps the most widely read book of Louverture in the nineteenth century, amplified Rainsford's sentiments, writing that Louverture "was a Great Man: and what one man of his race has been, others may be."[62] The image also crossed the Atlantic in one of Samuel Goodrich's popular illustrated textbooks for American children, *Lights and Shadows in American History* (Figure 5). Goodrich's artist took license in adding a beard to Louverture's face and all but eliminating the background scenery; nevertheless, the accompanying text translated Beauchamp and thus reinforced the heroic memory of Louverture: "the leader of the blacks, was one of the most extraordinary characters of modern times, and exhibited proofs of genius and elevation of character which gave him a high rank in the annals of great men."[63]

Rainsford's depiction of Louverture represents one of the three constructions of the great man of Haiti, which abolitionists fashioned in the half-century after his death. There was first and foremost the republican citizen soldier. Epitomized in Rainsford's drawing, it derived from the western tradition of virtuous citizens like the Roman Cincinnatus, who in times of war laid down their ploughs and abandoned their farms and families to defend the nation on the battlefield. They asked nothing in return for their patriotic sacrifices and after securing victory discarded their weapons and returned home to lives of peace and prosperity. Second, there was the sentimental slave, the nonthreatening and defenseless sufferer who required the intervention of others to save him from a desperate situation. A favorite of moderate abolitionists, it drew on the popular literary tradition of sentimentality that flourished among middle-class reading audiences and in particular women. Last, there was the revolutionary black bondman. The idol of only the most radical abolitionists and nightmare of white planters throughout the Atlantic world, he was the fearless chattel slave who through the effusive and effective use of violence sought to destroy slavery and any colony or nation that toler-

TOUSSAINT L'OUVERTURE.

Figure 5. Samuel Goodrich, *Lights and Shadows of American History* (1844). Courtesy of the Collections of the Library of Congress.

ated the institution. These symbolic Louvertures resonated loudly in American and Atlantic public culture throughout the antebellum period, and when the Civil War came, American abolitionists exploited each of them to secure their radical vision.

The Haitian Revolution had a profound effect on the United States throughout the first half of the nineteenth century. In an era that saw both the expansion of slavery and the growth of a movement to destroy the institution, it was both a resonant and polarizing symbol. At mid-century, when the Compromise of 1850 dramatically accelerated the sectional divide and the possibility of a violent confrontation grew imminent, one man noted its growing significance. "This insurrection having occurred so near to us, and being within the recollection of many persons living, who heard the exaggerated accounts of the day, has fastened itself on the public imagination, until it has become a subject of frequent reference." The speaker recognized the polarizing effect of these oral traditions on the growing sectional crisis, offering, "Southern twaddlers declaim about the Southern States being reduced to the condition of St. Domingo, and abolitionists triumphantly point to it as a case where the negro race have asserted and maintained their freedom."[64] In the next decade, Americans in both sections would increasingly deploy the symbols of the Haitian Revolution in public orations, printed texts, and visual images. During the Civil War, this surge of public memory became an explosion as politicians, pastors, soldiers, and slaves invoked the revolution and put its memory to various uses. What follows in an examination of the hotly debated contest that ensued.

PART I

Opening the Civil War of Words

"He patterned His Life After the San Domingan": John Brown, Toussaint Louverture, and the Triumph of Violent Abolitionism

IN 1822, A free black carpenter in Charleston, South Carolina, stood accused of conspiring to launch a massive slave insurrection.[1] According to evidence gathered by the Charleston Court of Magistrates and Freeholders, Denmark Vesey had organized hundreds of Charleston's free and enslaved black residents who planned to fire the city and murder the white residents, fill ships in the harbor with money and supplies, and sail for Haiti. Testifiers before the court revealed that memory of the Haitian Revolution infused Vesey's conspiracy. One bondman stated that Vesey "was in the habit of reading to me all the passages in the newspapers that related to St. Domingo, and apparently every pamphlet he could lay his hands on, that had any connection with slavery." Another witness recalled that Vesey promised followers they could "conquer the whites, if we were only unanimous and courageous, as the St. Domingo people were." When some of the conspirators protested the murder of white women and children, Vesey insisted, "it was for our safety not to spare one white skin alive, for this was the plan they pursued in St. Domingo." Vesey avowed that Haitians would provide military assistance, and, through a black cook employed on a schooner bound for Haiti, sent letters to the Haitian president informing him of the plot.[2]

There was another direct link between Vesey and the black republic. His army included a "company" of three hundred "French negroes" from Haiti, evidently refugees from the revolution. French-speaking representatives of the group testified before the court to both the willingness and ability of their "fully armed" contingent to provide spears, swords, bayonets, and firearms for the insurrection. If any harm came to these men, one accused blacksmith testified, there were other Frenchmen prepared "to rise and defend them."[3] It was perhaps the inclusion of these immigrants in the plot, or the belief that the Francophonic Vesey had been enslaved in Saint-Domingue, which led one Charleston editor to caution, "Let it never be forgotten, that our NE-GROES are truly the *JACOBINS* of the country."[4]

African American testimonials in the days and weeks surrounding Vesey's arrest and imprisonment confirm that the Haitian Revolution held a prominent place in the public memory of both free and enslaved black southerners.[5] As much of this testimony was coerced by white officials and inflected by the hysteria caused by the alleged conspiracy, we should consider the words of black men who walked the same streets as Vesey but played no discernible part in either the plot or the court investigation. Among them was David Walker, the fiery pamphleteer whose incendiary tract *Appeal . . . to the Coloured Citizens of the World* called on American bondmen to rise up and kill for their freedom. A recent biographer places Walker in Charleston just before the plot's discovery and posits that Walker knew Vesey and may have even volunteered as one of his assistants.[6] Walker's revolutionary ideology paralleled Vesey's in two respects. First, his reading of the Haitian Revolution convinced him of the American bondman's potential for revolutionary violence. Doubting the explosive potential of enslaved people made little sense, "when Hayti, the glory of the blacks and terror of tyrants, is enough to convince the most avaricious and stupid of wretches." Second, Walker believed that Haitians would assist African Americans in their quest for freedom by welcoming them within their borders. Walker wrote of the Haitian people that they "according to their word, are bound to protect and comfort us."[7]

Daniel Alexander Payne, the founder of Wilberforce University and first African American university president in the United States, was, like Vesey, a free black carpenter in Charleston in the 1820s. Also like Vesey, Payne used his freedom as a skilled artisan to gain literacy. In his biography, Payne recalled that while employed as a carpenter he "read every book within my reach." It was on reading many religious and historical texts that he decided upon his destiny: "Having heard of Hayti and the Haytiens, I desired to become a soldier and go to Hayti."[8] While some still doubt the willingness of black South Carolinians to kill for freedom, it is clear that white South Carolinians did not.[9] Consequently, Vesey and thirty-four other black men met a grisly end in the summer of 1822. The same cannot be said of the memory of the Haitian Revolution.

Soon after Vesey's execution, the American abolitionist movement breathed new life into public memory of the heroic narrative of the Haitian Revolution. Led by free black northerners and a small but committed group of white allies, American abolitionists exploited the vast technological and industrial advancements in printing and publishing and launched a cultural war against slavery. Joining the transatlantic commemoration of Louverture as a Great Man, they in lectures, books, articles, pamphlets, and illustrations offered him to an American audience as a symbol of both the virtue and potential of the black race. In addition to challenging the widespread belief in white supremacy, there is another reason why, in the aftermath of both the Vesey conspiracy and Nat Turner's undeniable slave revolt, American abolitionists, like their European counterparts, placed great emphasis on Louverture's character: to calm widespread fears of slave insurrection. By stressing Louverture's compassion, probity, and integrity at the expense of his militancy and defiance, they tried to soften the rock hard image of this indomitable black warrior and detract from the widespread fear of black bondmen. The strategy worked, for Louverture remained an antislavery icon among even conservative social reformers decades after his death. The convergence of European and American abolitionism around the memory of Haiti's preeminent founding father proved resilient. It was, however, only temporary.

An analysis of abolitionist oral, print, and visual culture reveals that in the decade before the Civil War African Americans and their white allies transformed Louverture into a symbol of black masculinity and violence that they deployed to bring about the destruction of slavery. They insisted that if slavery did not end immediately they would follow Louverture's example and employ violence to deliver freedom to their brothers and sisters in bondage. A look at radical abolitionism and in particular John Brown's raid on Harpers Ferry, Virginia, in October 1859 reveals the iconic stature of Louverture among American abolitionists; it moreover illuminates an important trajectory. The men who invaded Harpers Ferry joined their movement to a black revolutionary tradition that began in Haiti and, as the Vesey plot attests, survived throughout the antebellum period.

Historians once traced the beginning of American abolitionism to any number of important events in the United States in the early decades of the nineteenth century, chief among them the evangelical reform movement known as the Second Great Awakening.[10] Yet the devotion of Brown and his band of brothers to the violent tactics employed in the Haitian Revolution locates the American abolitionist movement beyond the geographical boundaries of the United States and firmly anchors it in the revolutionary eighteenth-century Atlantic world.[11] This is not to suggest that memory of the Haitian Revolution produced Brown's raid. By the middle of the nineteenth century, American abolitionists had for reasons unrelated to events in Haiti begun to abandon the tactic of moral suasion in favor of violent resistance.[12] Nevertheless, the resonance of the memories of Louverture and the Haitian Revolution among Brown and his men confirms their resiliency. It also underscores the radical-ization of the movement. Where abolitionists traditionally failed to transcend the virulent racism of their day, their identification with and adoption of a revolutionary black soldier and slave as a symbol of both their movement and their philosophy, indicates a significant transformation.[13] On the Civil War, abolitionists had not only shed their racialized past but were advancing a radi-cal racial ideology at least a century ahead of its time.

While the historiography of abolitionism in the United States is large and complex, there are important ideas on which historians now agree. First, the movement to abolish slavery in the United States was not monolithic. From religious dissenting Quakers in the colonial period, through north-eastern elites in the revolutionary and early national periods, and finally to the radical black and white immediatists of the antebellum period, there was not one single abolitionist movement. To the contrary, support for abolition waxed and waned unpredictably throughout various regions and communi-ties. Second, by the middle of the nineteenth century an increasing number of abolitionists embraced an increasingly radical philosophy. Abandoning the nonviolent tactics of their predecessors, they advocated the destruction of slavery through any means necessary. At the same time, they demanded and in many cases practiced racial equality.[14] Third, the struggle to abolish slavery in the United States was part of a much larger transatlantic movement, which centered on a number of key metropolitan hubs throughout Europe and the Caribbean that facilitated the international exchange of important ideas and tactics.[15] The British abolitionist crusade was extraordinarily influential in this regard, especially after the peaceful emancipation of all slaves through-out the empire in the 1830s. David Brion Davis writes, "While American politicians exploited a continuing tradition of Anglophobia, American liber-als, who prided themselves on their defense of freedom and human rights, were suddenly faced with the fact that the monarchic, aristocratic mother country, long blamed for 'forcing' slavery on the South, had taken the lead in liberating some eight hundred thousand colonial slaves."[16] Britain's abolition of slavery and the slave trade, along with its employment of African Americans in its military in both the American Revolution and the War of 1812, had a profound effect on black abolitionists, who saw in the British Empire an international ally of incomparable stature.[17]

The international character of American abolitionism is important for our discussion, as it helped entrench the heroic narrative of the Haitian Revolution in American memory. Throughout the first half of the nineteenth century, American readers because of limited economic and technological resources pored over foreign newspapers, periodicals, and books.[18] It was in these texts that the memory of Louverture survived among African Americans and their white allies. Samuel Cornish and John Russwurm's *Freedom's Journal*, the first newspaper owned and operated by African Americans, provides an example. Its pages included numerous accounts of the Haitian Revolution and the struggling independent black nation, and, in 1827, a three-part biographical sketch of Louverture, copied directly from the *Quarterly Review* of London, offered Louverture's character as proof of the equality of the black race.[19]

The same English article and other works from American, British, and Haitian authors inflected James McCune Smith's 1844 lecture in New York City. Like Marcus Rainsford's narratives and the article copied into *Freedom's Journal*, the oration included "a sketch of the character of Toussaint L'Ouverture." But this is where the similarities ended. Smith drew from the prominent works of American, British, and Haitian authors to offer a fresh perspective. Among the central ideas elucidated was that the French government did not emancipate the colony's enslaved people; it was rather something they seized "by force of arms." Led by a former bondman who "reached the prime of manhood, a slave," enslaved Haitians secured both individual liberty and national independence. Once free, "Like Leonidas at Thermopylae, or the Bruce at Bannockburn, Toussaint determined to defend from thralldom his sea-girt isle, made sacred to liberty by the baptism of blood."[20] The oration was a commentary on the efficacy of violence that anticipated a significant transformation in the memory of Louverture that would take place among American abolitionists on the eve of the Civil War. Considered alongside the articles in *Freedom's Journal* and the many other abolitionist accounts of the Haitian Revolution, it challenges those who have found a reticence among African Americans to invoke the Haitian Revolution in the antebellum era due to the images it evoked of race war and the failure of black government.[21]

Given the high regard that prominent African Americans gave to foreign accounts of the Haitian Revolution, it is to be expected that biographies of Louverture published in Europe infused American abolitionists' memory. Four widely read books published in England in the mid-nineteenth century deserve our attention especially, as they indicate an important modification of the symbol of Louverture. Henry Gardiner Adams, Wilson Armistead, John Relly Beard, and Harriet Martineau reinforced Louverture's construction as a Great Man. Beard ranked Louverture as among history's greatest men in his lengthy biography, writing, "If the world has reason to thank God for great men, with special gratitude should we acknowledge the divine goodness in raising up Toussaint L'Ouverture. Among the privileged races of the earth, the roll of patriots, legislators, and heroes, is long and well filled. As yet there is but one Toussaint L'Ouverture."[22] Armisted perhaps had a copy of Martineau's *Penny Magazine* article at his side when he wrote in his biographical sketch that Louverture "was, emphatically, a Great Man; and what he was, others of his race may equally attain to."[23] These writers continued to offer Louverture as proof of the equality of the races. Adams stated his objective for writing his biographical sketch explicitly: "It seems desirable to place before the public, in a cheap and easily accessible form, some of the most striking facts that could be collected, in refutation of the opinion, entertained, or at least urged, by some, that the Negro is essentially, and unalterably, an inferior being."[24] Beard claimed that his biography offered "the clearest evidence that there is no insuperable barrier between the light and the dark-coloured tribes of our common human species."[25] Armistead intended his anthology to prove "that the white and dark coloured races of man are alike the children of one heavenly father, and in all respects equally endowed by him."[26]

To demonstrate Louverture's exceptionalism, these writers emphasized his character at the expense of his revolutionary violence. They applauded his refusal to join the Saint-Domingue slave revolt in its early stages, his willingness to protect his white master, and his leniency toward vanquished foes. They recited his religiosity, his love of animals, and his monogamy. They repeated the oft-cited quotation that Louverture "never broke his word."[27] Louverture's domestic life was of special concern, and these writers wrapped him in gendered clothing when they embedded him firmly in the domestic sphere.[28] Adams wrote, "it is neither as the warrior nor to the legislator, great as he undoubtedly was in both these capacities, that we look upon Toussaint

L'Ouverture with the greatest admiration. Rather do we prefer to view him in his social and domestic relations as the attached and devoted servant, the tender and affectionate husband and father, the faithful friend."[29]

Martineau wrote in her popular "historical romance" *The Hour and the Man* that Louverture "was rather romantic, and did not like jesting on domestic affairs. He was more prudisih about such matters than whites fresh from the mother-country."[30] She describes a domestic scene that Beard depicted in one of the numerous illustrations included in his book (Figure 6). In the image, Louverture sits comfortably with his legs crossed in a square and sturdily constructed kitchen. His hat and jacket hang on a distant wall, while on his lap rests a thick, opened book, which has his attention. A feather and quill are ready for his use. Louverture is a bibliophile and an author. He is also a father. Two small children play at his feet, while their ball rests a short distance away. Louverture's turbaned wife prepares a meal with her hands, her sleeves rolled to the elbow. Two rows of beads circle her neckline. It is a scene of middle-class tranquility and domestic bliss, of a middle-aged man enjoying the company of his family. It is hardly the standard depiction of a revolutionary black soldier.

The image indicates an important aspect of the transatlantic abolitionist memory of Louverture at mid-century. Instead of amplifying the militancy and masculinity embedded in the Rainsford engraving, it evokes the "romantic racialism" that permeated the antebellum abolitionist imagination. According to George Fredrickson, reformers insisted on the vulnerability of slaves. They contended that African Americans were an inherently emotional and sentimental people. These traits rendered them powerless and submissive victims who were both incapable and unwilling to seek freedom through violent means.[31] British abolitionists' memory of Louverture demonstrates the multiple uses to which his memory could be applied. Targeting and eventually reaching a largely white, educated, middle-class audience, they stripped him of his sword and epaulettes and offered him as a passive and utterly nonthreatening sentimental slave. More than half a century after the violent end of slavery on Haiti, they remained committed to the conservative tactic of moral suasion. They placed great faith in the belief that evidence of a Great Man of African descent would convince slave owners throughout the Atlantic world of the potential of the black race and consequently the evils of bondage. They clung to the dream that slavery would end peacefully wherever it existed, in time.

American abolitionists had run out of patience. In remembering the Haitian Revolution, they revealed that their British counterparts were out of step with both their philosophy and their movement. In the 1850s, African Ameri-

Figure 6. John Relly Beard, *Life of Toussaint L'Ouverture, the Negro Patriot of Hayti* (1854). The artist depicts Louverture reading the work of the French abolitionist Abbé Raynal, who, predicting that an extraordinary bondman would liberate the enslaved people of the Americas, asked, "Where is he, this great man?" Courtesy of the Collections of the Library of Congress.

cans and their white allies delivered lectures on Louverture and the Haitian Revolution that set forth an exceedingly militant and subversive take on Haitian history. Moving beyond the standard models of Louverture as a republican citizen soldier and sentimental slave, these men of varying races and backgrounds emboldened him as a revolutionary black bondman who employed violence in the pursuit of freedom. If American abolitionists once hesitated to invoke the Haitian Revolution, now they eagerly deployed its memory and insisted upon its significance. The narratives of William Wells Brown, Charles Wyllys Elliott, James Theodore Holly, John Mercer Langston, and Wendell Phillips differed from those of British abolitionists in a number of respects. First, they were, like McCune Smith's New York oration, performed in public spaces. In the decade before the Civil War, Brown, a self-educated fugitive slave from Kentucky and Missouri, delivered "St. Domingo: Its Revolution and its Heroes" in London and Philadelphia. A year later, Elliott, a white author, reformer, and philanthropist, performed "Heroes are Historic Men. St. Domingo, its Revolution and its Hero, Toussaint Louverture" in New York City. Holly, a free black shoemaker, journalist, and church deacon from Washington, D.C., presented "A Vindication of the Capacity of the Negro Race for self-Government, and Civilized Progress, as Demonstrated by Historical Events of the Haytian Revolution" in New Haven, Connecticut. He later repeated the address in Ohio, Michigan, and Canada West, a haven for fugitive slaves from the United States in southern Ontario. John Mercer Langston, an Oberlin-educated lawyer of African, European, and Native American descent, gave an account of the Haitian Revolution in "The World's Anti-Slavery Movement; Its Heroes and its Triumphs," which he performed in Xenia and Cleveland, Ohio.[32] Finally, in 1857, Wendell Phillips, the radical Harvard-educated Boston Brahmin who often carried a copy of Martineau's biography of Louverture to the podium, began performing "Toussaint L'Ouverture: The Hero of St. Domingo."[33] Expunged from American memory of the Civil War today, it should, as we will see, be considered among the most popular orations of the time. Before the war, full-length copies of the lecture appeared in nearly every abolitionist newspaper, as well as such widely read publications as *Vanity Fair*, *New York Herald*, and the *New York Times*.[34]

Though American abolitionists like McCune Smith had lectured on the Haitian Revolution throughout the first half of the nineteenth century, the performances of Brown, Elliott, Holly, Langston, and Phillips subverted the traditional role of the orator as defender of the status quo.[35] By taking the Haitian Revolution out of the print media of books, newspapers, and periodicals and injecting it into the streets and open-air halls of the United States, Canada, and even London, these speakers fostered both the popularization of the memory of the Haitian Revolution and the radicalization of the American abolitionist movement. For the mnemonic device of oratory encouraged an immediate collective response from audience members who committed what amounts to a public display of abolitionist affection when they attended these lectures. That each address appeared later in print form amplified this process by making the lectures accessible to countless others. Consumption of these lectures in person or through print was a subversive act, for these orations not only celebrated the violent tactics that Louverture and innumerable enslaved Haitians used against whites to become free, but predicted and even called for their repetition in the United States. Though some who heard or read these lectures undoubtedly remained unmoved by the call of radical abolition, the aural and textual spectacle of a popular slave panegyric signaled a dramatic transformation taking place in public discourse.

Two of these performances in particular evidence their subversiveness. Twenty-year-old Charlotte Forten belonged to one of the nation's great abolitionist families. In December 1857, she recorded her impressions of Phillips's oration in Boston: "This eve. heard a splendid lecture on Toussaint by our noble Mr. Phillips. It was a glorious and well deserved tribute to the 'First of the Blacks.'" The young African American schoolteacher commented on the audience, which consisted primarily of men and women who ordinarily avoided antislavery lectures; presumably they were white. She seemed to take great pleasure in writing, "they had a grand dose of Anti-slavery and Anti-prejudice to-night."[36]

While Forten avoided comment on Phillips's race, Elliott's lecture captured the attention of the New York press, as white men did not ordinarily celebrate black men in public spaces. Even before the lecture, a writer in the *New York Times* confessed the daunting prospect of attending a lecture on such an unusual subject.[37] After the lecture, the paper reported that the lecture was "listened to with great interest. The audience applauded during his performance, and after its conclusion, tendered the speaker 'a unanimous vote of thanks.'"[38] Following the recital, various groups requested that Elliott repeat the lecture elsewhere, and the *Times* vouched for its value: "The great interest that attaches to the subject, the pleasing and attractive manner in which it is presented, and the agreeable address of the lecturer, will entitle him to large audiences, which we hope he may meet."[39] It is unknown whether any of the later performances took place.

We do know that the life of Elliott's lecture had only just begun. The New York Library Association published the speech as a pamphlet just one month after the original performance. That numerous media reviewed the text indicates that the lecture brought Elliott a degree of celebrity. The national periodical *Putnam's Monthly* dismissed the literary qualities of the piece, yet recommended it to its readers for the "spirited and deeply interesting account of the career of Toussaint L'Ouverture, the liberator of St. Domingo."[40] The *Times* suggested in a lengthy review that the lecture was most valuable for "its fearful historic lesson." The paper described the similarities between the causes of the Haitian Revolution and the reasons for America's sectional crisis and warned, "There is in these events of St. Domingo a deep lesson to the South." Bondpeople's songs and dances belied their discontent. The thirst for liberty "does not show itself now; it did not for long in St. Domingo. But it is there." The South sat atop a volcano. "It is possible that when the fatal time comes, not even a rumble or a quaking may warn us before." The lesson of Elliott's lecture was that for white southerners "Your TOUSSAINT may be now meekly enduring his bondage." Slavery would end in America just as it did in Haiti. The truth was "that you cannot safely hold a man a slave."[41] News coverage of the printed lecture is revealing when we consider the reaction of local media a decade earlier when the noted abolitionist John Jay also delivered an oration on Louverture in New York City. While the African American *Colored American* alerted readers to the event, the city's major papers were silent.[42] Now, on the eve of the Civil War even white papers took notice.

Another similarity of these American orations is the advocacy of violence to both end slavery and prove the masculinity of black men. Whereas British abolitionists accentuated Louverture's domestic and familial relations as evidence of his greatness, American radicals emphasized his military accomplishments. In doing so, they squared the gendered construction of Louverture with the evolving notion of manhood.[43] Brown summarized Louverture's accomplishments thus: "From a slave he rose to be a soldier, a general, and a governor, and might have been a king."[44] Elliott asserted that under Louverture's leadership Haitians were invincible. "The electric spark which fired his soul fired theirs." He then opined on the legitimacy of slaves' use of violence to both win freedom and vindicate their manhood. "Great is he who spends his blood and his life, fighting for liberty—but base is the man who kills and destroys for fame or plunder." On Haiti, black slaves defeated France's best soldiers and "proved themselves men."[45]

The orations underscored American abolitionists' growing faith in the use of violence to both secure liberty and prove the manhood of the race. Holly exhorted, "freedom and independence are written in the world's history in the ineffaceable characters of blood; and its crimsoned letters will ever testify of the determination and of the ability of the negro to be free, throughout the everlasting succession of ages." He then castigated those who qualified the outcome of the Haitian Revolution due to the racial bloodletting that occurred, and instead used violence as a trophy of black manhood. Using a gendered anvil, he shattered the symbol of Louverture as a passive, nonviolent, emasculated slave, remarking that the great general wished "every black to be immolated in a manly defense of his liberty, rather than the infernal and accursed system of negro slavery should again be established on that soil." Louverture "considered it far better, that his sable countrymen should be DEAD FREEMEN," rather "than LIVING SLAVES."[46] Langston said that as a husband and father Louverture "was altogether without fault, always exhibiting towards his wife the tenderest love, and towards his children the most affectionate and fatherly solicitude." As a friend, Louverture was both generous and magnanimous. But, the Ohio abolitionist insisted, "the character of this extraordinary man shines most brilliantly and beautifully in his conduct as a great military leader and hero." Langston admitted the Haitian Revolution was "full of blood, carnage, and death." He nonetheless justified "the struggle of a people who, driven to desperation by inhuman and intolerable oppression, made one last, mighty effort to throw off their yoke and gain their manhood."[47]

The third commonality of these lectures is the joining of the histories of Haiti and the United States. Judging the accomplishments of Louverture and his revolutionary army superior to those of George Washington and his, these radicals pointed out the failure of the American people to live up to the national ideals set forth in the Declaration of Independence and the Unites States Constitution. Brown argued, "Toussaint's career as a Christian, a statesman, and a general, will lose nothing by a comparison with that of Washington. Each was the leader of an oppressed and outraged people, each had a powerful enemy to contend with, and each succeeded in founding a government in the New World. Toussaint's government made liberty its watchword, incorporated it in its constitution, abolished the slave-trade, and made freedom universal amongst the people." On the other hand, "Washington's government incorporated slavery and the slave-trade, and enacted laws by which chains were fastened upon the limbs of millions of people. Toussaint liberated his countrymen; Washington enslaved a portion of his, and aided in giving strength and vitality to an institution that will one day rend asunder the UNION that he helped to form."[48]

Holly declared the Haitian Revolution a far greater event than that which resulted in the thirteen colonies winning their independence from England. He referred to it as "the grandest political event of this or any other age. In weighty causes, and wondrous and momentous features, it surpasses the American revolution, in an incomparable degree. The revolution of this country was only the revolt of a people already comparably free, independent, and highly enlightened." The greatest grievance of the American people "was the imposition of three pence per pound tax on tea, by the mother country, without their consent. But the Haytian revolution was a revolt of an uneducated and menial class of slaves, against their tyrannical oppressors, who not only imposed an absolute tax on their unrequited labor, but also usurped their very bodies." There was, Holly insisted, no comparison. "The obstacles to surmount, and the difficulties to contend against, in the American revolution, when compared to those of the Haytian, were, (to use a homely but classic phrase,) but a 'tempest in a teapot,' compared to the dark and lurid thunder storm of the dissolving heavens."[49] Langston was brief, invoking French historian Beauchamp in the *Universal Biography*: "Toussaint l'Ouverture was the most extraordinary man of his age, though he lived in an age remarkable for its extraordinary men;" enslaved for nearly a half century, he was "Superior to Napoleon and Washington as a great military leader."[50]

These descriptions of Louverture's superiority over Washington, of the importance of the Haitian Revolution over the American Revolution, constitute a fundamental departure from the standard abolitionist memory of Louverture. For a half-century abolitionists throughout the Atlantic world had labeled Louverture the "Black Napoleon" and the "Washington of St. Domingo." Now, African Americans and their white allies preferred the memory of Louverture and his revolution to these white revolutionary icons and their revolutions, something the legendary finale of Phillips's oration made clear. An Ohio abolitionist reinforced the growing status of the Haitian Revolution in abolitionist circles when in a letter published in the *Weekly Anglo-African* he urged readers to discontinue their celebrations of the First of August. For decades, American abolitionists gathered to celebrate the anniversary of the peaceful and gradual abolition of slavery in the British Caribbean.[51] Now, however, on the eve of the Civil War, this writer questioned the viability of a holiday for an enslaved people who did not fight for their liberation, writing, "I should prefer, therefore, commemorating the downfall of slavery, in St. Domingo."[52]

TOUSSAINT L'OUVERTURE, "THE FIRST OF THE BLACKS."

Figure 7. Francis Meriam was among the men who accompanied John Brown to Harpers Ferry. After escaping to Canada, Meriam returned to the United States during the Civil War to fight alongside former bondmen in the Union Army. He visited Haiti on the eve of the Civil War and brought back a portrait of Louverture, copied from this engraving. Just weeks after the outbreak of the Civil War, James Redpath published the image on the front page of *Pine and Palm*, his abolitionist newspaper that promoted African American colonization of Haiti. Courtesy of the American Antiquarian Society.

These historical lectures were part of a growing trend in which abolition-ists readily invoked the Haitian Revolution in speeches, newspapers, periodi-cals, and daily conversations. An examination of the men who participated in John Brown's invasion of Harpers Ferry illuminates the extent to which on the eve of the Civil War Louverture's name had become among American abolitionists a "household word."[53] Indeed, Brown's raid takes on a different character when we learn that both the men who marched into battle along-side him and those who backed the invasion financially shared Brown's admi-ration of Louverture as well as his dream of a second Haitian Revolution.

Francis Jackson Meriam, a white abolitionist from Massachusetts, visited Haiti just months before taking part in the raid. He accompanied the radi-cal abolition writer James Redpath, who intended to report on the progress of the nation and its people.[54] Among the items Meriam brought back to the United States from Haiti was an original portrait of Louverture.[55] The portrait, which shows a dignified and uniformed Louverture from profile, is copied from a well-known engraving (Figure 7).[56] That Meriam displayed his rare piece of artwork in front of his brothers-in-arms is likely, and it is tempting to envision Louverture's image peering over the shoulders of the men who in 1859 plotted the raid at Harpers Ferry. Numbers of Brown's close associates collected portraits of Louverture: Phillips owned a rare painting by a renowned Haitian historian;[57] George DeBaptiste, one of Brown's militant co-conspirators in Detroit, likewise owned a portrait;[58] James Redpath owned at least one portrait and during the Civil War became one of the first publish-ers to print an illustration of Louverture in an American newspaper.[59]

Visual representations of Louverture resonated with American abolition-ists on the eve of the Civil War. Just months before Brown's raid, Brooklyn educator and newspaper correspondent William J. Wilson recorded his im-pressions of a visit to a fictional portrait gallery. Visual images, he wrote, were more powerful pneumonic devices than the printed or spoken word. Pictures called "up associations and emotions" and produced thoughts "that paint the memory afresh with hues the most beautiful, touching, beneficial and lasting. A picture of a great man with whose acts we are familiar, calls up the whole history of his times. Our minds thus become reimpressed with the events and we arrive at the philosophy of them." A picture of Washington reminded Wilson of both the American Revolution and the birth of the Republic; one of Jefferson conjured memory of the Declaration of Independence.[60]

Yet another portrait seized Wilson's attention primarily. It was "a most beautiful portrait of one of the greatest men the world ever saw—TOUIS-

SANT L'Overture." Wilson confessed an inability to do justice to the image with either pencil or pen. "Some future historian in other times, will yet write the name of Touissant L'Overture higher and in purer light than that of any man that has lived up to to-day." The portrait reminded him of the accomplishments of this Great Man and the anonymous masses who followed him. "The whole history from the first to last of this Island and this people is so vividly brought before the mind, by merely this likeness of the inimitable Touissant L'Overture, that it is reimpressed with the extraordinary, *useful and touching lesson it teaches.*"[61]

It was not only the image of Louverture that inspired the men responsible for the attack on Harpers Ferry. John Brown's eldest son, John Brown, Jr., who served as his father's "special intelligence agent" for the raid, likewise demonstrated an affinity for Louverture.[62] In a letter that indicates the thinking of Brown's men regarding enslaved Americans and the likelihood of their participation in a violent revolt, Brown, Jr. wrote shortly after his father's execution that it was "only the body of Toussaint L'Ouverture which sleeps in the tomb; his soul visits the cabins of the slaves of the South when night is spread over the face of nature. The ears of our American slaves hear his voice in the wind-gusts which sweep over the prairies of Texas, of Arkansas and Missouri; his voice finds an echo in the immense valleys of Florida, among the pines of the Carolinas, in the Dismal Swamp and upon the mountain-tops, proclaiming that the despots of America shall yet know the strength of the toiler's arm, and that he who would be free must himself strike the first blow."[63]

Memory of Louverture and the Haitian Revolution buttressed the antislavery philosophies of the members of the Secret Six, a group of northeastern abolitionists who secretly funded Brown's attack. Gerrit Smith, the New York philanthropist and social reformer, referred to Louverture as a "noble" man in an "abolition speech" delivered in front of the U.S. Congress.[64] Francis Sanborn was a Massachusetts educator well versed in Haitian history and especially the life of Louverture. He read several histories of the revolution and biographies of Louverture, including Rainsford's, as well as Louverture's memoirs, which Joseph Saint-Rémy published in Paris in 1855.[65] In a sermon delivered at Music Hall in Boston, Sanborn revealed his high regard of Louverture, remarking, "I challenge all history to parallel the military genius and the statesmanship of this negro, who had been a slave all the best years of his life."[66] Thomas Wentworth Higginson, who cultural biographer David Reynolds calls "Brown's most ardent supporter," believed strongly in the effectiveness of violence in ending slavery.[67] The Transcendalist minister himself employed violence in an effort to liberate the fugitive slave Anthony Burns from a Boston courthouse and later wrote extensively on the history of slave revolts.[68] During the Civil War, he backed up his revolutionary rhetoric with action, serving as an officer of the Union army's first African American regiment. Higginson saw in African Americans great potential and on occasion drew comparisons between exceptional black Union soldiers and Louverture.[69]

Theodore Parker, one of Brown's more recognized accomplices, was a fiery Unitarian minister and orator who considered it the duty of all free citizens to aid bondpeople in gaining liberation. Jeffrey Rossbach suggests that it was William Wells Brown's lecture, "St. Domingo," which convinced Parker of the necessity and utility of violence.[70] In a letter explaining his radical stance, Parker admitted the bondman's aversion to violence, but added, "*there is a limit even to the negro's forbearance. San Domingo is not a great way off.*" Parker predicted the day was coming when enslaved Americans would no longer wait for the assistance of outsiders. "In the Slave States, there is many a possible San Domingo, which may become actual any day; and, if not in 1860, then in some other 'year of our Lord.'" Parker welcomed that day, explaining that it would expose the shortcomings of the United States and then enable the nation to realize its fundamental ideals. "We are always talking about 'Liberty,'" he began. "We continually praise our Fathers 'who fought the Revolution.' We build monuments to commemorate even the humblest beginning of that great national work. Once a year, we stop all ordinary work, and give up a whole day to the noisiest kind of rejoicing for the War of Independence." Parker concluded, "Do you suppose this will fail to produce its effect on the black man, one day?"[71]

James Redpath neither participated in Brown's raid nor assisted in its financing significantly; nonetheless, perhaps no other abolitionist had as great an impact on Brown's decision to launch a second Haitian Revolution. Born in Scotland, Redpath emigrated with his family to the United States in 1849 and quickly established himself as a successful printer and writer. After accepting a position with Horace Greeley's *New York Tribune*, Redpath traveled throughout the South, spending years in Bloody Kansas. In 1858 Redpath published *Roving Editor: or, Talks with the Slaves in the Southern States* , consisting of transcriptions of what the author claimed were his clandestine conversations with southern bondpeople. The interviews exposed much about slaves' discontent and their willingness to use violence. In the book, Redpath revealed his sympathy for violent slave resistance, writing, "I now believe that the speediest method of abolishing slavery, and of ending the eternal hypo-

critical hubbub in Congress and the country, is to incite a few scores of rat-
tling insurrections—in a quiet gentlemanly way—simultaneously in different
parts of the country, and by a little wholesale slaughter, to arouse the con-
science of the people against the wrong embodied in Southern institutions."[72]
Like many abolitionists on the eve of the Civil War, Redpath's abolitionism
was not just talk. As he traveled the South he aided more than a dozen slaves
in their escape and proposed an organization of radical abolitionists with the
name "apostles of freedom." He intended the group to aid in the liberation of
additional men and women in bondage. While in Kansas, Redpath formed
a close relationship with Brown and became an important "intermediary"
between Brown and the Secret Six.[73]

Haiti and its history fascinated Redpath, who credited Phillips's oration
with sparking his interest.[74] The Scottish immigrant wrote in a letter to Phillips, "your speech on Toussaint has had & will yet have a great influence on
my life."[75] It was because of the oration that Redpath visited Haiti in the
winter of 1859 and returned twice more in the next year. On his journeys, he
traded stories of Louverture with aged citizens and veterans of the revolution.
He spoke with men who had fought alongside the great black general.[76] During the Civil War, Redpath, who would remain one of the greatest advocates
of black emigration to Haiti, published a biography of Louverture with the
following impartation:

> The life which is described in the following pages has both a permanent
> interest and a permanent value. But the efforts which are now made to
> effect the abolition of slavery in the United States of America, seem to
> render the present moment specially fit for the appearance of a memoir
> of Toussaint L'Ouverture. A hope of affording some aid to the sacred
> cause of freedom, specially as involved in the extinction of slavery, and
> in the removal of the prejudices of which servitude mainly depends, has
> induced the author to prepare the present work for the press.[77]

That Redpath and Brown discussed the Haitian Revolution is apparent.[78]
Redpath's advocacy of slave insurrection was short-lived; nonetheless, no
other abolitionist surpassed his radicalism in the years leading up to the Civil
War, except perhaps John Brown.[79]

John Brown exploded on the national scene in October 1859 when he
and twenty-one devoted followers, including three of his sons and five African Americans, stormed the federal arsenal at Harpers Ferry, Virginia. They

brought with them hundreds of sharpened pikes, which they intended to distribute to local bondmen whom they expected to join the insurrection.[80] Within thirty-six hours, however, the attack was over, when a company of U.S. Marines under Colonel Robert E. Lee and Lieutenant J. E. B. Stuart stormed an engine house in which they had cornered Brown and a number of his men. Lee arrested a bloodied Brown, along with six of his followers. The state of Virginia tried, convicted, and hanged Brown and the remaining survivors. Of the other fourteen rebels, seven died in the attack and seven escaped. They had taken the lives of four people and wounded nine.[81]

No individual figures as prominently in the historical literature of the causes of the Civil War than John Brown. Popular and scholarly books and articles are devoted to nearly every aspect of his life, personality, and death. Today, most historians agree that Brown was not, as one scholar referred to him at a recent historical conference, "delusional"; he was a bold and defiant rebel who drew on a long tradition of slave and abolitionist resistance. David Reynolds writes, "If John Brown's efforts to wipe out slavery by raiding Virginia with a tiny band of men seems absurd when viewed as an isolated military act, it makes sense when seen in light of the slave revolts, guerilla warfare, and revolutionary Christianity that were major sources of inspiration for him."[82] Brown was at the forefront of a radical social movement that sought to end not only bondage but white supremacy as well.

Memory of Louverture fueled Brown's faith in revolutionary black violence. While we do not know whether Brown attended any of the lectures on Louverture described above, it is certain that he was aware of them. He throughout his life followed the abolitionist newspapers that kept alive the memory of Louverture—in his childhood, his father subscribed to William Lloyd Garrison's *Liberator*.[83] Brown drew inspiration from these articles, as well as books and conversations on the Haitian Revolution. Richard J. Hinton, one of Brown's allies, recounted that one evening Brown stopped to rest while helping eleven slaves escape from Bloody Kansas. At the home of a frontier abolitionist, Brown recounted the history of American slave resistance. He impressed Hinton by reciting the history of the Haitian Revolution. It was, Hinton remembered, a story Brown knew "by heart."[84] Richard Realf, an English immigrant and abolitionist journalist who also befriended Brown in Kansas, testified before a U.S. Senate investigating committee after Brown's arrest. Asked about Brown's motivations, Realf responded that Brown "had posted himself in relation to the wars of Toussaint L'Ouverture; he had become thoroughly acquainted with the wars in Hayti and the islands round about; and from all these things he had drawn the conclusion, believing, as he stated there he did believe, and as we all (if I may judge from myself) believed, that upon the first intimation of a plan formed for the liberation of the slaves, they would immediately rise all over the Southern States." It was because of Brown's study of the Haitian Revolution and wars of liberation that his plan emerged "spontaneously" in his mind.[85]

Brown once made similar pronouncements before a room full of black abolitionists in Chatham, Canada West, who gathered secretly to plot the end of slavery in the United States. One man suggested Brown reconsider his plan to provoke a slave insurrection, due to his concern that enslaved Americans might not rally behind an invading abolitionist force. According to one observer, Brown scoffed at the notion that American bondmen were "different from those of the West India island of San Domingo."[86] Enslaved Saint Domingans rose when the opportunity presented itself; Brown knew that enslaved Americans would too.

Additional evidence of Brown's desire to enact a second Haitian Revolution comes from testimony given years after his death. Four decades after the Civil War, Franklin Sanborn published a 600-page biography and anthology of his "old friend" that, in addition to cementing Brown's legacy as a divinely inspired freedom fighter, revealed the evolution of Brown's radical abolitionist philosophy. Brown was a "man of peace" who understood that "war had its uses." He often said, Sanborn recorded, "I believe in the Golden Rule and the Declaration of Independence. I think they both are the same thing; and it is better that a whole generation should pass off the face of the earth,—men, women, and children,—by a violent death, than that one jot of either should fail *in this country*." Brown was predictably a strong advocate of black soldiery, for it was only when bondmen stood on the battlefield "like men" that they would earn the nation's respect. According to Sanborn, Brown looked forward to a civil war over slavery, when black men would be "formed into regiments and brigades and be drilled in the whole art or war,—like the black soldiers of Toussaint L'Ouverture and Dessalines, in Hayti."[87]

One of Brown's Harpers Ferry jailors provided similar testimony. In an interview at the close of the century, Confederate veteran Colonel William Fellows remembered that Brown busied himself in the last days of his life reading the Bible, Thomas Carlyle's *French Revolution*, Edward Gibbon's *Decline and Fall of the Roman Empire*, "and a biography of Toussaint L'Ouverture." He further reported that Brown told him Louverture's life story and "put that poor black man alongside Socrates, Luther and John Hampden as the world's heroes." The quotation is instructive, as it evidences Brown's awareness of the abolitionist convention of ranking Louverture alongside history's Great Men. Brown shared with his jailor that "he had read and reread all the literature he could find about L'Ouverture for a dozen years," and he went to Harpers Ferry hoping to reenact a second Haitian Revolution with himself in the role of Louverture. Fellows insisted, "I know that he [Brown] patterned his life after the San Domingan and that he viewed his own death on the scaffold in the same light as the execution of L'Ouverture."[88] The ease with which the aging white abolitionist wrapped himself in the clothing of a revolutionary black soldier confirms the findings of John Stauffer, who holds that on the eve of the Civil War radical abolitionists lived blind to the socially constructed reality of racial distinctions. They were, despite the various shades of their skin color, all black men at heart.[89]

The movement that African Americans and their white allies built on the history and memory of the Haitian Revolution transcended section as well as race. Just months after the Harpers Ferry raid, one forgotten man used the revolution to finish the job Brown's men had started. In southern Virginia, a local grand jury indicted a man named Dodson for inciting slave insurrection. The evidence against him was damning. Local residents heard Dodson late at night telling slaves in their cabins of the Israelites who escaped bondage. He also told them "that the negroes of St. Domingo had overpowered their masters and set themselves free, and if they (the negroes of Virginia) would only be determined and show that they were in earnest, the North would send help." Dodson assured his brothers and sisters in bondage that upon rising there was also "500 men in this county who would help them, and that many of the remainder would do nothing against them, and that in a short time they could all be free."[90] Who was this mysterious figure? Was he black or white, free or enslaved? The record is silent; nevertheless, Brown's raid made it clear that this was not idle chatter. In fact, scholarship on the revolutionary black Atlantic underscores the likelihood of the existence of such a plot in southern Virginia.[91]

Public reaction in Haiti to Brown's execution further illustrates American abolitionism transcending geographic boundaries. Haitian newspapers filled columns with the news of Brown's life, trial, and hanging. The nation officially mourned his death for three days. Haitians flew flags at half-mast and hung black drapes from their windows. They raised some twenty thousand dollars for Brown's family and the families of the other dead rebels.[92] The government eventually renamed the primary thoroughfare in Port-au-Prince John Brown

Boulevard. An American living in Haiti described one funerary ceremony in which Haitians positioned a replica of Brown's casket in the center of a Catholic cathedral. They surrounded the casket with burning candles and incense, and on the front of the casket placed a piece of satin "on which was printed, in letters of gold, 'John Brown, heroic martyr for the liberty of the blacks.' "[93] The American Anti-Slavery Society reprinted several articles from Haitian newspapers in its annual report. One letter intended for American bondpeople underscores the transcendent appeal of violent abolitionism throughout the Atlantic world: "reassure yourselves, ye Slaves, nothing is lost; Liberty is immortal. Brown and his companions have sown this Slave-land with their glorious blood, and doubt not that therefrom avengers will arise."[94]

Throughout the first half of the nineteenth century, abolitionists on both sides of the Atlantic remembered Toussaint Louverture. In speeches, illustrations, and texts they celebrated him as a Great Man, a former slave who compared favorably to George Washington, Napoleon Bonaparte, and the other Great Men of the Age of Revolutions. It was a resilient image that survived in the United States throughout the early national and antebellum periods in spite of the triumph of white supremacy and the spread of plantation slavery across the American southwest. Public memory of Louverture influenced the American abolitionist movement for decades. But it had its greatest impact in the 1850s, because it was then that so many abolitionists abandoned their hopes of the natural and peaceful demise of the institution of slavery. Indeed, the passage of both the Fugitive Slave Law and the Kansas-Nebraska Act, in conjunction with the Supreme Court decision in the *Dred Scott* case, ensured both the expansion and perpetuation of the "peculiar institution." It was for this reason that African Americans and their white allies remembered Louverture. Frustrated with the nonviolent tactics of their movement, they understood the Great Man of Haiti as a revolutionary black bondman who willingly died and eagerly killed for freedom. Louverture was for them a symbol of the efficacy of violence in both ending slavery and redeeming black manhood. On the eve of the Civil War, abolitionists threatened to emulate Louverture by taking up arms and toppling the institution of slavery. Some, like John Brown, did.

"Contemplate, I beseech you, fellow-citizens, the example of St. Domingo": Abolitionist Dreams, Confederate Nightmares, and the Counterrevolution of Secession

THE VIRGINIA ATTORNEY who led the prosecution of John Brown for the crimes of murder, treason, and raising a slave insurrection understood the Harpers Ferry raid as a milestone in the history of the republic. It was, Andrew Hunter cautioned, "the beginning of a great conflict between the North and the South on the subject of slavery, and had better be regarded accordingly."[1] During the trial, Hunter stressed the urgency of the matter to both the court and the nation when he refuted those who dismissed Brown as either a political radical or a lunatic, declaring emphatically, "Brown was not a madman." Hunter argued that the invasion of Harpers Ferry was simply one part of an extensive northern abolitionist plot. Evidence abound that abolitionists had for months been plotting the murder of white southerners. The men who invaded Harpers Ferry were not extremists, but foot soldiers in a rising abolitionist army. Alongside Brown, they attempted to "usurp the government, manumit our slaves, confiscate the property of slaveholders, and without drawing a trigger or shedding blood, permit him to take possession of the Commonwealth and make it another Hayti."[2]

Hunter was not alone in interpreting Brown's raid as a second Haitian

Revolution. Punishment in retaliation for Brown's crime elicited similar comparisons in the days and weeks following the Harpers Ferry invasion. One man who witnessed Brown's hanging noticed the heightened alarm that gripped the South. There was, he surmised, only one explanation: "It was doubtless that deep sense of insecurity that widened into awful alarms at the suggestion of slave insurrections—the fact that society was permeated with the stories of West Indian wars of races, especially the traditions more terrible than history of the San Domingo horrors."[3] After the executions of Brown's co-conspirators, one Virginia writer reflected,

> Thus closes the retribution of one of the most unprovoked and demoniac plots of insurrection and invasion which was ever concocted against any community. Never, in the darkest and most infernal excesses of the French Revolution, was such scenes of horror perpetuated as the success of the Harper's Ferry outrage would have brought upon the fields and firesides of Virginia. All familiar with the scenes of unspeakable horror which occurred in St. Domingo, and of the atrocities peculiar to an African insurrection, may form some idea of the weeping and wailing, the fire and slaughter, the blood and defilement, which was destined by JOHN BROWN for every threshold in Virginia.[4]

John Brown's dream of a second Haitian Revolution was for most Americans a nightmare. For white southerners—especially those in regions with large populations of enslaved people—this nightmare was particularly horrifying.[5] Following the abolitionist invasion of Harpers Ferry, fear of a second Haitian Revolution turned to hysteria as writers, politicians, and ordinary men and women pondered the likelihood of racial Armageddon below the Mason-Dixon Line.[6] Through an examination of the explosion of public memory of the Haitian Revolution in southern public culture in the time period between John Brown's raid and the start of the Civil War, this chapter finds that the horrific narrative of the revolution played a critical role in both birthing the Confederacy and provoking the war. At the height of America's sectional conflict, the Haitian Revolution was a resonant symbol that sectional radicals exploited in an effort to win converts to their extreme political movement. Reminding white southerners of the likelihood of a repetition of the "horrors of St. Domingo" on American soil if the slave states remained in the Union, secessionist speakers and writers rooted their political movement in the counterrevolutionary philosophy of the eighteenth-century Atlantic world and at last achieved independence.

In spite of the long-held belief that the political philosophy of the Confederacy was steeped in the radical republican tradition of the late eighteenth century, secessionists openly professed the counterrevolutionary nature of their movement.[7] Perhaps none more clearly than James Henley Thornwell, a preacher, professor, and publisher who avowed, "We are not revolutionists—we are resisting revolution."[8] The white supremacist and proslavery philosopher George Fitzhugh was equally unambiguous, declaring that the southern separatist movement was "a solemn protest against the doctrines of natural liberty, human equality and the social contracts taught by Locke and the American sages of 1776." Northerners, he elaborated, were "radicals, rationalists, and destructives by inheritance. We, in like manner, are conservatives."[9] The combination of John Brown's raid and Lincoln's election made the counterrevolution ascendant. Yet it would be a mistake to trace the origins of the triumph of secessionism to either of these events. Manisha Sinha describes the radical secessionist movement that originated in South Carolina as having a much greater provenance. "Their cause was a part of the tide of reaction that followed the revolutionary era in the Atlantic world." Like Europeans in generations past who feared the "alleged excesses of the age of revolution," secessionists intended to stop the universal rights movement towards freedom and democracy in its tracks.[10]

Doing so was more difficult than once believed. More than a generation of separatists struggled to mobilize secessionist support outside the Deep South. William Freehling offers the best explanation of how they ultimately united various Souths and thus paved the way to war. In the second volume of his history of the secessionist movement, he describes how a minority of southern extremists, known as Fire-Eaters, convinced a majority of moderates of their radical beliefs by exploiting a number of unanticipated events. Chief among them were Brown's raid and the dialogue on slave insurrection the incident provoked. The northern response to the attack was especially maddening. "Yankees' applause for a murderous invader assaulted southern eardrums like amplified thunder," Freehling writes. Still, he goes too far when asserting that northern celebrations of Brown generated secessionist fervor more than did the renewed fear of slave insurrection: "Foreboding about blacks' violence, as usual, little involved expectations of a successful slave revolt or even an unsuccessful general uprising. Instead, lowcountrymen again worried that individual slaves might sabotage or kill."[11] While slaveowners undoubtedly feared the lone assassin who might lie in waiting, the Haitian Revolution left deep wounds on the psyche of both southern planters and their white neighbors, which Brown's raid opened and exposed to a deadly infection for which there was only one cure—secession.

That John Brown embarked upon a second Haitian Revolution is apparent. But to fully understand the depth of the fear that such an occurrence engendered in the minds of white southerners on the eve of the Civil War, we must consider the words of two of the most important architects of the horrific narrative of the Haitian Revolution, Bryan Edwards and Sir Archibald Alison. For decades, Edwards's graphic descriptions of black slaves maiming and massacring white colonists informed readers throughout the Atlantic world. In his proslavery polemic, which publishers printed in London, New York, and Charleston, South Carolina, more than a dozen times between 1797 and 1819, Edwards purported to describe the "horrors of St. Domingo" accurately. According to the Jamaican planter and proslavery apologist, Haitian slaves committed unprecedented acts of cruelty that nearly defied description. The most heinous occurred in the colonial capital Le Cap and the surrounding plantations, where rebel slaves sawed white men in half, spiked white infants on spears, and violated white women "on the dead bodies of their husbands and fathers." In spite of the graphic descriptions provided by Edwards, these were, he insisted, "horrors of which imagination cannot adequately conceive nor pen describe."[12] The images Edwards conjured resonated among the Americans people long after they first appeared.

This was something the eminent British historian Alison ensured with his mammoth multivolume *History of Europe, from the Commencement of the French Revolution in 1789, to the Restoration of the Bourbons in 1815,* which he completed in 1842. The tome was a smashing commercial success on both sides of the Atlantic. In the United States, readers purchased 100,000 copies of one edition alone. Alison placed great emphasis on the salience of the French Revolution in European history, as evidenced by the book's chronology and title. He had much to offer on the Haitian Revolution as well. When describing its "matchless horrors," he borrowed and at other times copied verbatim entire sections of Edwards's polemic. An example is his description of the battle of Le Cap, when "twenty thousand negroes broke into the city, and, with the torch in one hand and the sword in the other, spread slaughter and devastation around. . . . Neither age nor sex were spared." Most horrifying of all, "virgins were immolated on the altar; weeping infants hurled into the fires. Amid the shrieks of the sufferers and the shouts of the victors, the finest city in the West Indies was reduced to ashes."[13] For generations of Americans born after the Haitian Revolution, the words of both Edwards and Alison instructed them on the horrors of slave insurrection.

These words proved effective weapons in the war to win converts to the religion of secession. Nearly two decades before Brown's raid, one of the most important engineers of the movement to create a nation of slave states, legendary South Carolina Fire-Eater John C. Calhoun, urged white southerners to remember the Haitian Revolution when considering the consequences of abolition. The end of slavery, which he asserted was an emerging objective of the federal government, "would be followed by unforgiving hate between the two races, and end in a bloody and deadly struggle between them for the superiority. One or the other would have to be subjugated, extirpated, or expelled; and desolation would overspread their territories, as in St. Domingo, from which it would take centuries to recover."[14]

Where Calhoun and other antebellum radicals failed as proselytizers, John Brown proved remarkably efficient. This was something made evident immediately after the Harpers Ferry raid. While walking through the streets of Columbia, South Carolina, a Virginia militiaman encountered a local college professor who spoke of the widespread fear of slave rebellion that gripped the South. Defending the reaction of white southerners to the escalating crisis, the professor explained the need for his state to secede from the Union. There was no other option, he insisted, for if it failed to do so, "she was to be St. Domingois'd."[15] Seizing upon both the deep-rooted fears of slave revolt and the hysteria surrounding Brown's raid, southern speakers and writers who began building a case for secession put the Haitian Revolution to multiple uses. To illuminate the impact of the public memory of the revolution on the secessionist movement, what follows is an examination of each of the multiple functions that the memory of the revolution performed.

Secessionists deployed the revolution in public addresses and printed texts primarily as proof of a widespread abolitionist conspiracy to incite slave insurrections throughout the South. Brown's incursion was, they insisted, only the beginning of a revolutionary movement that promised to end in any number of the unspeakable acts that took place in Haiti. Contending that there were obvious similarities between the events that preceded the Haitian Revolution and the actions being advocated by northern abolitionists, they avowed that separation from the Union was the only way to insure that history would not, in this case, repeat itself. James De Bow, editor of *De Bow's*

Review, the most popular magazine published in the South, considered the advocacy of slave insurrection the greatest of many offenses committed by abolitionists. Abolitionists intended to bring upon the white men and women of the South a merciless race of "predatory, sanguinary, and lustful African negroes, whose known rule of warfare is not only an 'undistinguished destruction of all ages, sexes and conditions,' but one of beastly appetites, blood-drinking and cannibal horrors." History revealed no greater wrong than "the negroes of San Domingo, when, under the encouragement of the frenzied humanitarians of France, they rose against the white population. It was as if the fiends of hell, drunk with demoniac instincts and impulsions, were let loose on earth. 'An undistinguishable destruction of all ages, sexes and conditions,' was the least offence in scenes of dreadful outrage the pen may not indite, nor tongue utter." For years, abolitionists had encouraged among slaves "a harvest of blood and pollution." They delivered their "libelous and seditious tracts" to the South's slaves through the mail, and as a result "stirred up several limited negro insurrections," including the unforgettable revolt in Southampton, Virginia. Wherever the rebel slaves of Southampton traveled that fateful night, their trails "were marked with San Domingo scenes—an undistinguished destruction of all ages, sexes, and conditions. Infants, even, had been torn from their cradles by the heels, and their brains dashed out mercilessly against the walls."[16]

Brown's raid was the last straw. At Harpers Ferry, abolitionists again "unfurled the black banner of abolition." With a "notorious horse-thief and murderer" in the lead they "boldly invaded the States of Maryland and Virginia, seized upon the United States Arsenal at Harpers Ferry, and invited the slaves throughout the South to rebellion and a feast of blood and rapine, necessarily to terminate, if successful, in the overthrow of the governments of the Southern States, and the extermination of their white proprietors."[17]

Prominent southern writers and politicians amplified De Bow's thinking, noting the similarities between northern abolitionists and those in Europe at the end of the eighteenth century, whom they blamed for igniting the Haitian Revolution. In a widely successful tract that sold tens of the thousands of copies, South Carolina state senator John Townsend, a lowcountry patriarch who owned nearly three hundred slaves, warned an audience of the "ignominy and degradation" they faced upon submitting to an impending abolitionist revolution.[18] Townsend insisted that there was no difference "whether our lives and fortunes were controlled by Red Republican France, or Black Republican Massachusetts; whether we are to be the victims of the

Pharisaical self-righteousness of Old England philanthropy, of the Puritanical self-righteousness of New England philanthropy? France had her Santhonox; England her Clarkson and Buxton; and the North have their Giddings, their Wilson, their Seward, and their Sumner." As abolition had produced such horrific consequences elsewhere, Townsend questioned whether white southerners were prepared to take the necessary steps to escape its effects. He recalled that at the turn of the century French radicals took the ideas emanating from such texts as the *Rights of Man* beyond Europe and delivered them throughout the empire to its colonies where they were "inapplicable." These actions doomed Saint-Domingue, which became a theater of indescribable scenes of horror. The black republic was a stark reminder of the consequences of abolition: "there she stands—a Degraded Thing—a monument of 'warning' to all peoples, to take their government into their own hands, and not to permit themselves to be governed by another and a hostile people!"[19]

In a proslavery anthology published in 1860, University of Virginia professor Albert Taylor Bledsoe offered a narrative of the Haitian Revolution to illustrate the parallels between its origins and the events that were presently flaming the sectional crisis. He began, "May it never be forgotten that the 'Friends of the Blacks' at Boston had their exact prototypes in 'les Amis des Noirs' of Paris." Of the latter group, "Robespierre was the ruling spirit, and Brissot the orator. . . . By the dark machinations of the one, and the fiery eloquence of the other, the French people—la grande nation—were induced, in 1791, to proclaim the principle of equality to and for the free blacks of St. Domingo." Consequently, one of the world's most beautiful islands, the "brightest and most precious jewel in the crown of France," became the first of the West Indian colonies in which abolitionists embarked on the dreadful experiment of racial equality. French radicals knew of the "horrors into which it would inevitably plunge both the whites and the blacks of the island." Nevertheless, they remained firm and resolute in their course. Aware that abolition might detract from the wealth of these colonies, Robespierre, declared, "Perish the colonies rather than sacrifice one iota of our principles!"[20]

Northern abolitionists, Bledsoe warned, shared these same ambitions. The parallels were obvious. As Robespierre announced to the free blacks of Saint-Domingue that they were entitled to all the rights and privileges of citizens, Seward announced the same policy to northern free blacks, so they would propagate the same doctrines among their brethren in the South. Like in the eighteenth-century French colonies, American slaves "would be instigated, in every possible way, to claim their natural equality with the whites;

and, by every diabolical art, their passions would be inflamed." Still, abolitionists were unconcerned. Poverty, ruin, and death were small items that
rarely entered into their calculations. "The dangers of a civil war—though
the most fearful the world has ever seen—lie quite beneath the range of
their humanity," Bledsoe opined. "We should expect our argument from
the consequences of emancipation to be met by a thorough-going abolitionist with the words,—'Perish the Southern States rather than sacrifice one
iota of our principles!'" Abolitionists forgot how Haiti's white population
"melted, like successive flakes of snow, in the furnace of that freedom which
a Robespierre had kindled." The lives of white southerners depended on
their never forgetting.[21]

Objection to the elevation of Abraham Lincoln to the presidency was
the second use to which secessionists put the memory of the Haitian Revolution in the aftermath of Brown's raid. Southern conspiracy theorists argued
that among abolitionists' primary aims was placing a candidate in the White
House who shared their ambition to launch a second Haitian Revolution.
Secessionist John Thrasher elucidated in a proslavery speech delivered in Port
Gibson, Mississippi, which began with a recital of the history of the French
Jacobins during the French Revolution. These extremists, Thrasher argued,
were ultimately responsible for "the bloody scenes on St. Domingo, the destruction of the white race, and the relapsing into barbarism of the black
race." Their fanatical philosophy, which originated in England had since
spread to the North. American abolitionists sought similar results, and they
would use the Executive Office to ensure it. White southerners had no choice
but to interpret Lincoln's election as "a declaration of war against slavery and
the South."[22] A writer from Georgia expressed grave concern about the unity
of white southerners should Lincoln gain the presidency. "We may not succeed, as, unfortunately, there are some in our midst who, shutting their eyes
to JOHN BROWN's raid in Virginia—to the incendiarisms and insurrections in our sister States—to the murder and poisoning of our unoffending
people—to the exclusion of our property from the territories acquired by
common blood and a common pursue—to the *irrepressible conflict* doctrines
of the Republican party—and to the military organizations at the North—
still counsel the timid and the wavering to await an OVERT ACT—who
cry peace when there is no peace; who suggest delay when the consequences
are that the Abolitionists, gaining strength by our irresolution, will bind us,
hand and foot, and give our homes and families to the horrors of another St.
Domingo." While it was suicidal to wait for either Lincoln's election or his

subsequent inauguration, the occurrence of either was welcome, as it would undoubtedly unify white southerners. The "baptism of blood will cement a Southern union stronger and dearer to the hearts of the people then all the paper resolves and parchment records of a thousand Conventions."[23]

Benjamin Morgan Palmer used the pulpit of the First Presbyterian Church in New Orleans on Thanksgiving Day to warn of the revolutionary horrors resulting from the ascendancy of the abolitionist party in the presidential election of 1860. There was historical precedent, Palmer explained. The Jacobin abolitionists of France cried out, "liberty, equality, and fraternity" and consequently "converted St. Domingo into a howling waste." In the South, these slogans translated as "bondage, confiscation and massacre." Worst of all, the election of an abolitionist president was not the consummation of abolitionists' aims, but simply "the beginning of that consummation." If history was honest, then "there will be cohesion enough till the end of the beginning is reached, and the dreadful banquet of slaughter and ruin shall glut the appetite." Palmer spoke of slave revolution with great authority. Decades earlier, in Charleston, South Carolina, he had visited Denmark Vesey and other suspected insurrectionists in their cells and accompanied some of them to the gallows. Perhaps it was here that Palmer came to believe in the revolutionary capability of American bondmen, for according to one scholar of the Vesey plot, Palmer "neither questioned nor ever expressed doubts about Vesey's guilt."[24]

Palmer's 1860 address resonated with white southerners. Requests for prints of the sermon poured in, and immediately publishers copied it in newspapers and in pamphlet form throughout the South. One scholar estimates the number of copies published in New Orleans alone at nearly 100,000.[25] Jon Wakelyn calls the sermon "a famous contribution to the secessionist cause."[26] William Freehling ranks it "first among preachers in disunionist impact."[27] Offering a glimpse into the mental world of white southerners on the eve of the Civil War, the sermon is among the essential documents of the story of secession.

The equation of Abraham Lincoln's election with the commencement of a second Haitian Revolution was easy arithmetic for white southerners, who upon learning of his election warned of the dangers expected to visit the South. A writer in the *Montgomery Advertiser* remarked that the government and all its political and institutional strength rested firmly "in the hands of the enemies of the Southern States. Henceforth, the Abolitionists will undertake to govern States." There was only one possible outcome: "Look at

St. Domingo."[28] Lincoln's election convinced one Gulf Coast resident of the inability of the nation to remain intact, which led him to advocate secession to protect the "institutions of the South." While he did not want violence, he maintained that the South would never allow the federal government to make the United States "another S'Domingo." When war came, "the South will choose to be exterminated to the last man, rather than submit to such a state of things."[29]

One native South Carolinian imagined such a scenario in *Black Gauntlet*, a racist, proslavery polemic written by Mary Howard Schoolcraft in response to Lincoln's election. In the book, fictional abolitionists of the "Ethiopian equality party" thought the election was the "hour of triumph." It was instead the "hour of trial." Before Lincoln even assumed the presidency and took any substantive action, a massive slave insurrection erupted and spread "from the waters of the Chesapeake to those of Apalachicola." It was "sudden, desolating, and bloody. . . . From Delaware to Louisiana and Texas, the negroes, led on by the most rabidly fanatic of the abolitionists, rose up in a secret and well-concerted plot against their masters." No slave state avoided the horrors. Whole families were murdered. "Fire, massacre, and barbarian cruelty and treachery, marked every plantation; and for a season the extermination of the white race seemed inevitable. San Domingo fiendish cruelty gloated itself with blood on the first outbreak of this servile war." The southern states of Howard's imagination responded swiftly to the racial Apocalypse. Uniting "in a Southern confederacy," they defeated the abolitionist invaders, and "In a few months a million of negroes were put to the sword."[30]

Andrew Pickens Calhoun, who on the death of his father took up the mantle of secession, spoke similarly of the effects of the election of an "Abolitionist" president in a speech that lacked the reassuring distance of fiction. He predicted that Lincoln's election would damage the South irreparably. It would "place the power of this Government—its fiscal—physical and moral force—against us, so potentially, that a long and tumultuous struggle must ensue, before we could disentangle the serpent—like coils that would twist themselves around the limbs of the South." When that happened, the South would mirror St. Domingo, where "shortly after the great and radical revolution in France, the ideal and fanciful words, liberty, equality and fraternity, each roseate with blood, swept over the earth, more deadly and lasting than any epidemic that ever devastated the moral nature of man." Calhoun argued that those three words lost meaning in Haiti, and they meant even less in the South now. "Strange to say, no three words in any language have so little sense and meaning when submitted to analysis." The French arrested the impact of these words on their side of the Atlantic. "But when the storm passed over, the wrecks of a higher civilization lay around. The negro in Hayti . . . arose, with all the fury of the beast." Such an unthinkable scene, Calhoun reminded his audience, abolitionists "would delight to see re-enacted now with us."[31]

Comparisons of eighteenth-century European radicals with northern abolitionists, and dire predictions of a South oppressed by an extreme abolitionist government, served an additional purpose besides promoting secession. As Calhoun's oration attests, they buttressed proslavery arguments, which white southerners had erected on the ideology of white supremacy. The insistence that the Haitian Revolution was the result of outside agitators and that northern abolitionists were required to launch southern slave revolts—the third use to which secessionists put the Haitian Revolution—affirmed the proslavery argument that slaves were neither desirous nor worthy of freedom.[32] That enslaved Haitians broke their bonds prior to the French government's formal decree of emancipation meant little to secessionists, who proved more intent on demonstrating the positive good of slavery than recording accurate history. A writer in the *Charleston Mercury* recalling the Haitian Revolution explained, "We believe that there is not in the world, a more harmonious population than the white population of the Southern States."[33] Bledsoe declared that both Haitian and American slaves were "contented in servitude." Only with encouragement from abolitionists, did they clamor for "their inalienable rights." Should American slaves have the same opportunity as Haitian slaves, the result would be "the most horrible civil war the world has ever witnessed."[34]

For secession to take place, it was incumbent upon leading southern intellectuals to reconcile the history of revolutionary black violence in Haiti with the alleged contentedness of American slaves. The Apostle of Secession Edmund Ruffin, who would fire one of the first shots of the Civil War at Fort Sumter, South Carolina, commented on the rarity of slave insurrections throughout history in a disturbing secessionist novel published on the eve of the war.[35] "Among hundreds of slaveholding nations, and in the course of thousands of years, there have been some insurrection of slaves, and some few servile wars, of sufficient importance to be recorded in history," Ruffin wrote. Of these, "the only one which was not quelled by their masters, was the servile war of St. Domingo." But this was not a real rebellion. It "was both instigated and reinforced by the abolition fanaticism of the Jacobin government of revolutionary France." Similar outside influences threatened the

South. "Such instigation and encouragement, and, indirectly, the promise of the future aid of armed support, are offered to our slaves by our 'northern brethren.' But they have a very different people to deal with; and they will equal the emancipators of St. Domingo only in intention and effort."[36]

On the floor of the U.S. Senate, Jefferson Davis continued this line of thinking, only one week before resigning his position and assuming the presidency of the Confederate States of America. In a vituperative on northern aggression, Davis denied slaves' yearning for liberation, explaining, "Governments have tempered with slaves; bad men have gone among the ignorant and credulous people, and incited them to murder and arson; but—of themselves—moving by themselves—I say history does not chronicle a case of negro insurrection." The Haitian Revolution, "so often referred to, and so little understood, is not a case where black heroes rose and acquired a Government. It was a case in which the French Government, trampling upon the rights and safety of a distant and feeble colony by sending troops among them, brought on a revolution, first of the mulattoes, and afterwards of the blacks. Their first army was not even able to effect this." A second army was required. "Do you wonder, then, that we pause when we see this studied tendency to convert the Government into a military despotism?" White southerners remembered "the conduct of France, and that those troops were sent with like avowal, and quartered on plantations, and planters arrested for treason—just such charges as are made to-day against southern men—and brought away that insurrection might be instigated among their slaves?"[37]

Former Florida governor Richard K. Call invoked the Haitian Revolution in a public letter on secession to support his extreme racial theories. It is perhaps in this document that the plasticity of the memory of the revolution is best illuminated. In what must rank among the most explicit declarations of white supremacy published in the Civil War era, Call maintained that the events that took place in Haiti were an anomaly, incapable of occurring in the United States. Africans were an inferior people, Call avowed, and this was why he slept every night with the doors to his house "unlocked, unbarred, unbolted, when my person is accessible to the midnight approach of more than two hundred African slaves." Call maintained that the failure of John Brown's raid was the result of the unwillingness of enslaved people to come to Brown's aid, and it was this failed attempt at insurrection that proved the "total incapacity" of the slave to undertake a second Haitian Revolution in the United States. That "murderous insurrection" resulted from special circumstances, "its limited territory, its isolated situation, the peculiar character of both races of the islanders, one cruel, the other savage, the vastly superior number of slaves, and the unfriendly relations existing between the Spanish and French divisions of the island." Such a thing had never and could never take place in the United States, provided the institution of slavery remained untouched, and that slaves were allowed to continue living "comfortably and happily with their masters." Should the North intervene on behalf of the slave, however, Call avowed that secession was the antidote. The ex-governor urged caution, and he hoped that white southerners would embrace separation only as a "last resort." But once the bloody sectional battle began, he was confident "that every Southern man will be ready and willing to die rather than yield to a proposition so unjust, so abhorrent, and so dishonorable."[38]

Call's confidence in the eagerness of southern white men to fight to the death, suggests the fourth use to which secessionists' put the Haitian Revolution. While secessionists' fears of a second Haitian Revolution stemmed largely from the anxiety of white men losing their lives to their former slaves, they also derived from their fears of losing their patriarchal authority over white women. Stephanie McCurry describes a South in which white yeoman farmers and planters shared "in a definition of manhood rooted in the inviolability of the household, the command of dependents, and the public prerogatives manhood conferred."[39] This helps explain why secessionists filled their speeches and writings with alarming predictions of the sexual violence black men would exact against white women on the realization of a second Haitian Revolution. An editorialist on the front page of the *Charleston Mercury* opined on the ultimate consequence of life in the South should abolitionists finish what Brown started: "A war of races—a war of extermination—must arise, like that which took place in St. Domingo." When the second Haitian Revolution began, "The midnight glare of the incendiary torch, will illuminate the country from one end to another; while pillage, violence, murder, poison and rape will fill the air with the demonic revelry, of all the bad passions of an ignorant, semi-barbarous race, urged to madness by the licentious teaching of our Northern brethren."[40]

Citizens from Bibb County, Georgia, forwarded a resolution to the state legislature in which they blamed the sectional conflict on northern abolitionists who fomented slave insurrections. While John Brown failed to ignite a southern race war, there were many others remaining in the North who shared his ambitions. They stole slaves and provided them safe passage to the North, ignored federal laws regarding the capture and return of these fugitives, and attacked and even killed southern citizens who sought the return of their property. Worst of all, northern abolitionists threatened the ability of southern white men to protect white women. They published and circulated literature that "recommends to the slaves the indiscriminate massacre of their masters, and the re-enactment of the horrors of St. Domingo upon our wives and daughters."[41]

Secessionist commissioners amplified the patriarchal fears of these concerned citizens. Georgia Supreme Court justice and slaveowner Henry L. Benning warned an audience in Virginia of the impending doom of the South should it remain in the Union. Upon the abolition of slavery he predicted that the region would become a second St. Domingo. Benning shared his horrific vision with his audience. "By the time the North shall have attained the power, the black race will be in a large majority, and then we will have black governors, black legislatures, black juries, black everything." While these comments elicited laughter from his listeners, his next remark drew silence: "We will be overpowered and our men will be compelled to wander like vagabonds all over the earth; and as for our women, the horrors of their state we cannot contemplate in imagination."[42] Alabama commissioner Stephen Hale, in a speech Charles Dew calls "required reading for anyone trying to understand the radical mind-set gripping the lower South on the eve of the Civil War," catalogued the numerous injustices that northerners committed against the South in the name of both abolition and racial equality.[43] Taken together, these crimes constituted "a solemn declaration, on the part of a great majority of the Northern people, of hostility to the South, her property, and her institutions; nothing less than an open declaration of war." The philosophy of the Republican party, "this new theory of government," he argued, would lead inevitably to the destruction of southern property. It would, "lay waste her fields, and inaugurates all the horrors of a San Domingo servile insurrection, consigning her citizens to assassinations and her wives and daughters to pollution and violation to gratify the lust of half-civilized Africans."[44]

The fifth and final use to which secessionists put the Haitian Revolution was as a unifying symbol around which disparate southern people could find common cause. Uniting white men and women who were divided along both provincial and economic lines would remove perhaps the most stubborn obstacle to secession. A New Orleans editorialist who acknowledged the diversity of the South's various "slaveholding communities" entreated the citizens of the border states to secede. There were, he maintained, few other choices available. These territories could "make themselves a powerless appendage to

Northern territory." On the fringe of an abolitionist skirt, they would befriend neither North nor South. In this no-man's land, the future was bleak. Caught between two millstones, they would eventually "be ground into atoms." Now was the time to cast their lot with the Confederacy, before it was too late. The writer urged the men and women of the border states "to contemplate the fate of St. Domingo . . . as prophetic of their own."[45] A writer in Louisville, Kentucky, who advocated secession expressed solidarity with the wealthier cotton states to the South. There was no end in sight to the war against slavery now developing in the North. It was only a matter of time. Wherever slavery existed, attachment to the Union would mean "a war of life and death, sooner or later terminating in a repetition of all the horrors of St. Domingo." In an instant, the most successful and affluent states, "whose exports constitute the wealth of the nation," would transform into "an uninhabited and habitless desert!" With the destruction of the South's wealthiest states, the fate of its poorer ones was sealed.[46] One Alabama official addressed the Missouri State legislature in an attempt to convince the voters of this pivotal border state of the necessity of secession. He warned that the Republican Party intended to stop the expansion of slavery, "causing an increase of slaves in the Southern States, which would prove extremely dangerous." Under this policy, "the time would arrive when the scenes of San Domingo and Hayti, with all their attendant horrors, would be enacted in the slaveholding States."[47]

Fear of a second Haitian Revolution served to unite white southerners of varying economic classes as much as it did those from different locations. In an essay arguing the interest of non-slaveholders in slavery, James De Bow described the likely effect of abolition on poor whites, "of which class, I was myself until very recently a member." It was essential that non-slaveholders remembered the Haitian Revolution, for on Haiti the men from the lowest ranks of society were "massacred equally with the rich."[48] Mississippi's former governor and U.S. senator Albert G. Brown insisted that a violent revolution over slavery threatened all whites, even those who did not own slaves. If secession failed, the rich would flee the country leaving those unable to own slaves fending for themselves. In time, "The Negro will intrude into his preserve . . . insist on being treated as an equal." He would then "go to the white man's bed, and the white man his." Subsequent to this, his son would "marry the white man's daughter, and the white man's daughter his son." Ultimately, the former slaves would demand and receive equality. "Then will commence a war of races such as has marked the history of San Domingo."[49]

A writer in the *Charleston Mercury* refuted those outsiders who perceived southern class conflict. "It is the error of all northern Abolitionists—that there is an antagonism between the slaveholders and the non-slaveholders of the South:—that hatred and hostility, with a desire to liberate the negroes, and not confidence and respect, exists between them." It was incumbent on nonslaveholders to remember the Haitian Revolution. "Where are the white non-slaveholders of Hayti? Slaughtered or driven out of that grand paradise of Abolitionism." What would come of the South if it remained in the Union? Once more, the wealthiest would abandon the country. "None will remain, but those who are unable to leave it, or who do not realize the fearful terrors of their condition." A conflict would arise between the former slaves and white southerners who remained, "compared with which, the atrocities and crimes of ordinary wars, are peace itself. The midnight glare of the incendiary torch, will illuminate the country from one end to another; while pillage, violence, murder, poisons and rape will fill the air with demoniac revelry." The fear of such a situation realizing was something Americans beyond the boundaries of the slave states "cannot, or will not, understand." The writer ended with an affirmation of white racial solidarity and southern nationalism, declaring slaveowners and non-slaveowners "one in sympathy, interest, and feelings. They have equal rights and privileges—one fate. They will stand together in defence of their liberties and institutions, and will yet exist at the South a powerful and prosperous confederation of commonwealths, controlling the welfare and destiny of other nations, but controlled by none."[50] A writer from Georgia, in an emotional plea to nonslaveholders written on the eve of Lincoln's election, encapsulated the various functions—race, status, class, gender—that the memory of the Haitian Revolution performed for secessionists: "IN FOUR YEARS BY ABOLITION ENACTMENT THE NEGRO WILL BE TURNED LOOSE, AS YOUR EQUAL AND MY EQUAL, and the tragedy of St. Domingo will be enacted upon the soil of our beloved Georgia—you, I, the common classes of society will be the sufferers, by being reduced to a state of perfect degradation, and more than probably inhumanly butchered. Our mothers, wives, and daughters, debauched and murdered, our children slain, and our humble cottages reduced to ashes."[51]

Whether warning of an abolitionist conspiracy, Lincoln's election, and the horrors awaiting white women upon the end of slavery, or attempting to prove white supremacy and unify all white southerners in spite of their heterogeneity, secessionists invoked the "horrors of St. Domingo" above all else to prove the necessity of launching what James McPherson called a "preemptive counterrevolution."[52] A confederation of slave states was, they insisted, the only guarantee of avoiding a second Haitian Revolution. Advocates of secession filled influential southern periodicals with passionate appeals for a southern union. A writer in *De Bow's Review* calling himself "Python" wrote "there is but one sure mode of escape, and but one position of safety for the South, and these are, Secession and a new Confederation." While Northerners used the Constitution as a vehicle for the destruction of the South, southerners sat by passively and observed. They took no action. Their refusal to act meant "a civil and servile insurrection, the devastation of their country, the slaughter of their wives and children, the unspeakable horrors of another San Domingo." Secession was a matter of "LIFE AND DEATH."[53] In the *Southern Literary Messenger*, William Henry Holcombe, a medical doctor who traced his bloodlines to a veteran of the American Revolution, argued that the drift of the United States towards abolitionism meant the ruin of the South. The alternative to building a separate nationality, a "slave-holding republic," was the Africanization of the South. Fortunately, he avowed, "St. Domingo is before us with its bloody teachings."[54]

Calls for secession rang out from nearly every corner of the South. Florida governor Madison Perry urged the state legislature to convene in order to take all necessary measures to ensure that peace and prosperity continued in the South. Perry understood the hesitancy of some to embrace the movement, but he insisted on the worthiness of his cause, warning, "If we wait for such an overt act our fate will be that of the whites in Santo Domingo."[55] Benjamin Morgan Palmer warned Louisianans of the likely results should they refuse secession: "We may, for a generation, enjoy comparative ease, gather up our feet in our beds, and die in peace; but our children will go forth beggared from the homes of their fathers . . . Sapped, circumvented, undermined, the institutions of your soil will be overthrown; and within five and twenty years, the history of St. Domingo will be the record of Louisiana." The choice was clear. "If dead men's bones can tremble, ours will move under the muttered curses of sons and daughters. . . . Under a full conviction that the salvation of the whole country is depending upon the action of the South, I am impelled to deepen the sentiment of resistance in the Southern mind, and to strengthen the current now flowing towards a union of the South, in defense of her chartered rights." Though unsought, "it was a duty which I shall not be called to repeat, for such awful junctures do not occur twice in a century."[56]

In South Carolina, Andrew Calhoun maintained that secession would remove any desire among slaves for freedom, and thus eliminate all possibilities of a second Haitian Revolution: "The action of the South with promptness will dispel this idea and reduce the negro to unconditional quiet and submission, if the disentanglement from the North is complete, thorough and radical. . . . The only haven of security to the South must now be entered through a dissolution of the Union."[57] John Townsend wondered whether the South would "remain a passive victim, and, like the timid sheep, allow itself to be bound whilst the butcher is preparing the knife for its destruction; or will she not rather throw off, at once, her degrading sloth and cowardice, and, summoning up her ample powers, throw off a government which is about to be taken possession of by her deadly enemies?"[58] Disunion was the only alternative. For those still harboring attachment to the Union, Townsend expressed a sense of urgency: "Fortunately for the South, history has recorded for our warning the fatal consequences of such folly. Contemplate, I beseech you, fellow citizens, the example of St. Domingo."[59]

While John Brown's raid fueled white southerners' fears of a second Haitian Revolution, the effect of this fear is difficult to prove. We could argue that the speeches, pamphlets, and articles in which whites exposed their distress were simply droplets in a tidal wave of words that southerners used to debate secession. From the vantage point of nearly a century and a half, we could also dismiss these fears as the trivial ramblings of sectional demagogues, political extremists with vivid imaginations and political axes to grind. However, there is evidence to suggest that there was good reason for white southerners to treat these alarms with great concern. Indeed, proof abounds that the makings of a second Haitian Revolution were already afoot. In the days and weeks surrounding the opening of the Civil War, reports surfaced that Abolitionists were conspiring with free blacks in the North, Canada, and Haiti to launch a military invasion of the South. A writer quoting an unnamed source reported that the well-known abolitionists James Redpath, Frederick Douglass, Gerrit Smith, and John Brown, Jr., were at the center of the plot. The men had traveled to Canada and Haiti in search of black recruits. Redpath's well-advertised sojourn to Haiti to promote colonization was, this writer insisted, a ruse. His real purpose for visiting the black republic was to obtain military assistance from the Haitian president. The "daring scheme" consisted of an abolitionist army numbering in the thousands arriving from Haiti on the coast of Georgia or Florida. Here they would "strike the slave line, with their colored cohorts, somewhere in the neighborhood of the Mississippi, march in a body and directly for the Gulf, through the portions of the South most thickly populated with slaves, stir up insurrections among these as they go, force or induce slaves to join them, pillage, plunder, murder, and burn,—leaving their track as desolate as the desert, and black with ruin."[60]

Other than unreliable newspaper accounts such as this, there is little evidence to suggest that after John Brown's execution abolitionists conspired to launch a massive slave insurrection throughout the lower South with the aid of armed Haitians.[61] Indeed, the apocryphal nature of the scheme prompted one publisher to question the veracity of these sensational accounts, offering, "We do not undertake to say how much reliance is to be placed in the information respecting a projected raid from Hayti. Readers can form their own conjectures and conclusions."[62] The unlikelihood of a second Haitian Revolution does not detract from the fear it engendered among white southerners in the aftermath of the attack on Harpers Ferry. It was, Alfred Hunt reminds us, "as if the lessons they had learned, the stories they had been told, were all coming true."[63] The ubiquitousness of the "horrors of St. Domingo" in secessionist speeches, newspapers, and pamphlets suggests that memory of the Haitian Revolution offered more than convenient and effective rhetorical devices for unifying white southerners. It rather provided a combustible cultural agent that secessionists could readily ignite and inflame.

In the end, secessionists exploited the widespread fear of slave insurrection that Brown's raid exposed in order to win converts to their radical cause. Arguing that their movement to build a new and independent nation harkened to the days of the founding fathers, they insisted that the Civil War was a second War for Independence and that they were the Washingtons, Jeffersons, and Madisons of a new age. The words they used to achieve nationhood, however, belie these assertions. Secession was not a revolutionary crusade for political liberty and social equality; it was rather a militant campaign to conserve and perpetuate a counterrevolutionary movement begun in the eighteenth-century Atlantic world. The objective was not simply to achieve nationhood; it was primarily to maintain the status quo regarding slavery, and avoid, at all costs, the horrors of a second Haitian Revolution.

PART II

A Second Haitian Revolution?

CHAPTER 4

"Liberty on the Battle-field":

Haiti and the Movement to Arm Black Soldiers

IN DECEMBER 1861, Wendell Phillips delivered "Toussaint L'Ouverture" in New York and Boston in front of large and boisterous crowds. It was the first time he had delivered the panegyric in nearly two years, and though the text of the lecture remained largely the same, the audiences had changed. After eight months of war, the men and women now listening were familiar with talk of the impact that runaway slaves, or "contrabands," were having on the war, and conversations on black soldiers were familiar to them. There is little doubt that Phillips and the men and women in front of him envisioned American bondmen dressed in the blue jackets and pants of Union soldiers when he declared, "there never was a race that, weakened and degraded by such chattel slavery, unaided, tore of its own fetters, forged them into swords, and won its liberty on the battle-field, but one, and that was the black race of St. Domingo."[1] Phillips, as we have seen, had lectured on Louverture in New England before the war to mixed reviews. But after the start of the war, he repeated "Toussaint L'Ouverture" in cities and towns across the United States, from Boston, New York, and Philadelphia, to as far west as Chicago and as far South as Washington, D.C. In each of these places, audiences celebrated both the lecturer and the lecture. One of Phillips's earliest biographers explained the source of the newfound popularity of the oration: "It proved to be, to many people, a conclusive answer to the absurd talk of those who affirmed that the negroes would not fight."[2]

It was no coincidence that the fame of the "Toussaint L'Ouverture"

peaked at the same time Americans furiously debated the issue of black soldiery. Indeed, it was the debate over the enlistment of African Americans
in the Union Army, which provoked such public discourse. The American
people greeted the opening of the Civil War with great élan. Both northerners
and southerners rallied behind the flags of their respective nations, yet neither
anticipated the horrors the long-anticipated contest would bring. Opening
battles made it clear to both sides that victory would come neither quickly
nor easily, and circumstances forced both Union and Confederate armies to
begin conscripting men to fill their thinning ranks. The war would be a long
and bloody ordeal, a war of attrition. In spite of the tremendous source of
bound laborers available to the Confederacy, southern leaders did not consider the possibility of arming black soldiers until the very last moments of
the war. In the North, African Americans and their white allies immediately
called on president Abraham Lincoln and the federal government to put mus-
kets in the hands of both northern free blacks and southern bondmen. This
revolutionary proposal—unthinkable just months before—sparked one of
the most contentious debates of the war.

In an effort to achieve a public policy of black soldiery, abolitionists
from the opening of the Civil War deployed the heroic narrative of the
Haitian Revolution in public speeches and printed texts, asserting that by
arming African Americans the ranks of the federal army would swell with
motivated, disciplined, and patriotic black men. The soldiers abolitionists
envisioned were not the revolutionary black bondmen that John Brown and
his radical band of brothers had dreamed of emulating. Instead, these were
republican citizen soldiers, patriots who yearned to spill their blood in the
twin causes of freedom and nation. Led by Wendell Phillips, advocates of
black soldiery in lecture halls and theaters, newspapers, pamphlets, and
books amplified the transatlantic abolitionist memory of Louverture to win
converts to their cause. They contended that African Americans if given the
opportunity to fight would live up to the incredible martial standard set
by Louverture and the tens of thousands of black men who followed him
into battle. That the men and women who used the heroic narrative of the
revolution to endorse the enlistment of African Americans represented a
cross of the American people—they were black and white, rich and poor,
northern, southern, and western—indicates that in addition to promoting radical public policy, something more subversive took place as well.
Abolitionists who seized upon the symbols of Louverture and the Haitian
Revolution not only sought the integration of the armed forces. Insisting

on the relevance of both a great black man and an important milestone in
African American history at perhaps the most decisive moment in the history of the United States, they endeavored to transform the republic into a
free and equal society, one that accepted African Americans equally as both
soldiers and men.

Immediately after the firing on Fort Sumter, groups of northern free blacks
organized militias and with the assistance of their abolitionist allies lobbied
the president, politicians, and public for permission to serve in the armed
forces. Though African Americans had served honorably in both the American Revolution and the War of 1812, Lincoln rejected these overtures. In spite
of his strong anti-slavery sentiments, the president, like most white Americans,
questioned whether black men had either the will or ability to fight.[3] According to John David Smith, Lincoln considered the issue of black soldiery with
great deliberateness, charting "a far more linear course toward freedom than
his nineteenth-century critics and modern historians have recognized."[4] It
was thus an inauspicious beginning for the proponents of black soldiers. The
prospect of persuading Lincoln, the federal government, and the American
people of the military potential of black men was daunting. Nevertheless, abolitionists in crowded halls and auditoriums and in widely read newspapers,
books, and pamphlets deployed one of the irrefutable historical examples of
the efficacy of black troops.

   Louverture and the Haitian Revolution were potent weapons that abolitionists exploited to win a policy of black soldiery. It would be a mistake,
however, to credit abolitionists' strategic deployment of these weapons for
eventually securing such a policy. As the authors of a study of the use of
black soldiers throughout history maintain, the United States eventually employed black troops during the Civil War for the same reasons Europeans
had traditionally armed Africans throughout the Americas, "because the pre-
dominately white population was unable to continue filling the ranks that
commanders needed to settle the conflict."[5] Indeed, while the pragmatic and
calculated considerations of a wartime commander in chief do little to satisfy
Lincoln enthusiasts who want to remember the president as a transforma-
tional figure whose racial outlook transcended his time and place, it is hard to
imagine a scenario whereby Lincoln would have armed black men were it not
for the military necessity. This fact does not diminish the powerful influence
of the memory of the Haitian Revolution on the debate over black soldiers. Its
amplification by abolitionists in the first two years of the war played a pivotal

role in preparing the nation for a radical transformation in military policy, which circumstances encouraged and the president eventually embraced.

Abolitionist promotion of the heroic narrative of the Haitian Revolution began the moment the war commenced. In an item published in multiple print media in the first months of the war, Elizur Wright testified to the salience of Haitian history. In *The Lesson of St. Domingo: How to Make the War Short and the Peace Righteous*, the abolitionist editor and co-founder of the American Anti-Slavery Society encouraged Americans to remember Haiti's revolution, as it was the only event on record "parallel to our own present crisis." Wright explained that, with the rebellion of the Confederacy now under way, "the teachings of history are unspeakably important to our government at this moment." He summoned the memory of St. Domingo so that his country would not repeat the errors committed by the rulers of the French colony more than a half-century earlier, writing, "The pride and prejudice of race and color may be great luxuries, but St. Domingo can teach us what they cost." Wright drew an analogy between the black man's military record in St. Domingo and his potential to fight in the United States. Referring to African Americans as "as raw military power," he asked, "What is the lesson of this history? . . . Though the black material may be very raw, under proper guidance, it may soon be made effective." The lesson that Wright took from the Haitian Revolution was vital to the American republic: "You that have read, reflect! for, in history, as in physics, like causes produce like effects."[6] Wright's piece attracted numerous responses in the northern press, including a published letter from A. Tate, a captain in the Haitian Presidential Guard. "The History of Hayti, is," Tate wrote, "unhappily, too little known by Americans." This was fateful, for the parallels between the present condition of the United States and that in Haiti before the revolution were unmistakable. It was time to learn the lesson of the Haitian Revolution, "which God seems to have placed expressly in view of the Americans, to save their beautiful and flourishing country from the ruin and desolation with which slavery threatens it."[7]

The serialization of a lengthy article on the Haitian Revolution in the *Atlantic Monthly*, one of the most recognized periodicals in the nineteenth century, indicates the rising status of the revolution, which coincided with the debate over black soldiers. In "The Horrors of San Domingo," John Weiss played on the trope made familiar by generations of paranoid white slaveowners. The Unitarian minister and author understood the power of memory, explaining that northerners and southerners were the combatants in a longstanding history war. "In the two decades between 1840 and 1860 the American Union was seldom saved by a Northern statesman without the help of San Domingo," Weiss wrote. At the same time, "Southern men of intelligence had the best of reasons for understanding the phenomena of San Domingo, and while the 'Friends of the Black' were dripping with innocent French blood in Northern speeches, the embryo Secessionists at Nashville and Savannah strengthened their convictions with the proper rendering of the same history." Weiss recognized the impact of the Haitian Revolution on the sectional crisis over the decades. "San Domingo was helping to destroy the Union at the South while it was trying to save it at the North." Now, however, there was only one possible outcome. "Slavery will continue to be the great unimpaired war power of Southern institutions, till some color-bearer, white or black, in the name of law and order, shakes the stars of America over her inland fields." Weiss demanded historical revision, insisting that the "horrors of St. Domingo" in reality consisted of the brutal and bloody acts white planters committed against enslaved men and women. African Americans naturally shunned violence, but the "valor and fighting qualities" they displayed in the Haitian Revolution "were nourished by the wars which sprang from their own necessities." For slaves, "learning to fight was equivalent to learning to live." History taught a valuable lesson that Americans could not at this crucial time ignore: in Haiti bondmen fought their former masters for freedom and in the end emerged victorious.[8]

Eminent abolitionists throughout the Civil War weighed in on the debate on black soldiers by reprinting antebellum histories and biographies of the Haitian Revolution that highlighted the military success of black soldiers. New York City's lone black publisher, Thomas Hamilton, published William Wells Brown's *The Black Man: His Antecedents, His Genius, and His Achievements*, a collection of short biographies of fifty-eight of the greatest black men and women in history, including four soldiers of the Haitian Revolution: Louverture, his generals Henri Cristophe and Dessalines, and the mulatto leader Rigaud. Only the entry on Nat Turner exceeded in length that on Louverture. In *Toussaint L'Ouverture: Biography and Autobiography*, John Brown's loyal confidant James Redpath reprinted John Beard's 1853 biography of Louverture, along with a translation of a recently discovered transcript of Louverture's memoirs. Redpath stated in the introduction his reasoning behind the reprint: "*Are the Negroes fit for Soldiers?*" Only those who were "Ignorant of the history of Hayti, which forever settled the question," still had doubts. "'*Are Negroes fit for Officers?*' We are entering on the debate now. The Life of Toussaint may help to end it."[9]

The abolitionist press welcomed the new publications and enthusiastically promoted their distribution. William Lloyd Garrison's *Liberator* carried advertisements for Redpath's book. The editor considered the volume worthy of "a wide circulation—now that the employment of negro soldiers for the suppression of the Southern rebellion is the settled purpose of the Federal Government."[10] The *Boston Commonwealth* likewise noted the parallels between the events described in Redpath's biography and the current conflict. "For years the abolitionists of Europe and America have seen that we were coming in this country, to a repetition of some of the extraordinary incidents of Haytian history, and they have dwelt with emphasis on the career of Toussaint, the greatest military genius ever produced on this side of the ocean." Still, the paper maintained, no one on either side of the Atlantic "exhausted, or even approached the magnitude of their subject. It is impossible to dwell on the story of Toussaint without wonder approaching to credulity,—for certainly no man in modern days ever had such an astonishing career." Continuing the tradition established on the eve of the Civil War of maintaining the superiority of Haiti's founding father to those of the United States, the paper continued, "The difficulties against which Washington and our fathers contended were as nothing, when compared with those which this unlettered slave overcame." The review concluded with a direct plea for the relevance of the memory of Louverture and the Haitian Revolution: "It is of especial importance at this time, that these things should be known, and this prodigious page of history studied with care. We are performing, on the immense stage of a continent, the drama which went through its island-rehearsal in Hayti in the last decade of the last century. The capacity of the negro—*unassisted by the white man*, to raise, arm, discipline, command and conquer with great armies, was fully proved in the wars of Toussaint and Dessalines." The outcome of the present war was unknowable. Yet it was likely that "a chief like Toussaint may rise among our own Negroes."[11]

Louverture and the Haitian Revolution were for the advocates of black soldiery irresistible symbols of black valor. In the second year of the war, the *New York Evening Post* copied on its front page a letter to the editor that soon appeared in other papers. In it, John Weiss responded affirmatively to the question, "Will the Blacks Fight?" Citing the published memoirs of a French soldier who had fought against Louverture's army, Weiss testified to the bravery of black men in combat. Enslaved Haitians fought admirably and the same could be expected of enslaved Americans if given the opportunity. Weiss asserted, "The history of Hayti shows that the blacks will fight with enthusiasm whenever they are led by whites or by men of their own color, provided their steps never point again in the direction of slavery."[12] A New England writer responded to the same question with the following: "There is no instance, that we remember, of regular and protracted warfare between negroes and whites, save in the island of Hayti. We shall not now discuss the political aspects of the Haytien Revolutions, but barely examine them, to discover what light they shed on the question which has been raised." In Haiti, "The negroes manifested fortitude, courage and enthusiasm through the long war. They were intrepid in attack, steady and unflinching when assailed." They took on the best troops in the world and proved themselves worthy adversaries. "The history of the Haytien Revolution is positive proof that negroes *have* made good soldiers."[13]

The Haitian Revolution emboldened abolitionists to continue hammering away at the ideology of white supremacy, which suggested that black men lacked the masculine virtues inherit in combatants. Redpath in his biography described how Louverture in response to Napoleon's massive invasion that intended to return slavery to Haiti in 1802, decided on a policy of armed resistance and revealed his manly courage in the face of death declaring, "If I must die, I will die as a brave soldier, as a man of honor. I fear no one."[14] J. Miller McKim, founder of the Port Royal Relief Committee, responded in a widely disseminated public letter to an inquiry as to whether the black man possessed "the spirit—the *pluck*—to do his proper part in maintaining the status now, or hereafter assigned to him." Admitting southern slaves' aversion to insurrection, McKim suggested that in certain cases "it would not be safe to count confidently on their fighting qualities." Nevertheless, he asserted that black slaves had always, "when occasion required it" shown themselves "capable of the arts of war." The slave's record in Africa, the United States, "and in the history of San Domingo, furnish ample illustrations of this fact."[15] Insisting on the manhood of black men, Philadelphia minister Jonathan Gibbs recalled the glorious history of black soldiery, avowing, "What has made the name of Haiti a terror to tyrants and slaveholders throughout the world, but the terrible fourteen years' fight of black men against some of the best troops of Napoleon—and the black man wiped them out. There are some fights that the world will never forget, and among them is the fight of black men for liberty on the Island of Haiti."[16]

No author was as unyielding on the issue of whether the Haitian Revolution proved black manhood as William Wells Brown. The former bondman explained his motivation for publishing an anthology of great black men thus: "If this work shall aid in vindicating the Negro's character, and show that he is endowed with those intellectual and amiable qualities which adorn and dignify human nature, it will meet the most sanguine hopes of the writer." According to Brown, Haiti's founding fathers demonstrated the essential qualities of manly soldiers, even the "savage" Dessalines. "A more courageous man than he never lived," Brown wrote. Though exceeding the bounds of civilized warfare, Dessalines was worthy of emulation, for having scorned "effeminacy" and avenged centuries of cruelty. "Of all the heroic men which the boiling cauldron of the St. Domingo revolution threw upon its surface, for the purpose of meeting the tyrannical whites, of bringing down upon them terrible retribution for their long and cruel reign, and of vindicating the rights of the oppressed in that unfortunate island, the foremost place belongs to the African, the savage, the soldier, the general, the president, and lastly the emperor Jean Jacques Dessalines." Brown reserved even more laudatory language for Louverture, but in an effort to indicate the fighting qualities of ordinary men, he asserted that the bondmen who followed Louverture into battle were equally brave warriors. For years, they toiled slavishly for the benefit of others, but when the opportunity presented itself they "awoke as from an ominous dream, and demanded their rights with sword in hand." Upon the commencement of a terrible civil war, "the blacks were victorious in nearly all the battles." There was no reason to doubt that given a similar opportunity, American bondmen would perform equally.[17]

Anonymous letters published in northern newspapers during the Civil War promoting black soldiery illuminate the ascendancy of the heroic memory of the Haitian Revolution. The authors of these letters, whether they cited Louverture's accomplishments or those of the nameless and faceless black bondmen who fought alongside him, used the revolution to refute the racial myths put forth by the opponents of black soldiery. A writer in the *Salem Observer* remarked on the supposed docility of African Americans: "For ourselves, we have not much faith in the fighting qualities of the negro. His nature seems to be too kindly and mellow for such work." If African Americans were a fighting race, their bondage would have ceased long before. "But yet, Toussaint was a negro, and it was a black army which, in Hayti, routed and destroyed in field fights and in regular sieges, the best legions of France, fresh from the most famous fields of Europe." Memory of the Haitian Revolution led this skeptic to conclude, "the negro may make a fine soldier after all."[18] A Rhode Islander cited a long list of accomplished Africans as evidence of the military potential of African Americans. The cursory historical overview then gave way to a discussion of more recent events: "In view of these facts, no one can reasonably doubt that a large portion of the blacks of the South, as well as of the North, are capable, not only of working, but of being trained so as to render valuable service as soldiers." Black soldiers performed admirably on American battlefields before. The examples were numerous. "Gen. Jackson found black soldiers so brave and efficient at the battle of New Orleans, that he bestowed upon them a high public expression of praise. One of the greatest military heroes that ever appeared in connection with the history of this continent was Toussaint, a negro, who, in Hayti, led his army of blacks to victory in field fights and regular sieges against the veteran soldiers of France."[19]

A chaplain in the Union army who witnessed the organization of black regiments in Beaufort, South Carolina, struggled to contain his enthusiasm for the experiment that was occurring before his eyes. African Americans were finally going to take their place alongside the world's fighting races. In a letter published in the *Weekly Anglo-African*, he predicted that the enlistment of black men "will mark an epoch in the history of this civil war, and the effects upon the nation will continue for generations to come." It was well known that in colonial Saint-Domingue and then in Haiti black bondmen "fought and slaughtered the English, the French and Spanish with a courage, and—it must be admitted—a ferocity scarcely ever equaled." Such facts were "sufficient to prove that the fighting element is in the negro character; that in this respect he is like his fellowmen, and not an exception to all the other nationalities and tribes of earth. That he has suffered himself to be the victim of a most cruel and oppressive servitude is admitted; but that fact proves nothing against his spirit and manhood." Centuries of bondage had assuredly tested the spirit of the black man, but "if the incubus of slavery were removed, he would put on such a garb of manhood as would challenge our respect."[20]

Testimonials of revolutionary black violence were double-edged swords that required deft maneuvering. Given the stories and legends of the "horrors of St. Domingo," such evidence had the potential of discouraging support for the very public policy the advocates of black soldiery hoped to secure. Consequently, abolitionist speakers and writers made a concerted effort to amplify the construction of Louverture as a Great Man. His name was not commonly associated with the horrible acts of vengeance that Haitian slaves committed against white colonists; thus, abolitionists readily deployed it in an effort to conjure the more positive and comforting image of disciplined, orderly, and effective black troops. Wells Brown wrote that Louverture, "by his superior knowledge of the character of his race, his humanity, generosity, and courage, had gained the confidence of all whom he had under his command. The rapidity with which he travelled from post to post astonished every one. By his genius and surpassing activity, Toussaint levied fresh forces, raised the reputation of the army, and drove the English and Spanish from the island."[21] According to Phillips, Louverture was a man who manufactured an army out of what some called a

> despicable race of negroes, debased, demoralized by two hundred years of slavery, one hundred thousand of them imported into the island within four years, unable to speak a dialect intelligible even to each other. Yet out of this mixed, and, as you say, despicable mass, he forged a thunderbolt and hurled it at what? At the proudest blood in Europe, the Spaniard, and sent him home conquered; at the most warlike blood in Europe, the French, and put them under his feet; at the pluckiest in Europe, the English, and they skulked home to Jamaica.[22]

Louverture's biographers avowed that even after decades of servitude he bore no resentment toward whites. Wells Brown wrote, "One of his chief characteristics was his humanity. Before taking any part in the revolution, he aided his master's family to escape from the impending danger." He entered the army only "After seeing them beyond the reach of the revolutionary movement."[23] Redpath explained that in the opening years of the revolution "Conflagration raged everywhere. The mountains, covered with smoke and burning fragments, borne upwards by the wind, looked like volcanoes. The atmosphere, as if on fire, resembled a furnace." The signs of devastation were everywhere: "demolished edifices, smoldering embers, scattered and broken furniture, plate, and other precious articles overlooked by the marauders; the soil running with blood, dead bodies heaped the one on the other, mangled and mutilated, a prey to voracious birds and beasts." In this destruction, "Toussaint could take no part. Faithful to his owner, he, during a whole month, protected the plantation, at the head of the negroes, whom he greatly contributed to keep in obedience, and prevented the insurgents from setting the fields of sugar-cane on fire." As whites fled from the island, Louverture protected the lives of his former owners and overseer. Upon rising in the ranks of the revolutionary army, he then used his influence to allow them to emigrate."[24]

Abolitionists had always celebrated Louverture's effective use of violence. In the debate over black soldiery, however, it was just as important to remember that under his leadership armed bondmen responded to military discipline and rule. Louverture's attitude and actions were communicable, abolitionists insisted. One editorialist offered, "Before L'Ouverture gained the command, the blacks fought in predatory, guerilla bands, plundering, burning, and murdering; but he organized them into regular military organizations, disciplined them, and curbed their fierce and vindictive passions."[25] In the *Atlantic Monthly*, Weiss quoted Marcus Rainsford, who after witnessing a review of fifty thousand Haitian soldiers, recorded that the troops went through their routines "with a degree of expertness seldom witnessed, and performed equally well several manœuvers applicable to their method of fighting."[26] With the sound of a whistle, "a whole brigade ran three or four hundred yards, then, separating, threw themselves flat on the ground, changing to their backs or sides, keeping up a strong fire the whole of the time, till they were recalled; they then formed again, in an instant, into their wonted regularity." The men performed this exercise with unequaled facility and precision. "Such complete subordination, such promptitude and dexterity, prevailed the whole time, as would have astonished any European soldier." In the *New York Evening Post*, Weiss quoted Lacroix: "It was remarkable to see the Africans, half naked, with musket & sabre, giving an example of the severest discipline. They set out for a campaign with nothing to eat but maize, established themselves in towns without touching anything exposed for sale in the shops or pillaging the farmers who brought things to market. Supple & tremble before their officers, respectful to citizens, they seemed only to wish to obey the instinct for liberty which was inspired in them by Toussaint."[27] The point was clear. Under proper guidance, black men would not only fight; they would obey orders and refrain from committing wanton acts of violence.

The explosion of public memory of the Haitian Revolution that attended the debate over black soldiery indicates the extent to which Americans were reconsidering both their ideas on race and the future of the nation for which bondmen yearned to fight and, if necessary, die to preserve. The response to Phillips's oration "Toussaint L'Ouverture" was extraordinary. The *Boston Commonwealth* recommended to readers "This great speech giving the history of the NEGRO ARMIES OF ST. DOMINGO." Phillips's "noble panegyric" was the best account of Louverture's wonderful career, and it provided the ideal "answer to the absurd talk of those who say the negroes will not fight."[28] The *Weekly Anglo-African* alerted readers, "It will be instructive to read it in these times when men are praying for an insurrection, but doubting the military capacity of the Negro."[29] A writer in the *New York Tribune* avowed, "no subject could be more appropriate to the hour. We are debating whether we will let the Negro help save the Republic—whether he has courage to fight and capacity to be a soldier—and since that discussion is conducted on the other side by help of shrieks over the 'Horror of San Domingo,'" it was now more critical than ever that the public learn the "real history of the revolution in that island." The pro-slavery narratives of the revolution, which slandered Louverture "as the savage leader of a bloody insurrection," were fallacious. "Let those who believe him such, and those who doubt whether his race is worthy to fight for its own and the Nation's salvation, listen to-night to Mr. Phillips's brilliant eulogy of this Representative Negro as soldier, statesman, and patriot."[30]

Two performances of the lecture in New York City illustrate its reception. Advertisements filled prominent local papers in the days before both talks as well as on the days the addresses took place. The starting time for Phillips's first lecture, to take place on 11 March 1863 at the Cooper Institute, was 8 o'clock, with the doors opening a little after seven. The *New York Tribune* listed three agents who sold two hundred advance tickets for fifty cents, making the price of admission double that before the war. For those who waited to buy at the gate, the cost was half—but there was no guarantee that they would get a good seat or in the door at all.[31] The next night Phillips delivered the address again, this time at the Brooklyn Academy of Music. An additional number of vendors offered tickets, including the local branch of the Young Men's Christian Association, the lecture's official sponsor. Numerous papers reported on the lectures in the following days. The *New York Tribune* described "immense audiences" at both lectures, and following the second, concluded, "The heroic virtues, the military genius, and the statesman-like sagacity of Toussaint were illustrated, and his noble personal traits described in glowing eulogy by the orator. The enthusiastic applause of the audience showed how completely they sympathized with his opinions and convictions."[32]

A writer by the name of Junius reported his first-hand observations of the Brooklyn lecture in the *Christian Recorder*. "Desirous of hearing the silver-tongued orator on his favorite theme, I found my way there through a dense concourse of people. I looked eagerly to see if there were many colored persons present." Junius estimated the number of African Americans present at fifteen. "But the dense mass of whites were like bees, filling every place. The lecture was grand, and was well worth listening to."[33] Junius censured blacks for not attending the lecture in greater numbers. However, what we know about the readership of Garrison's *Liberator* and other abolitionist publications indicates that African Americans were among the largest consumers of "Toussaint L'Ouverture" in print form.[34] Nevertheless, Junius's account is revealing. In the decades before the Civil War, public memory of Louverture was to a great extent constricted within the parameters of black newspapers, homes, and meeting places. By the second year of the war, however, memory of Louverture spilled beyond the boundaries of African American culture. Now, when Wendell Phillips celebrated the life of the onetime Haitian bondman, white spectators filled the seats "like bees." And when Phillips placed Louverture's name above Washington on the list of history's Great Men they stood and applauded.

The reaction to Phillips's oration testifies to a Civil War culture that revolved around the memories of the Haitian Revolution, for the approbation the address received in concert halls and auditoriums paled in comparison to the reception audiences awarded it in print. In a remarkable transformation, book and newspaper publishers converted the panegyric into a mass-produced, widely consumed, and commodified piece of print culture. The ubiquitousness of "Toussaint Louverture" in Civil War-era print media has led some to overestimate the number of times Phillips actually delivered the lecture. One literary scholar contended it was "spoken more than a thousand times during the war years 1861–1865."[35] This was not the case. Yet its widespread circulation in print certainly makes it appear so. James McPherson's estimation that Phillips gave the speech "dozens of times" is accurate.[36]

The abolitionist press provided reproductions of the lecture in print form through the duration of the war. Just weeks after the war began, the address appeared in Thomas Hamilton's New York City *Weekly Anglo-African* and James Redpath's *Pine and Palm*, which he published simultaneously in Boston and New York.[37] The first issue of Redpath's paper included a detachable supplement entitled, "TOUSSAINT L'OUVERTURE: AN ORATION, BY WENDELL PHILLIPS."[38] It was a large full-page sheet, convenient for display. Redpath printed the lecture—which he copied from a version published in the *New York Herald* a year earlier—in its entirety, the last column reduced in size in order to fit on the paper. The public's demand for the supplement caught the editor by surprise, so much so that six months later the paper delivered the following plea: "If any of our readers have copies of the first number of The Pine and Palm, containing Wendell Phillips' speech on Toussaint L'Ouverture, they will confer a great favor by sending it to us. We printed 6,000 copies of that issue, but not one remains, even for our files."[39]

As the war progressed, publishers printed hundreds of thousands of editions of "Toussaint L'Ouverture." The popular abolitionist papers *Boston Commonwealth*, *National Anti-Slavery Standard*, and *Liberator* all published the lecture.[40] The *New York Tribune* likewise published the oration. No ordinary anti-slavery paper, it had a daily circulation in the tens of thousands and is regarded as the most widely read paper of the time.[41] Papers that reprinted "Toussaint L'Ouverture" provided readers with a tangible form of the lecture, a material piece of Phillip's oration. The articles, supplements, and extras allowed individual readers to share in the experience of the lecture and bring the revolutionary black icon into their shops, offices, and homes, even if they could not afford to attend a lecture. It also made the lecture available to those in rural areas outside the traditional lyceum circuit, where celebrities like Phillips rarely if ever performed. While only several hundred spectators saw Phillips lecture in New York City in March 1863, when the *Liberator* reprinted the speech as a part of its weekly publication, and later as a supplement, it expanded his audience immeasurably.

In addition to printing thousands of copies of Phillips's lecture, northern newspapers and periodicals secured its widespread distribution. The *Liberator* provided readers with the address of the anti-slavery office where they could obtain copies of the oration and remarked, "It has been delivered in many places, before crowded audiences, exciting intense interest and the highest gratification. Now let it be scattered broadcast." The paper encouraged other newspapers to reprint the speech "that the people may be able to read it." It also sold a "sheet" of the lecture individually for three cents, or by the "dozen or more" for two cents each.[42] Both the daily and semi-weekly edition of the *New York Tribune* included the oration and offered the following, "No more interesting reading can be sent to soldiers who are fighting our battles, and every person who has friends in the army should see that they are supplied." The paper advertised the bulk sale of prepackaged supplemental copies for five cents apiece, or three dollars per hundred." The price rose to four dollars if customers wanted delivery. The paper also provided the address where interested patrons could obtain copies in bundles of one hundred.[43] The *Boston Commonwealth* reprinted the lecture in its entirety, telling readers "it should be circulated every where." The paper additionally printed the speech as an extra, and offered it to consumers at two cents per copy, thirty cents per dozen, and $1.50 per hundred.[44] Uninformed consumers walked into the offices of the *Weekly Anglo-African* and paid 10 cents apiece.[45]

The preponderance of these newspaper extras makes it is easy to imagine standing on a crowded thoroughfare in any Northern city during the war and seeing among the cacophony of standard visual eye candy of the day— commercial advertisements, recruiting posters, and national flags—copies of "Toussaint L'Ouverture" displayed in public squares and in the windows and on the walls of restaurants, shops, and parlors. It is a striking portrait of northern popular culture during the Civil War. The panegyric of one of the greatest black men in history had moved from beyond the public culture of the lyceum and into the hands and homes of readers across the Union, from oral and print to material and visual culture.[46]

Phillips's delivery of the oration in Washington, D.C., in the spring of 1862 on the eve of the abolition of slavery in the nation's capital, underscores the transformation that was taking place in the collective consciousness of the American people. That a number of African Americans attended the lecture at the Smithsonian Institution and thus broke the institute's color bar further testifies to this metamorphosis. The lecture was, in the words of Michael Conlin, the "most anticipated" lecture of the year.[47] A Washington paper announced that those who wished to hear the lecture on "the States-man and Patriot of San Domingo" must arrive early, "or it will be impossible to gain admittance."[48] It was widely reported in the abolitionist press that Phillips met with the president on the day of the lecture, though, biographer James Brewer Stewart points outs, the two actually met earlier.[49] Whether the subject of the lecture came up in their conversation is unknown. We do know that John Hay, the president's private secretary, attended the lecture and recorded his impressions in his column, which appeared regularly in the local press:

> Wednesday evening was an epoch at Washington for those who believe that free discussion is the surest way to gain victory for great truths. The lecture hall of the Smithsonian was packed with attentive listeners— among them not a few of Southern birth—to hear Wendell Phillips, one of the pioneer-leaders of abolition, narrate the life of Toussant L'Overture, and endeavor to prove him superior to the leading white men of his time. Mr. Phillips is an orator, indeed; although apparently, at first glance, a calm, passionless Saxon. Yet when he begins to speak, his countenance glows with varied expression, his gesticulation is [as] graceful as the play of a golden willow in the wind, and the cadence of mournful music alternates with the gushes of power, as he gradually raises with affecting pathos, deep feeling, withering scorn, and biting

sarcasm, the negro-slave of St. Domingo to a position far higher than mortal man, of any color or race, has ever yet occupied.[50]

While scholars have acknowledged "Toussaint L'Ouverture" as one of Phillips's preeminent speeches, they have underestimated the cultural work it performed.[51] The oration impressed a generation of Americans who experienced the Civil War. One observer called it "the most magnificent specimen of eloquence to which any man of the present generation has given utterance."[52] Another remarked, "it was a vision of lofty inspiration under masterly control. And the assembled throng was powerless except to thunder its applause."[53] Nearly half a century after the war, George Edward Woodberry wrote of his youth, "I knew more about negro rights than Latin grammar, Santo Domingo better than the Peloponnesus." Regarding Phillips's oration, he continued, "I can remember the hour and the place when in my boyhood I discovered Shakspeare, Byron, Shelley, Carlyle, Scott, Tasso, Virgil, Homer; but there are some names I seem always to have known. The Bible, Washington, Whittier, Milton, William Tell, Algernon Sidney, Garibaldi, Toussaint L'Ouverture . . . I suppose I owe Toussaint L'Ouverture to Phillips."[54]

The lecture cemented Phillips's stature among America's men of letters, and gave him, in the words of one biographer, "the ear of the North as he never had before."[55] It also enabled his celebrity and professional status. Autograph collectors hounded him and audiences routinely filled auditoriums beyond capacity.[56] In the winter of 1861–1862, he received roughly two hundred invitations to lecture on Louverture and other subjects.[57] Horace Greeley indicated the market demand for Phillips's orations when commenting on a published anthology of Phillips's speeches that included "Toussaint L'Ouverture," "I doubt that any other living layman's collected speeches would sell so well as these."[58] Phillips was a committed reformer who sought change, not profit; nonetheless, his popularity indicates the commodification of the public memory of Louverture and the Haitian Revolution.[59] The popularity of "Toussaint L'Ouverture" during the Civil War motivated some years later to credit Phillips with steering the nation toward emancipation. Chauncey Depew was a successful New York lawyer and politician when Abraham Lincoln issued the Emancipation Proclamation. In a speech on his birthday in 1894, he recalled the halcyon days of the American Lyceum, noting the "lecture platform was at one time the place where a popular with convictions could express those convictions with effect, and have them reach the remotest corners of the earth." In the middle of the century, the nation's greatest orators "inculcated the most unpalatable truths of liberty." On the streets, men like Wendell Phillips were subjected to the mercy of the mob, "but on the lecture platform, in describing the life and deeds and the death of Toussaint L'Ouverture, he could drop the seeds of that truth which bore fruit upon the plains of Kansas and flowered in the Emancipation Proclamation of Abraham Lincoln."[60]

Richard Wheatley was an ordained minister and frequent contributor to postbellum Christian journals who also remembered the powerful effect of the oration. He never forgot that during the war Phillips "advocated liberation of the blacks as a war measure, and then enfranchisement of the emancipates as an act of national justice and self-defense. Like General Grant moving on Richmond, he was bent on fighting out the battle on that line if it took all time to do it, and like him he changed movement from front to flank as emergency required." The road to emancipation was "slow and halting," Wheatley explained, but "Phillips paved the road to consummation of hope by his marvelous lecture on *Toussaint L'Ouverture*, the Negro creator of the Haytian republic."[61]

Perhaps the greatest indicator of the bearing Phillips's lecture had on wartime public culture is the number of imitators it inspired. As Phillips was unable to quench Americans' thirst for the history of Louverture and the Haitian Revolution, a variety of writers, publishers, and orators responded to the call. Recognized abolitionists were among those who joined Phillips in talking about the Haitian Revolution during the war. William Wells Brown continued to perform his lecture on the Haitian Revolution, while William Lloyd Garrison and Frederick Douglass addressed the subject at length in public addresses. Lesser-known abolitionists likewise lectured on the Haitian Revolution. In New York City, grammar school principal and noted orator Alan M. Bland gave a series of lectures on Louverture. One observer noted that Bland's mastery of the facts of Louverture's life story made it appear "that he must have been a contemporary," and quoted Bland on the significance of Louverture's memory: "Toussaint needs no eulogy. No massive monument of finest Italian marble need rear its lofty pile to remind his country and the itinerant stranger that beneath its foundation stones are all of the once peerless Toussaint." The Haitian's "heart is his sepulcher, and his epitaph is engraven thereon. . . . To forget the noble Toussaint with his imperishable virtue, will be to forget the immortality of the soul."[62] Another reviewer encouraged readers to attend a performance of Bland's lecture, as the oration afforded "an opportunity to compare the black man's with the white man's thoughts on the renowned Haytien hero."[63] As far west as the Colorado Territory, William J. Hardin delivered a "masterly" oration on Louverture in the cities of Central and Black Hawk. It was a lecture especially appealing to the "intelligent people of color of the two cities on account of the prejudice existing in the mountain cities."[64]

Black women joined the chorus of male voices celebrating Louverture. Oneda DeBois, an American-born slave educated at Oberlin College who emigrated to Haiti and then returned to the United States, performed "Hayti and the Haitians" throughout the Northeast, from Philadelphia to Maine, in an effort to raise funds for Haitian schools.[65] In 1863, she crossed the Mason-Dixon Line and delivered the oration in Baltimore and Alexandria, Virginia.[66] In these southern locales, she performed under the name Oneda Woods, no doubt to conceal her status as a runaway. Performing in front of large audiences, she quoted Phillips's oration at length. Struck by the novelty of DeBois's nationality and gender, William Lloyd Garrison interviewed the talented speaker and described her as "highly intelligent and of pleasing address."[67] A writer in Philadelphia wrote that her oration was "exceedingly touching and elegant." It was a vindication of the black race, its soldiers, and "a well-deserved panegyric" on the Haitian Revolution.[68] The *Christian Recorder* asserted, "She was not a whit behind Wendell Phillips, in his great address on that sable personage."[69] DeBois was not the only woman to lecture on the Haitian Revolution. In New York City, Louisa DeMortie treated a large gathering of a local literary society to a reading of John Greenleaf Whittier's celebrated poem "Toussaint L'Ouverture."[70]

That high-ranking Union officers invoked Louverture and his army in public speeches advocating black soldiery underscores the entrenchment of the heroic narrative of the Haitian Revolution in northern memory. General Benjamin Franklin Butler invoked the Haitian Revolution in the defense of black soldiery in a speech delivered before a large and supportive audience in New York City. Commenting on the role that emancipated slaves might play in the Union Army, Butler added that no international law governed the employment of liberated slaves as soldiers. When asked, "Will the negroes fight?" he responded that he had no personal experience with freed slaves, but knew of their use as soldiers throughout history. He recalled how bondmen fought admirably in both the American Revolution and the War of 1812. If these national examples failed to convince listeners of the capacity of African Americans to fight, Butler added, "Let the veterans of Napoleon I under Leclerc, who were whipped out from San Domingo, say whether they will fight or not. . . . If you want to know more than that, I can only advise you to try them." According to one newspaper correspondent, the crowd responded to Butler's boast with "Great Applause." For those unable to attend the address, publishers quickly made the speech available in newspapers as well as in pamphlet form.[71]

In July 1862, an estimated 100,000 New Yorkers gathered in Union Square to demonstrate their support of the Union. A local writer described the patriotic scene: "From the hotels and housetops, and from the churches, the stars and stripes were displayed with the utmost profusion. The windows looking from the residences upon all sides of the Square were thrown up, and the balconies facing them filled with ladies and children, whose presence served greatly to add to the animation of the scene below. Broadway and the other thoroughfares leading to the Square were thronged with the multitudes who had closed their stores and workshops to attend the meeting." The diversity of the crowd was striking. "Every class and trade were represented. The wealthy millionaire, who had left the luxuries of a well-filled tables and dashed up in a splendid equipages, had come prepared to counsel with the hard-fisted laborer who had left mattock and spade, crow-bar and barrow, to devise means for maintaining the Union; and the voices of both were unanimous that 'it must and shall be preserved.'" In front of this enthusiastic and partisan throng, which according to one bystander "had no parallel on this continent," Colonel James Fairman stood at Stand No. 5. A well-known Unionist and member of the Seventy-Third New York Volunteers, also known as the Second Fire Zuoaves, Fairman urged those in front of him to remember the Haitian Revolution, when black slaves "under the leadership of a man born a slave, hurled the disciplined troops of two of the most warlike nations of Europe, quivering from their shores." This army of slaves never submitted. It was only through "a meanly contrived stratagem of the great Napoleon, and by it getting the person of L'Overture in his power, could France temporarily subdue the little island of Hayti."[72] It was the largest American crowd to hear someone talk about Louverture.

In spite of both the frequency and popular appeal of these addresses, it is important to remember that many northerners remained unconverted to abolitionism. Nevertheless, condemnation of Phillips and his oration does not detract from their significance. To the contrary, the public rejection of the lecture on Louverture underscores the subversiveness of his memory. Two examples will suffice. After the *New York Herald* published a copy of "Toussaint L'Ouverture," an editorialist questioned the decision of the paper to reproduce a speech that exalted a bondman "above Washington and every other historical hero in the world." Phillips lifted up Louverture as "a black deity, for the idolatrous worship of the republican party." What did Phillips really know of the real Louverture? There was no way to tell. Irrefutable was the present state of the black nation: "the negroes of the island have changed their humane white masters for cruel black ones, and private servitude for a military despotism. Disorder, revolution and civil war are their normal condition." Consequently, "to worship Toussaint as a hero and statesman superior to Washington is not more rational than to worship the bull of the ancient Egyptians as a deity superior to Christ."[73]

In front of an estimated crowd of 25,000 at a Democratic rally in Indianapolis, one speaker railed against abolitionists: "Fellow citizens, what is it these mad people will not do?" The founding father of the United States, "our own Washington, was placed below a barbarous, brutal and treacherous negro by Wendell Phillips." Referring to the oration recently given in Washington at the Smithsonian Institute, the speaker continued, "Mr. Phillips concluded with a glowing eulogy upon Toussaint L'Ouverture. He would call him a Cromwell, but he was a greater statesman than Cromwell; he would call him a Napoleon, but he did not make his way over broken oaths like Napoleon; he would call him Washington, but the great Virginian held slaves. Above all was the soldier, statesman, martyr Toussaint L'Ouverture." Phillips and his associates slandered "the brightest characters that illustrate the pages of our history. No character, however estimable, is safe from their attacks."[74]

When the enemies of abolition repeated Louverture's name in public lectures and orations, they recalled a defiant black man who conquered white armies and led a nation of slaves to freedom and national independence. When in newspapers and pamphlets they removed Louverture's name from atop those of Washington and Napoleon and placed it far beneath these two eminent white generals, they nonetheless acknowledging the existence of the name of a former bondman on the short list of the world's Great Men. Echoing Louverture's name in speeches and texts, those who steadfastly refused to join the march toward black freedom and equality traded in a revolutionary currency, which generations of abolitionists throughout the Atlantic world had used to build their movement to destroy both slavery and white supremacy.

Immediately after the commencement of the Civil War, African Americans and their white allies launched a public offensive to convince Lincoln, the federal government, and the American people of the military capability of black men. Though never donning the uniform, these abolitionist speakers and writers proved effective soldiers in the civil war of words. While their role in winning black soldiery is indeterminable, the widespread dissemination of their message indicates that a radicalization of public sentiment regarding African Americans' martial potential had taken place. The Civil War forced many Americans to reevaluate their ideas about race and nation, and Louverture's explosion in American popular culture suggests the widespread acceptance of the abolitionist narrative of the Haitian Revolution.

Abraham Lincoln was undoubtedly the most prized convert to abolitionism. With the number of battlefield casualties rising, sagging morale, and no end to the violence in sight, on 1 January 1863 he issued the Emancipation Proclamation. While the edict technically did little to effect the liberation of southern bondpeople, it nonetheless represented the most decisive stand ever taken by an American president against slavery.[75] Often overlooked is that the proclamation did something else as well. Lincoln wrote, "I further declare and make known, that such persons of suitable condition, will be received into the armed service of the United States to garrison forts, position, stations, and other places, and to man vessels of all sorts in said service."[76] With that, the United States government welcomed black men into the armed forces. It was this gesture, James McPherson maintains, which secured the revolutionary character of the war: "The organization of black regiments marked the transformation of a war to preserve the Union into a revolution to overthrow the old order. Lincoln's conversion from reluctance to enthusiasm about black soldiers signified the progress of this revolution."[77] In the next two years, more than two hundred thousand African Americans—the majority of them bondmen or former bondmen—served in the United States Army and Navy.[78] Not since the Haitian Revolution had so many black men waged war. The United States had in a very short time taken a dramatic turn, and increasingly the sectional war over slavery mirrored the other war over slavery that took place in Haiti at the turn of the nineteenth century.

"Emancipation or Insurrection":
Haiti and the End of Slavery in America

THE EMANCIPATION PROCLAMATION was not the first abolition of slavery in the Americas by executive fiat. Six decades earlier the radical French Jacobin Commissioner Léger Félicité Sonthonax arrived in Saint-Domingue and promised freedom and citizenship to all bondmen in rebellion who joined the French republican army. A year later, the French government affirmed Sonthonax's declaration and officially abolished slavery in the embattled colony and throughout its empire. It was an extraordinary turn of events, a watershed in the long history of slavery. More than a half-century later, one man cited this, the first federal abolition of slavery in the Americas, in an effort to manufacture a second. In *The War Powers of the President, and the Legislative Powers of Congress in Relation to Rebellion, Treason and Slavery*, William Whiting asserted that the French government's actions in 1794 established a precedent that the war powers of a commander in chief included the right to end slavery; consequently, Abraham Lincoln had similar authority.[1] It was an argument that many Americans bought, both figuratively and literally. *War Powers* went through ten editions in its first year of publication, and within a decade more than forty editions appeared. Readers purchased 30,000 copies of one edition alone, leading one writer to commend the book for the "profound impression it has made and is still making on the public mind in all parts of the country."[2] The book impressed Lincoln, who shortly after viewing the volume appointed Whiting solicitor of the War Department.[3] According to the portraitist Francis Carpenter, it was the president's frequent resort to the text in the days and months leading up to the Emancipation that prompted him, with Lincoln's approval, to include the book in his famous painting of the first reading of the Emancipation Proclamation.[4]

Whiting was not alone in using the Haitian Revolution during the Civil War to affect governmental policy regarding emancipation; however, most abolitionists employed a different tactic. Working under the assumption that a groundswell of popular support for abolition would move officials to embrace their radical agenda, they targeted the hearts and minds of ordinary Americans by delivering lectures and publishing pamphlets and articles, which warned of the danger of a second Haitian Revolution. While we have seen that memory of the "horrors of St. Domingo" was a potent weapon in the proslavery arsenal, our focus now turns to an exploration of how during the Civil War abolitionists seized the horrific narrative of the Haitian Revolution from the proslavery opposition in an attempt to convince the American people of the necessity of immediate emancipation. Abolitionists asserted that while American bondmen could make heroic and patriotic contributions on the battlefield, they also had the capacity to become uncontrollable and bloodthirsty rebel slaves. Enslaved people in the southern states patiently awaited the right opportunity to rise in unison, and every day that the war continued the likelihood of a violent upheaval increased. Thus, abolitionists insisted, the alternative to insurrection was emancipation.

Given the fear of revolutionary slave violence there were limits to the effectiveness of a strategy that relied so heavily on the prospect of a second Haitian Revolution. Consequently, abolitionists asserted that enslaved Americans would if emancipated become peaceful and effective free laborers, just as they had done in Haiti. Louverture proved the antidote to the widespread trepidation over the conduct of freed slaves, for it was understood that under his leadership nearly a half million freed people returned to their plantations, cultivated crops, and refrained from committing violent acts of vengeance upon their former white masters. Abolitionists promised nothing less of emancipated Americans. While they did not expect the freedmen to equal the greatness of Louverture, they were confident that under proper governance and guidance they would emulate Haiti's free and productive workforce at the close of the eighteenth century.

The use of Louverture to demonstrate the tractability of American bondpeople might suggest that abolitionists valued Louverture primarily as a safe and cautious symbol that reinforced the status quo. This, however, was not the case. The embracement of a militant black icon amid a terrible war that rang the death knell of slavery in the republic indicates that a revolutionary transformation was taking place. Louverture's preeminence in the wartime public discourse on emancipation illuminates how abolitionists successfully used his memory to shape popular perceptions of enslaved people. The construction of African Americans in the popular culture of the war in the image of a Great Man of African descent marked a transformative moment in which the American people imagined the United States as a new nation, one that would receive African Americans as free and equal members.

The avalanche of printed and spoken words of Louverture and the Haitian Revolution that the debate over emancipation triggered is anomalous. It challenges the historical literature, which suggests the limited effect of the revolution on the abolition of slavery over the Atlantic world. Prominent historians of slavery have observed the extent to which the revolution failed to secure abolition beyond its borders and instead provoked slaveowners to take measures to ensure the survival of the institution for decades. Seymour Drescher in his study of British abolition finds the revolution's impact on abolition negligible, concluding, "Whatever the primacy of St. Domingue's resistance in precipitating the first French emancipation, this formulation fails to demonstrate just how the revolution in Haiti generated British abolition or any of the subsequent emancipations by other Continental powers."[5] David Geggus contends, "An event of unique significance does not necessarily have uniquely significant repercussions," while David Brion Davis goes so far as to call independent Haiti "a godsend for the abolitionists' opponents."[6] The international impact of the revolution on the end of slavery is difficult to determine. Yet there is much to be gained by adjusting the vantage point from which historians have traditionally observed the revolution's influence. Focusing our lens on the middle of the nineteenth century and examining the war that ended slavery in the United States reveals a much clearer and sharper image.

When the Civil War came, abolitionists capitalized on the fear of a second Haitian Revolution to destroy slavery. It is not surprising that one of John Brown's former accomplices took the lead. Harvard-educated Transcendentalist Franklin Sanborn shared Brown's admiration of slave insurrection, and became on the eve of the Harpers Ferry invasion one of his most devoted followers and fundraisers. Years later, Sanborn published a 600-page biography and anthology of his "old friend" that reinforced the author's commitment to revolution.[7] Ironically, the book made no mention of Sanborn's rejection of slave violence in the aftermath of the Harpers Ferry raid. Following Brown's arrest, Sanborn denied having assisted Brown in preparing the Harpers Ferry invasion, fled to Canada to avoid arrest, refused to testify before a Senate committee investigating the raid, and discouraged other abolitionists from attempting to liberate Brown from jail. Though some of Sanborn's closest allies condemned these acts as desperate and cowardly, many of them shared his sudden lack of faith in Brown's tactics. Sanborn and other abolitionists were, as Jeffery Rossbach has shown, ambivalent about insurrection.[8]

Just days before the Confederate bombardment of Fort Sumter, Sanborn delivered a "sermon" at Music Hall in Boston entitled "EMANCIPATION," which the abolitionist press quickly disseminated and in at least one instance reprinted as a full-page supplement. Sanborn began, "I propose to preach to you to-day on Emancipation, the only safe Compromise, enforcing what I say by referring to the history and position of Hayti, the African Republic of the Antilles." He asked his audience whether they wished to see a repetition of the "horrors of St. Domingo" in the South. To avoid such a catastrophe, he argued, required emancipation. Without it, the South would receive "the dreadful punishment of St. Domingo." Sanborn insisted on a nation without slavery, for if it continued so did violent slave resistance. "Emancipation or insurrection," he avowed, were "the two alternatives." He spoke of Haiti as a nation "whose history teaches wisdom by the most trenchant example." The violent end of slavery in this French colony always mattered to the United States, but now it was especially important, as "our own slave states may act over the tragedy of St. Domingo,—now, of all times, we ought to study carefully these terrible chapters in that book of doom." Sanborn asked, "Has the story any moral for us?" The answer was yes. "The history of Hayti is set before us as a warning—as an example, too, could we have the wisdom and the courage to understand it." Sanborn demanded of his audience, "Read it, if you have the heart, in the sickening pages of St. Domingo's history." Slavery promised a race war, like the one in Haiti that resulted in the extermination of the "feebler white" race. He exhorted, "O my countrymen of the South!— brothers still, though steeped in the defilement of your inherited sin—will you not listen to these voices from the Past, from the graves of dead nations from the oracles of the living God?" He then offered an ultimatum: free your slaves, or face their wrath; learn from history, or repeat it.[9]

One of Sanborn's Harvard classmates amplified this argument in a widely read book that defended both the morality and legality of emancipation. Often overlooked by scholars of the abolitionist movement, Moncure Daniel Conway's story is extraordinary. The son of a prominent Virginia slaveowner, the precocious student moved to Boston, where he graduated from Harvard University and traveled in renowned Transcendentalist circles. Conway then found employment as a Unitarian preacher in Washington, D.C., a crucible of slavery, the internal slave trade, and the Underground Railroad.[10] Conway's time in the nation's capital was brief, for on expulsion from the proslavery First Unitarian Church for his radical views, he returned to the North to focus on abolition. Conway took the title of his influential book, *The Rejected Stone; or, Insurrection vs. Resurrection in America*, from the biblical verse, "The stone which the builders rejected is become the head of the corner. And whosoever shall fall on this stone shall be broken; but on whomsoever it shall fall it will grind him to powder" (Psalm 118:22).

For Conway, slavery was a grinding stone that threatened to pulverize the South. In a chapter on emancipation written in the form of a letter addressed to the president of the United States, Conway entreated Lincoln to abolish slavery so that the nation would forever link "its destiny with that of Universal Freedom." The world waited to see inscribed on the national standard, "IMMEDIATE AND UNCONDITIONAL EMANCIPATION." A policy of abolition was legal, constitutional, and moral, Conway asserted; without it, white southerners faced a horrible disaster. "There is, indeed, a possibility that 'the scenes of St. Domingo' may be repeated upon this continent; and it is not hard to foretell on whom the responsibility of their occurrence shall rest in such an event." In this highly idealistic tract that dreamed the republic would soon live up to its lofty ideals, Conway addressed a more pragmatic benefit of emancipation, writing of the southern bondman, "He *may* presently become a blind insurrectionist, and his wrath sweep like a conflagration through the land." Only then would the American people learn "that it was a false mercy to the South, and a great injustice to the whole country, that he was not (as he may be now) transformed into a controllable power and subject of the nation."[11]

Republican Party leader George Boutwell reminded an audience at Boston's Tremont Temple that even they had a vital interest in removing the threat of a second Haitian Revolution taking place in the South. The former Massachusetts governor delivered an impassioned address in which he called for the immediate abolition of slavery, and in anticipation of the response of his critics, asked, "What will you do . . . if you emancipate the slaves?" His response was, "My friend, what will you do if you don't?" The audience erupted. Boutwell then invoked Thomas Jefferson's familiar remark that if slaveowners did nothing about slavery they would become the murderers of their own children. Boutwell considered these "Terribly prophetic words! Terrible in the possibility of their fulfillment!" Abolition was both necessary and inevitable. Slaveowners would liberate their slaves peacefully, or slaves would take their freedom in their own bloody hands. Boutwell knew whether white southerners preferred peaceful emancipation like that in Jamaica, or the violent variety that occurred in the adjacent French colony? The answer was obvious. So instead he inquired of the northerners who sat before him, "after the sacrifices you have made in the service of slavery, the expenses in which you are involved, the just and righteous hatred you have for these leaders in the rebellion—I ask you if, after all this experience, you ought not to choose an emancipation such as took place in Jamaica, rather than reserve this question of slavery until emancipation takes place as it did in St. Domingo."[12]

Oberlin-educated teacher and writer Sara Stanley underscored the inevitable fate of any society built on the bedrock of slavery in a lengthy narrative published in the *Weekly Anglo-African*. "The St. Domingo struggle stands upon the historic page a dark, stern, terrible monitor to oppressors," she affirmed. "The uncomplaining slaves, who had so meekly and submissively worn their fetters, singing merry songs, under the burning sky while at their unrequited toil, and gaily dancing by moonlight in the orange and citrongroves to the sound of the castanet—suddenly, without a word of warning, threw off the delusive semblance of contentment and happiness they had so long maintained; and in fearful earnestness, with the violence and devastating fury of a hurricane, entered upon their bloody retaliative work." Once begun, there was no way to stop them. "In such a conflict the most vindictive passions were necessarily aroused; goaded to desperation by the accumulated wrongs of years, men thought only of their *allegiance to liberty*, of the tyranny which had outraged and virtually annihilated every prerogative of manhood, which supreme intelligence had declared sacred and inviolable; and the loud sanguinary cry went up from the ranks, LIBERTY FOR US, OR DEATH FOR YOU." There was no denying what then took place. "Barbarities which shock humanity were unhesitatingly practiced, tragedies the most terrible and revolting were enacted, and death and desolation followed in the footsteps of the infuriated, avenging army."[13]

Scare tactics were part and parcel of the abolitionist argument for emancipation. Instead of downplaying or even contextualizing the violence of the Haitian Revolution, they played it for all it was worth. Underscoring the likelihood of slave revolt to justify emancipation was a dangerous practice that occasionally polarized abolitionists into two camps. A writer in the *Weekly*

Anglo-African chastised James Redpath for so readily invoking the horrific narrative of the revolution in his abolitionist newspaper and asked, "Cannot our contemporary, the 'Pine and Palm,' see the gross impropriety of filling the fences and walls our city, and the advertising columns of our daily papers with "The Horrors of St. Domingo, while the public mind is considering the propriety and necessity of emancipating the Southern slaves?" The writer, a vocal opponent of black emigration to Haiti, wondered if Redpath's paper, "could not select, from all languages, three words which would do more to check a public feeling in favor of emancipation. Or, does it with cool diabolism, thus advertize the 'horrors' of emancipation, unaccompanied with expatriation—thereby hoping to drive grist into its own mill?"[14]

To counter the use of heavily racialized stereotypes of savage and violent black slaves, abolitionists went to great lengths to explain and qualify the troubling events that took place in Haiti. Defending the enslaved Haitians who many believed perpetrated the "horrors of St. Domingo," they reassured the public of fear of bondpeople. Among them was William Lloyd Garrison, who since 1831 had saturated nearly every page of every issue of the *Liberator* with his uncompromising stance on immediate emancipation; nevertheless, even his radicalism had limits. Garrison denounced violent abolitionism, and as numerous historians have shown, he throughout his career showed a strong aversion to slave insurrection.[15] In one of the first issues of the *Liberator*, Garrison acting as a spokesperson for American abolitionists declared, "We do not preach rebellion; no, but submission and peace." After denying abolitionist complicity in sparking violent slave resistance, he continued, "the possibility of a bloody slave insurrection at the south fills us with dismay."[16]

A near assassination and more than two decades of abolitionist agitation did little to affect Garrison's commitment to nonviolence. By 1859, however, his views began to change. The passage of the Fugitive Slave Act in 1850 and the Kansas-Nebraska Act in 1854 drew him and other abolitionists out of the pacifist camp. By the time of John Brown's raid, Garrison was reasoning that the end of immediate emancipation justified all means. Garrison saw the Harpers Ferry raid as a "misguided, and wild, apparently insane" venture. Still, he admitted a changing philosophy: "our views of war and bloodshed, even in the best of causes, are too well known to need repeating here; but let no one who glories in the revolutionary example of 1776, deny the right of the slaves to imitate the example of our fathers."[17]

The Civil War completed Garrison's transformation. In the summer of 1862, before an audience at Williams College in Massachusetts, he defended those in Saint-Domingue who shed blood in the zealous pursuit of liberty. What perturbed the editor especially was the racial double standard applied to the history of the Haitian Revolution; there was great irony in the fact that citizens of a nation founded on the universal rights of all men invoked the revolution in Haiti to warn against emancipation. Garrison wondered, "While every other people who have ever gallantly defended their rights and liberties when menaced, are esteemed and applauded, on what principle of justice are the unconquerable freemen of St. Domingo to be excluded from general approval and admiration? Gracious Heaven! to think of their brave but desperate efforts to save themselves and their posterity from yokes and fetters being held up, in this boasted land of freedom, in order to subserve the interests of Southern slavery, as attempts of emancipated slaves to cut their master's throats, in consequence of their liberation from bondage!" Though frustrated by the proslavery claim, he believed that such "historic falsification" would only contribute to the abolitionist cause: "The solemn and impressive lesson taught by St. Domingo is this—not the danger of letting the oppressed go free, but the madness and folly of seeking to turn freemen into slaves! It serves to make the position of the Abolitionists all the more impregnable, and to illustrate all the more strikingly the ignorance and folly of their opponents."[18]

U.S. Senator Charles Sumner agreed with Garrison on the portents of the Haitian Revolution. Shortly after Lincoln issued the preliminary Emancipation Proclamation, which gave the seceded states one hundred days to rejoin the Union or face the federally mandated abolition of slavery, Sumner vilified the opponents of the measure. In a speech at Faneuil Hall that enjoyed widespread distribution in newspapers and in pamphlet form, Sumner listed the most common objections to the proclamation and rebutted each of them. Atop the list were the effects the measure would have on both the border states and white soldiers in the Union Army and the idea that slavery was only a secondary issue in the war. Next on the list was "SLAVE INSURRECTION." Regarding this prevalent fear, Sumner with great sang froid offered the following: "God forbid that I should fail in any duty of humanity, or tenderness even; but I know no principle of war or of reason by which our rebels should be saved from the natural consequences of their own conduct." Confederates deserved whatever came. "When they rose against a paternal government, they set the example of insurrection, which has carried death to so many firesides. They cannot complain if their slaves, with better reason, follow it." Fear of slaves, according to Sumner, derived from a false impression of the bondman. "The story of St. Domingo, so often quoted against him, testifies to his humanity. It was only when Napoleon, in an evil hour, sought to re-enslave him, that those scenes of blood occurred which exhibit less the cruelty of the slave than the atrocious purposes of the white man. The African is not cruel, vindictive or harsh; but gentle, forgiving, and kind." Raised by a father who shared stories of his visit to Saint-Domingue at the close of the eighteenth century, Sumner concluded with authority, "Such is authentic history."[19]

James Redpath joined the chorus of abolitionist voices who contested the favorite bugaboo of the enemies of emancipation. He avowed that emancipation did not cause the "horrors of St. Domingo." Slavery did. *"Horrors of St. Domingo!"* was a cry that had "long been fraudulently used to excite the apprehensions of the ignorant and unthinking, and to prejudice society against a measure just in itself, and imminently politic, as well as humane." In the first year of the Civil War, Redpath's newspaper serialized M. St. Amand's sympathetic *History of the Revolutions in Hayti*, "In order that this pro-slavery bugbear might, as far as lay in our power, be set before the public, in the light of history, and stripped of that adventitious terror with which excited imaginations are accustomed to invest its vague outlines as they loom up through the mists of perverted traditions and exaggerated statements." Redpath accepted the dark side of Haitian history, explaining that the revolution was "stained with excesses equal in horror to those which two years desolated France and terrified the world—excesses unequalled in the sad catalogue of violence." There was for the "impartial student of history," however, a simple explanation. "For nearly three hundred years the blacks and their descendants had been the victims of the cruelest oppression and degradation that human ingenuity could devise." It was a "harvest of horrors" that "were attributable to the persistent refusal of the whites to ameliorate the wretched condition of the slaves, and not to the naturally ferocious disposition of their long suffering, and hitherto submissive victims." Redpath's qualification continued. When the colony's slaves rose against the white population, "they were as *merciful* as their oppressors had taught them to be." Even so, they only partially repaid the cruel debt that had accrued over time. "They merely cancelled the interest, leaving the principal to be liquidated by the impartial adjustment of God's providence." Redpath considered it a perversion of history to "cite the destructive effects of a vicious social condition as a reason for its reproduction and maintenance." The *"Horrors of St. Domingo,"* instead of proving the depravity of the black race, furnished the best argument for the eradication of slavery. Redpath concluded, "The lesson to be learned from that celebrated catastrophe is the folly of attempting to violate with impunity the laws which the Almighty has established for the well being of man."[20]

Abolitionist author and activist Lydia Maria Child recalled that the violence in Haiti was the result of the unwillingness of white colonists to grant rights to the colony's large black population. In *The Right Way the Safe Way*, the renowned abolitionist poet and writer asserted that the effort of the French to restore slavery was what provoked slave violence. "Whenever immediate emancipation is urged, the 'horrors of St. Domingo' are always brought forward to prove it dangerous." This was absurd. "All the disasters to the whites came in consequence of *withholding* those rights, in the first instance, and afterward from a forcible attempt to *take them away*, after they had long been peacefully and prosperously enjoyed under the protection of French laws." To prove the positive effects of emancipation in the United States, Child invoked the famous eyewitness account of the French general Pamphile Lacroix, who remarked of post-emancipation Saint-Domingue, "The Colony marched, as by enchantment, toward its ancient splendor; cultivation prospered, and every day furnished perceptible proofs of progress." She concluded, "SUCH WAS THE EFFECT OF EMANCIPATION IN ST. DOMINGO!"[21]

Articles published in some the nation's most widely read newspapers and periodicals, which qualified the bloodshed of the Haitian Revolution, played a key role in manufacturing public opinion on emancipation in the United States. The *New York Tribune* challenged those who employed the "Historical Bugaboo" of the Haitian Revolution to defend slavery. The author maintained that the screams of "St. Domingo" demonstrated clearly how "History is abused." The paper acknowledged that a racial bloodletting had taken place: that Haitian slaves "took ample revenge is not denied"; however, they acted within reason. "What caused them—who was in the right, and who was in fault—whether the Blacks did anything to be praised instead of blamed—these are minor considerations, unworthy of the attention of men who know absolutely nothing of that sad history, and who could not, for their lives, upon a cross-examination, tell us whether Toussaint was a black man or a white one, what he did while living, or where, or under what circumstances, he died." The French proclamation of emancipation did not provoke the slaves to insurrection; it instead allowed them to return to their plantations. It was not until the French army attempted to reenslave the population that the freedmen sought vengeance. "Such is the case of St. Domingo. Admitting all that the advocates of Human Bondage say of it, it proves nothing against Emancipation."[22]

A writer in *Harper's Weekly* likewise confessed the difficulty of interpreting history accurately. This was especially the case when examining an
event "that happened in another country many years ago, when the object
of the representation is the gratification of a malignant purpose, and when
the vehicle in which it is made is notoriously mercenary and untrustworthy,
every reader ought to remember that he is probably reading the grossest falsehoods." Writers ordinarily subjected the history of the Haitian Revolution
to the "most stupendous and malicious falsehoods." Here was the truth: enslaved Saint-Domingans revolted only after seeing "the whites and mulattoes
ferociously fighting, the one party for equal rights, the other for exclusive
privilege." It was undoubtedly a terrible insurrection of slaves, "but it was not
the result of emancipation, for they were not freed; it was the consequence of
slavery." It was during the ensuing period of anarchy that the French abolished slavery throughout the colony. Emancipation led not to chaos but to
order. Louverture recalled the fugitive planters and converted the former
slaves into wage laborers. "The island became once more peaceful, prosperous, and happy, as every state must be where justice is the fundamental law."
The "horrors of St. Domingo" took place only when the French army arrived
in 1802 to reenslave the freedmen. The paper implored, "Let it be constantly
remembered, then, that 'the horrors of St. Domingo' began three years before
the slaves were emancipated, and began because they were not liberated. They
ceased with freedom, and they revived with the attempt to restore slavery."
The truth was that "The trouble of insurrection springs from slavery, and not
from liberty." The similarities between the events on Haiti and in the United
States were undeniable. "The point for us all to remember, as men and citizens, is that it is always more dangerous to the public peace to treat men as
brutes than as human beings."[23]

While pondering the vicissitudes of history, the editor of *Harper's New
Monthly Magazine* arrived at a discussion of the Haitian Revolution. "There
are historical points the truth of which we are in a position to determine,
which are almost universally misrepresented and misused," the column
began. "One of these misrepresentations in just now very current in this
country. The story of the Saint Domingo insurrection is constantly told, and
told untruly." This was important to acknowledge, for such falsification could
easily be exploited toward pernicious ends. "The usual understanding is that
the slaves of that island rose against their masters, and, under the lead of
Touissaint L'Ouverture, committed nameless horrors until the island was virtually depopulated and the earth shook with horror." Who was responsible?

"It is a question that all of us will have to answer in the next ten years; and it is one with whose correct answer we ought to be familiar." Standard histories of slavery in both the French and British West Indies explained why the real story of the emancipation was still, in fact, unfamiliar. "The real authorities upon the subject are not Bryan Edwards and the English planters, but, rather, indifferent French eye-witnesses, who report what they saw. Dallas, who wrote the, 'History of the Maroons,' was a West Indian by birth, and Bryan Edwards lived there for many years. Of his history, which is one of 'no-gentleman's-library-without,' kind, the cool Mc'Culloch says that is shows 'a disposition to extenuate the cruelties that were too often inflicted upon the slaves.'" The French and Haitian historians Victor Schoelcher and Ardouin, "with the French memoirs of the time and place, are the proper sources of information." The controversy offered a valuable lesson on emancipation: "In our country the question involved in the matter is shifting from a question of slavery to that of the colored race; and no man who wishes to think and act as every honest man should, that is to say, with intelligence, upon the subject, will allow himself to be swept away by any generalizations of men whose immediate interest prompts them to cherish prejudice."[24]

Invocations of Louverture in the national publications of the preeminent New York City publishing firm Harper and Brothers suggest the ascendancy of the heroic narrative of the Haitian Revolution in American memory, which coincided with the Emancipation Proclamation.[25] It moreover demonstrates Louverture's elevated status in American public culture—never before had so many Americans acknowledged his greatness. A reviewer of Redpath's biography *Toussaint L'Ouverture* maintained that it was imperative to remember Louverture as the nation prepared to receive the freedmen as both free and equal members. Though his name was "vaguely known through the century," his autobiography was now "of the profoundest interest to all of us." Louverture "was born a black African slave, and he died the victim of the jealousy and falsity of Napoleon Bonaparte, after having drawn order and peace out of 'the horrors of St. Domingo.'" There was, nevertheless, great value in his life story. "Whoever would know exactly what those horrors were must read this book; and he will learn, as no well-informed student longer doubts, that they sprang from the baseness and selfishness of the whites, and not from the savage blood-thirstiness of the blacks. A more instructive and tragical tale was never told." Of Redpath's book the writer concluded, "We commend it to every thoughtful American citizen."[26]

In a nation divided by war amid a social and political revolution, memory of Louverture survived, like that of most Great Men, as a reassuring symbol of reason and moderation. Sanborn remarked that following the initial slave revolt of 1791 and the subsequent emancipation of the slaves, the situation was grim in Saint-Domingue until "an old plantation slave" rescued the colony and returned it to its former greatness. He quoted Rainsford at length, concluding that under Louverture slaves worked, obeyed laws, and thrived under a written Constitution. Had he lived, "St. Domingo would have continued to grow in wealth and power, and would have become a century sooner what it must yet be—a great nation of civilized Africans."[27] Redpath called Louverture's Code Rural the "most successful solution of the difficulties in the way of emancipation, ever yet attempted anywhere." Louverture bore no resentment toward the white planters. "This negro, himself a freed slave, brought back the whole laboring class of freed slaves from the forced idleness of civil war to the faithful service of their old master. They worked for pay, but they worked as well as under the whip of the overseer. Prosperity returned to the decimated Island. Her trade increased wonderfully; her people were strictly governed, but they were happy, and they were rising in civilization."[28] The *National Anti-Slavery Standard* recounted that after securing peace Louverture turned his attention to establishing both law and order. It was a difficult task, "far worse than a similar work would be in our Southern States." A decade of civil war was poor training for the "semi-barbarous" freedmen of Saint-Domingue. Fortunately, "Toussaint, by a well-devised code of labor, brought them back to the service of their old masters, and in a few years had well nigh restored the former prosperity of the colony."[29]

The construction of Louverture as a republican citizen soldier is evident in these descriptions. He was a Great Man who, after claiming victory on the battlefield, restored law and order. But it was Louverture the sentimental slave that abolitionists readily put forth when imagining the revolutionary transformation of former slaves into free laborers. In an effort to shape the attitudes and behavior of freedmen, abolitionists resurrected the romantically racialized bondman constructed by moderate British abolitionists before the war. Those who packed their bags and traveled south to aid the freedmen during the war brought the memory of Louverture with them in an effort to assist the freedmen in the transition from slavery to freedom. Motivated in part by their own fears of a repetition of the "horrors of St. Domingo," they encouraged his memory among the former slaves in an effort to remake them as free people in his image. Though Louverture set a standard that few slaves could attain, abolitionists were confident freedmen and freedwomen in the South could mimic their counterparts in Haiti, who prospered under his leadership. The use of Louverture as a symbol of moderation is revealed in a novel published in 1865, when a plantation mistress addresses a crowd of freedmen and implores, "Be patient and strive in the humble ways, for there are Toussaint L'Ouvertures innumerable, among your people, who are worthy the martyr's crown, or, better still, the laurel of liberty. The good God's day has not yet come for your perfect emancipation, but the blush of its dawn is upon you. Be patient!"[30]

Public celebrations of emancipation presented an ideal occasion for abolitionists to revive the public memory of Louverture among the freedmen. More than three thousand abolitionists, soldiers, educators, dignitaries, and freedmen gathered in Charleston, South Carolina, to celebrate the first anniversary of emancipation. The event was resplendent with marches, speeches, and ceremony. At Camp Shaw, a flag bearing the stars and stripes floated above a series of large arches above the speaker's stand, alongside the names of America's greatest men, "Washington, Lincoln, Toussaint L'Ouverture, John Brown, Shaw and Adams." On hand for the event were members of the Fifty-Fourth Massachusetts, including Toussaint L'Ouverture Delany. "It was," wrote one witness, "a great day for the sable sons of Africa, who reigned supreme, demanding and receiving the adoration of their white brethren."[31]

In Washington, D.C., a local Contraband Relief Association hosted an emancipation celebration at the Fifteenth Street Presbyterian Church. William E. Matthews of Baltimore spoke of the ancient tradition of commemorating significant events. Intimating that the Fourth of July was still not a legitimate holiday for African Americans, he offered alternatives. "The colored people should celebrate the birthdays of their great men." In addition to the birthdays of the African soldier Hannibal and the Maryland mathematician Benjamin Banneker, they should observe the birth of Louverture, "who worked successfully the greater than mathematical problem that they who would be free must strike the first blow." It was essential that African Americans never forget the name of the man who "turned Hayti from a hell of slavery to a paradise of freedom."[32]

Some reformers who relocated among the freedmen were especially qualified to disseminate the memory of Louverture and the revolution among the freedmen. They had been to Haiti and could speak with certainly of the legacy of freedom among the Haitian people. There was Hamilton Wilcox Pierson, an agent for the American Tract Society, who before the war traveled to Haiti to distribute French-language Bibles. When prospects for Bible distribution diminished, he returned to the United States and continued proselytizing in Kentucky. During the Civil War, Pierson relocated to Washington and then northern Virginia, where he taught both contrabands and black soldiers. By February 1862, Pierson oversaw the distribution of 100,000 pages of literature to contrabands at Fort Monroe in Hampton, Virginia, and Port Royal in Beaufort, South Carolina.[33] Frances Dana Gage also spent time in Haiti as a missionary and later moved to the South to aid the freedmen. Throughout the war, her articles regarding life among the contrabands were widely circulated in the abolitionist press.[34] It is likely that both Pierson and Gage shared their tales of the Haitian people and their history with the freedmen.

Charlotte Forten had never been to Haiti, but as an autodidact of Haitian history she admired the men and women who penned the prominent works on the Haitian Revolution—among them Wendell Phillips, William Wells Brown, Lydia Maria Child, and Harriet Martineau—and eventually befriended all of them. Evidence that Forten's interests informed her teaching when working as a teacher among the freedmen in South Carolina comes from an entry in her journal that reads, "Talked to children a little while to-day about the noble Toussaint." The students showed great interest. "It is well that they sh'ld know what one of their own color c'ld do for his race. I long to inspire them with courage and ambition (of a noble sort,) and high purpose."[35]

Like Forten, Sara Stanley never visited Haiti. Nevertheless, in her narrative of the Haitian Revolution that appeared in the *Weekly Anglo-African*, she celebrated the extraordinary rise of Louverture, who was formerly "A negro slave, a mere chattel, an automatic thing! Despised, execrated, brutalized!" Death did little to erase the accomplishments of this Great Man and the men and women in Haiti who freed themselves from bondage, Stanley avowed. "The name of Toussaint L'Ouverture coruscates upon the page of history a prefiguring symbol, a stern prophecy of the future; more radiant, far than any name inscribed thereon—as the greatest spirit among the only race of slaves, who have demonstrated their ability to effect their own enfranchisement by individual power, unaided by any extraneous influence." Stanley closed with the famous sonnet of the British poet William Wordsworth:

"Toussaint! thou has left behind
Powers that will work for thee; air, earth and skies,—

There's not a breathing of the common wind,
That will forget thee: thou hast great allies.
Thy friends are exultations, agonies
And love, and man's unconquerable mind."[36]

There is little doubt that when Stanley taught freedmen in Virginia, Missouri, Kentucky, and Alabama, she shared her admiration of Louverture with her students, and encouraged them to aspire to his greatness.[37]

Schoolbooks distributed among the freedmen revealed that the white race did not have a monopoly on Great Men. Lydia Maria Child's *Freedmen's Book* and the American Tract Society's *Freedman's Third Reader* filled the boxes and crates of printed matter that northern abolitionists sent south in order to educate the freedmen. Instructing readers on how to become productive citizens, both offered short biographies of the Haitian founding father, as he was an ideal model for the freedmen to emulate. Child explained in the introduction to the *Freedmen's Book*, "I have made this book to encourage you to exertion by examples of what colored people are capable of doing. . . . Probably none of you will be called to govern a state as Toussaint L'Ouverture did; for such a remarkable career as his does not happen once in hundreds of years." Though few African Americans could equal the accomplishments of Louverture, Child nevertheless insisted on the importance of his memory at this critical time. "Well may the Freedmen of the United States take pride in Toussaint l'Ouverture, as the man who made an opening of freedom for their oppressed race, and by the greatness of his character and achievements proved the capabilities of Black Men." The *Third Reader*, the third installment of the American Tracts Society's educational primer, included a three-part biography of Louverture. The piece, which exceeded in length the other biographies of Great Men except that of Abraham Lincoln, opened with a translation of the oft-repeated opening line from Michaud's *Universal Biography* that Louverture was "one of the most extraordinary men of an age when extraordinary men were numerous." To assist the freedmen in remembering this name, the text included its phonetic spelling: "Toussaint L'Ouverture, pronounced Toosang Loo-ver-ture."[38]

What separates these biographical sketches from most published by abolitionists during the Civil War is their construction of Louverture as a sentimental slave. Like the biographies by Henry Gardiner Adams, Wilson Armistead, John Beard, and Harriet Martineau published before the war, these texts emasculated Louverture by depicting him as a moderate, deferential, and accommodating former rebel slave whose motto was "No Retaliation." Child especially admired Louverture's refusal to aid in the initial outbreak of violence in 1791, and though he eventually joined the slave uprising he "resolved not to take part in their barbarities." He ultimately became a leader not for any personal gain, but "that he might protect the ignorant masses, and restrain those who were disposed to cruelty."[39] The *Third Reader* described Louverture as a slave who because of good conduct and superb character earned the esteem of his master. During the revolution, he joined his brethren in arms, but he had no feelings of revenge to gratify. He remained the "same amiable and charitable person as ever." His devotion to his master outlived the insurrection, for he risked his life to aid his master's family and send them to America. Louverture rose in rank, and "The first use which he made of his power was to establish order and discipline among the blacks. To this they readily submitted; and peace and prosperity in that beautiful island were the result of his incessant and most benevolent labors."[40]

Avoiding a discussion of Louverture's use of violence, both books revised his biography to inculcate in the freedmen the middle-class virtues of economy, industry, and family. Child noted that, in spite of his fame, Louverture dressed simply and deferred to others. "His food consisted of vegetable preparations, and he drank water only." According to the *Third Reader*, Louverture was "simple in his dress, his food, and all his habits. Cakes and fruit, with a glass of water, made him a good meal." Because of his rule, the colony prospered. On the plantation, the freedmen worked faithfully, and "upon receiving the wages of their labor, were contented, obedient, and industrious. They submitted to wise regulations and necessary authority; and, being free, were satisfied and happy." According to both volumes, Louverture's manhood derived not from his military prowess, but rather from the love and respect for his wife and family. Child noted, "No trait in the character of Toussaint Breda was stronger than his domestic affections . . . he was always clean in his manners and language." The *Third Reader* noted Louverture's great contentment both at home and in the field. He married at an early age and remained "faithful and affectionate," and wrote of his life on the plantation, "We labored in the fields, my wife and I, hand in hand, and were scarcely conscious of fatigue. Heaven always blessed our toil, giving us not only an abundance for our own wants, but the pleasure of bestowing food on our fellow-blacks who needed it. This I greatly enjoyed." The Sabbath was a special day for Louverture, as he always attended church with his family. He lived a life of great probity and abstemiousness, and this example taught a nation of former slaves "that virtue, order, industry, and necessary self-restraint, were, under God, the only and sufficient guaranty of civil and social liberty."[41]

In the earliest days of the federal offensive to assist the freedmen that became known as Reconstruction, the discipline and order Louverture demanded of former slaves at times provided a defense for the army's imposition of harsh restrictions on the South's newly freed black population. Writing in the *Liberator*, the renowned Spiritualist Levi Judd Pardee contended that with assistance from the North, freedmen would rise like Louverture "from the glooms of social obscurity and the house of bondage." In the wake of emancipation, the question now was labor, and the man responsible for providing answers was Nathaniel Banks, the former Governor of Massachusetts and recently appointed Commander of the Department of the Gulf. That some vilified Banks' disciplinary measures among the freedmen troubled Pardee, who noted, "No man jumps into manhood." Pardee wondered, "Should the late Governor of this noble Commonwealth be blamed for that which the inspiration and insight of Toussaint himself, once a slave, under almost similar circumstances, though not so complicated, suggested and advised?" The history of Haiti provided the answer. "Let the right arm of military power, wielded as a parent and friend should wield it, be extended over the emancipated. As many of the blacks as have gone beyond its adaptation will readily, peacefully glide from it." Pardee concluded, "For one, I am satisfied with the past, and rest secure in the assurance of the future."[42]

Banks himself used Louverture to justify firm rule. Having spent a considerable amount of time among the freedmen, he felt secure explaining their needs. What the slave "asks and what he demands is, that his children shall be educated, that his family shall be held sacred, and his wife and children relieved from the hardship of field labor as soon as possible. That is what he demands, and nothing more than that." These were reasonable requests, and granting them was not a new idea. "It has been tried for three-quarters of a century. Toussaint L'Ouverture tried the experiment himself, for his own countrymen, in the West India Islands, and there is nothing different in his system from that which we have adopted, except that his was infinitely more severe than ours." Louverture forced laborers to return to the plantations of their masters and required them to stay put. To leave required the consent of either a magistrate or an employer. Louverture placed men in command who were both tyrannical and violent, and, under his orders, hanged any laborer found guilty of the smallest crime "as an example to the rest." The actions of the U.S. army regarding the employment of the freedmen were, Banks asserted, tame in comparison.[43]

The appropriation of Louverture to justify an oppressive post-emancipation labor system seems to indicate a conservative strain that may have underpinned Reconstruction. In fact, the opposite is the case. Eric Foner writes that Banks's plan was "an anomaly born of the exigencies of war, ideology, and politics." Though deeply flawed, the "compulsory system" of labor "substantially increased wages and required planter to supply laborers with garden plots, permitted the freedmen to choose their employers, and allowed black children to attend schools financed by a property tax."[44] Considering this, we can conclude that the use of Louverture to support Banks's controversial free labor system reinforced the subversiveness of his memory. Whenever soldiers, officers, and officials rooted their arguments for various strategies to aid former slaves in the history of the Haitian Revolution, they accelerated the transformation of the United States into a new republic that welcomed African Americans not only as soldiers but also as citizens. In the final analysis, Louverture's iconicism indicates an important radicalization of public sentiment that accompanied both emancipation and the beginning of Reconstruction. For, as we have seen, his greatness not only undermined slavery, it subverted the white supremacist ideology upon which Americans had built the institution.

While the symbol of Louverture resonated in transatlantic abolitionist culture for decades, in both volume and intensity the explosion of popular interest in Louverture during the Civil War was unprecedented. In the days, months, and years surrounding the Emancipation Proclamation, speakers and writers immortalized Louverture in American popular culture. Publishers sold his memoirs and reprinted and serialized versions of popular biographies of him written by respected authors. Editors inserted biographical sketches of Louverture in widely read anthologies, periodicals, and newspapers. Louverture's reach extended beyond print culture to material and visual culture, as collectors of autographs, portraits, and other ephemera vied for valuable pieces. Biographies of Louverture published during the war included reproductions of his autograph and made the inclusion a part of their commercial advertisements. One trade circular described the auction of a collection of rare autographs owned by Edward M. Thomas, an African American who had for years worked as a messenger to the House of Representatives. Among "the most important" signature's was that of Louverture, which sold for $5.50, a price that equaled that of a signed letter by Thomas Jefferson.[45]

Louverture's image appeared on the pages of newspapers, magazines, and books. In 1864, Jacob Snider, Jr., of Philadelphia presented a portrait of Louverture to a committee established to raise funds for the family of a recently deceased abolitionist. The paper assured that the image did justice to Louverture's blackness, writing that it was "unmistakably that of a pure African." The paper further testified to the portrait's authenticity by detailing some of its physical markings. "On the back of the frame there are wax impressions of three seals, one bearing his [Louverture's] own effigy."[46] In order to obtain the portrait, Snider traded a painting he owned of George Washington with John Bigelow, who, in addition to being a fanatical student of Louverture and the Haitian Revolution, was a prominent abolitionist and associate of Abraham Lincoln who during the war served as U.S. consul in Paris.[47] The barter among friends reminds us that during the Civil War some preferred even the image of Louverture to Washington.

In Detroit, newspaper correspondent Toussaint L'Ouverture Lambert praised the "colored women of the city" who had formed the Ladies Freemen's Relief and Educational Society to aid the freedmen and organized a fair to raise funds. As word spread of the event, white women joined the group, which then decided to make the event a large State Fair. Following the suggestion of "one of the colored members of the Committee," the group reinforced its biracial character by promising to direct proceeds towards white refugees in the South, in addition to the freedmen. The Society held the fair at Merrill Hall in the third week of March. Among the exhibitors were Barnum's Museum and the Post Office. Two large paintings suspended from the ceiling greeted patrons in the main Hall. "One was a powerful portrait of Col. Shaw of the 54th Mass, who fell at Fort Wagner, painted and donated to the fair by Mr. L. T. Iver, the other was a portrait of the celebrated 'Toussaint L'Ouverture,' hero of St. Domingo, painted by Koal of Paris." Lambert exhibited a degree of satisfaction that the portrait of his namesake sold for $300. Shaw's went for $75.[48]

The clamor for visual representations of Louverture transcended boundaries of race and gender. Alice Fahs describes the transformation of visual representations of African Americans in popular literature over the course of the Civil War. Though avoiding a discussion of the image of Louverture, its prevalence in the visual culture of the war reinforces her argument that while at the outset of the conflict African Americans appeared normally in popular media as racial caricatures, "in the months leading up to and following emancipation, particularly as more and more Northerners argued for the employment of black men as soldiers, such images gave way to illustrations that articulated and celebrated black manhood and even, occasionally, black heroism."[49] In addition to inflecting the debate on emancipation, the images, words, and relics of Louverture that Americans produced and consumed during the Civil War helped shape popular conceptions of the millions of men and women in bondage whose liberation the war produced. Though exceptional, Louverture provided a model of the constructive ways that millions of newly freed bondpeople would respond to freedom. He was a reassuring symbol of the new role that African Americans would play in a society without slavery.

The amplification of the memory of a Great Man of African descent in the popular culture of the Civil War is significant for another reason as well. It suggested the unlimited possibilities that had opened to United States since it had finally cleansed itself of the original sin of slavery. Memory of both Louverture and the enslaved people he guided toward freedom and equality, equipped the American people with powerful symbols that allowed them to imagine the United States as a new nation, one that would extend the opportunities of citizenship to all people, regardless of race. Abolitionists' use of Louverture in the debate over emancipation amplifies the findings of the previous chapters that the seeds of the Civil War were planted in the revolutionary eighteenth-century Atlantic world. That the first terrible war over slavery in the Americas would greatly effect the second is expected. But during the Civil War, memory of the Haitian Revolution influenced the American people in various ways beyond the highly charged political issues of slavery, secession, black soldiery, and emancipation. In the following chapters, we consider its impact on the construction of several collective identities, which following the war impeded the development of a transcendent national identity and instead set the stage for various conflicts that would plague the reunited republic in the postwar years.

PART III

Nations Within a Nation

CHAPTER 6

"Many a Touissant L'Overture Amongst us": Black Identity

FREDERICK DOUGLASS WHEN enslaved on the Eastern Shore of Maryland was a serial runaway who eventually succeeded in securing his freedom. But it was always his decision to fight the vicious overseer Edward Covey that he credited with making him a man: "I was a changed being after that fight. I was nothing before; I WAS A MAN NOW."[1] Douglass's faith in masculine violence made the Haitian Revolution an attractive symbol to him and countless other black men, because in Haiti hundreds of thousands of bondmen employed violence to win their freedom and disproved the theory of white supremacy.[2] Douglass revered the black republic and identified with its people. He especially admired Louverture, a man many compared to Douglass himself.[3] Douglass invoked Haiti's founding father in a popular oration delivered on the antebellum lyceum circuit, insisting, "In an age of great men he [Toussaint] towered among the tallest of his times."[4] Only a month before the start of the Civil War, Douglass wrote in his monthly paper, "A dream, fondly indulged, a desire, long cherished, and a purpose, long meditated, are now quite likely to be realized." The future United States ambassador to Haiti was to sail for the black republic, "the theatre of many stirring events and heroic achievements, the work of a people, bone of our bone, and flesh of our flesh." Having nearly given up on his dream of making the United States a land of liberty and equality for all, the long-time opponent of colonization planned to explore Haiti's prospects as a location for black emigrants, including himself. Only the start of the war kept him from making the trip.[5]

During the war, Douglass exploited the public memory of the Haitian Revolution among African Americans in an effort to increase the number of black volunteers in the Union army. In "Men of Color, to Arms!" Douglass exhorted black men to redeem their manhood, for "Liberty won by white men would lose half its luster."[6] Though failing to mention the Haitian Revolution explicitly, "Men of Color, to Arms!" relied heavily on African American memory of the event.[7] Historical and biographical narratives of the Haitian Revolution published just prior to, and during the Civil War, for example, invoked Douglass's battle cry, "To Arms!" Charles Wyllys Elliott's New York lecture revealed that during the revolution " 'Liberty!' and To arms! To Arms!" were on the tongue of every rebel slave.[8] John Relly Beard's biography of Louverture, which James Redpath reprinted in Boston during the Civil War, copied a letter in which Louverture explained how armed bondmen nearly destroyed one Haitian town, but for the calm and discipline of black officers. Louverture wrote, "there arose a cry 'To arms!' . . . [and] had a single musket fired, the city would have perished."[9] The narrative revealed further that bondmen charged into battle behind Louverture singing the Marseillaise, the inspirational anthem of the French Revolution, which called on revolutionary citizens to resist their enslavement and commanded, "Aux armes!" During the Civil War, African Americans knew the revolutionary French anthem and sang it in public gatherings.[10] In addition to these accounts, some also would have recognized the exclamation "Aux armes!!!" from the last line of Alphonse de Lamartine's dramatic poem "Toussaint L'Ouverture."[11] With broadsides emblazoned with the slogan "Men of Color, to Arms!" strewn about the streets of crowded cities and towns, the connection between the Civil War and the Haitian Revolution was evident. The front page of a black French-language newspaper in Louisiana revealed in bold letters the long reach of Douglass's clarion call: "AUX ARMES! c'est notre devoir."[12]

The transformation of both free and enslaved black men into soldiers amplified African Americans' identification with Haiti and its preeminent founding father. During the American Civil War, Louverture's name was for African Americans the touchstone of a transatlantic identity, one that transcended both time and space as it joined their violent struggle for freedom and equality to the black revolutionary movement that began in Haiti. White abolitionists played an important role in reinforcing this identification, for when they saw armed and uniformed black men they likewise imagined American Toussaints, committed, disciplined, and talented slave soldiers who were eager to both die and kill for freedom. African Americans' longstanding racial identification with Haiti was an enduring bulwark, which subverted the racist ideology that attended the rise of the white republic. Though white supremacy was firmly entrenched in the bedrock of the American experience, it failed to stop the advance of the powerful symbols of racial equality and black manhood provided by the Haitian Revolution, symbols that continued to resound among African Americans long after its conclusion.

The academic conversation on black identity dates back at least a century to W. E. B. Du Bois's effort in *The Souls of Black Folk* to describe a collective consciousness among black people. This endeavor culminated years later in the aftermath of the Civil Rights movement in the publication of various scholarly works, which argued that African Americans shared a common culture and unique worldview that could be traced back to the southern plantations of the antebellum South and ultimately to the African continent.[13] The appearance of Sterling Stuckey's *Slave Culture: Nationalist Theory and the Foundations of Black America* cemented the belief that black nationalism derived from the opposite side of the Atlantic Ocean and opposed the predominant European American culture of the United States. Stuckey concluded of African Americans, "Their very effort to bridge ethnic differences and to form themselves into a single people to meet the challenge of a common foe proceeded from an impulse that was Pan-African—that grew out of a concern for all Africans—as what was useful was appropriated from a multiplicity of African groups even as an effort was made to eliminate distinctions among them."[14]

More recently, Patrick Rael has elucidated the shortcomings of the prevailing paradigms through which scholars of black identity continue to operate, while exploring black protest in the antebellum North within the framework of an American political culture.[15] In the end, we are left with a nationalist-assimilationist binary of black identity that fails to explain the evidence developed in this chapter. The explosion of public memory of Louverture and the Haitian Revolution during the Civil War among African Americans indicates the existence of a collective consciousness that was neither nationalist nor assimilationist. In the middle of the nineteenth century, African Americans were part of a transatlantic culture that was neither exclusively African nor American. They instead occupied the middle ground between these two poles, immersed in a transatlantic, or "black Atlantic" tradition, which defied political, geographical, and temporal boundaries.[16]

Douglass's reliance on the memory of the Haitian Revolution is only Exhibit A in a large collection of evidence that testifies to the existence of a transatlantic identity among African Americans during the Civil War. For he was not alone in appropriating Louverture and the Haitian Revolution to endorse black military service. One call for recruits maintained that the army provided black men the "opportunity to display those qualities which the experience of this war, as well as the history of Toussaint's Battles, has shown him to possess."[17] A correspondent of the *Weekly Anglo-African* writing from Washington, D.C., implored

> Men of color, my fellow-citizens, do not stop to ask the question: "What are we going to fight for?" but enlist, buckle on your armour, and with strong arms and brave hearts go into this war and fight for your rights. Did Toussaint L'Ouverture stop to ask that question? Did his followers stop to ask that question?" The answer was "No, no, not at all. They rose up with all their strength and struck blow after blow for freedom, and this day their posterity are enjoying the fruits of their victories.

The author called on African Americans to repeat the success of their Haitian brethren, concluding, "Let us as a people emulate their example."[18]

Another writer envisioned the revolutionary possibilities for black men as the result of military service, arguing that by copying Louverture they would open the door to both freedom and equality. African Americans had served in the U.S. army before and the government had denied them their rights, but now the interests of black men were paramount. The author's affinity for both Haiti's founding father and the United States is revealing: "Every young man of this blood should prepare himself for the glorious destiny of sharing in the duties and honors of the then only free and great nation in the world. Let him study and emulate this greatest of Africans [Toussaint] and not a whit behind the greatest of men." Whites must also acknowledge genius, the writer continued, "whatever be the color of the skin that enwraps it; and they must prepare themselves to welcome to the leadership of our armies and our Senate . . . black Toussaints, who, by their superior talents and principles, shall receive the grateful homage of an appreciative and admiring nation."[19] The United States needed American Toussaints to redeem both the nation and the black race. Once accomplishing this, the possibilities were endless.

African Americans identified with Louverture, and when the opportunity presented itself they enlisted in the Union army intent on reenacting his extraordinary accomplishments. The record of the Fifty-Fourth Massachusetts Regiment is illustrative. Immortalized in scores of soldier narratives,

Augustus Saint-Gaudens's Shaw Memorial in Boston, and the popular motion picture *Glory*, the Fifty-Fourth holds a special place in American memory of the Civil War.[20] The regiment's longstanding popularity rests on several factors. First, its location and organizers made the regiment a favorite of the local abolitionist press. Organized in New Bedford, Massachusetts, the regiment's supporters included Frederick Douglass, Wendell Phillips, and the black radical abolitionist Martin Delany. Second, the regiment's famous assault on Fort Wagner, under the direction of the white commander Robert Gould Shaw, lent itself to celebration by white abolitionists. After all, one of their own gave his life for the movement. Third, the Fifty-Fourth's story was palatable for northerners, as it fit squarely into the narrative of northern exceptionalism. Writers told the tale of a regiment of free black men—northerners—going south to end slavery, a despicable and peculiarly southern institution. It is not the story of enslaved people taking up arms, fighting and killing whites in battle. Yet most soldiers of the Fifty-Fourth did not live in Massachusetts. They came from nearly every northern and border state as well as Canada and the West Indies. More than 300 were from states that joined the Confederacy. Edwin S. Redkey suggests that perhaps as many as half of these men were formerly enslaved. Nearly all had family or friends in bondage.[21]

The Haitian Revolution inspired the men of the Fifty-Fourth. One of the most celebrated soldiers of the regiment was Sergeant William H. Carney, a former Virginia bondman.[22] At Fort Wagner, Carney suffered injuries to his legs, chest, and arm while holding the American flag aloft, and because of his heroism became the first African American to receive the Congressional Medal of Honor. What is less known is that when Carney and the rest of C Company stormed Battery Wagner, they went by the name of the "Toussaint Guards." The company nickname is something historians of the Civil War overlook, though contemporaries rarely failed to mention it.[23] Originally, the company went by the name "Morgan Guards," in honor of one of the regiment's most loyal supporters, a wealthy New Bedford merchant.[24] However, in March 1863 the *New Bedford Mercury* reported the changing of the name to the "Toussaint Guards." According to the paper, the change occurred "in compliance with the very proper suggestion of our townsman S. Griffiths Morgan, Esq."[25]

While it is tempting to credit this elite white benefactor with the name, there is reason to believe the soldiers themselves were responsible. The rank and file of the Fifty-Fourth remembered the Haitian Revolution. Sergeant Frederick Johnson made sure of it, regularly distributing among the regiment copies of the *Weekly Anglo-African*, which more than any other wartime newspaper regularly discussed and debated the history of the revolution in its columns.[26] Frederick Douglass's two sons served in the Fifty-Fourth. Lewis Douglass, the eldest, served as sergeant major, and historian Joseph Glatthaar has noted, "few white soldiers in the Union army, officers or enlisted men, possessed" his "writing fluency."[27] Lewis grew up in the offices of his father's newspapers, the *North Star* and *Douglass' Monthly*, where he learned the printer's trade and assisted in the writing, editing, and printing of articles on Haiti that appeared in both papers.[28] Douglass's sons and the other men of the Fifty-Fourth fought alongside Martin Delany's son Toussaint L'Ouverture Delany, and doubtless they were all aware of his namesake.

One member of the Fifty-Fourth revealed a particularly strong affinity for the black republic. Rhode Island native Charles E. Greene had for years held sacred the memory of the Haitian Revolution and hoped to see the day when he could partake in the violent end of slavery in America. Greene joined the Fifty-Fourth in February 1863 and lost his life a year later in Beaufort, South Carolina. Two years earlier the Union army had refused the services of this man because of his complexion. Consequently, Greene and other black Rhode Islanders formed an independent military company and began drilling. After learning of a growing conflict between Haiti and residents on the eastern side of the island in Spanish Santo Domingo, Greene forwarded a letter to Redpath's *Pine and Palm*, in which he offered his services and that of several other men from his unit to aid the Haitians. "We would like to know," Greene inquired, "if we could go as a military body. If so, we go to *fight*."[29] Greene's abolitionism transcended oceans and boundaries. It is likely that he and the other regular members of the Fifty-Fourth played a part in the renaming of the company.

Greene was not the only man who in addition to serving in the United States Colored Troops offered to fight in Haiti. William H. Johnson of the Eighth Connecticut Volunteers hoped to travel to Haiti to assist in the war with Santo Domingo, but first there was a war to fight at home. Johnson wrote to Redpath, "I am at present engaged to follow this war against the slave propagandists of the South. We will conquer. Slavery will finish." After avenging John Brown, Johnson explained, "I will be able to go to the Haytian war against despotic Spain, and carry with me a practical knowledge of modern warfare, and a contingent of intellect and military strength."[30] H. Ford Douglas, the noted Midwest orator and former runaway slave who went on to serve in both a white and a black Union regiment, remarked on the new threat to Haitian independence: "If there is to be any fighting in the island . . . please count me in."[31] Neither Greene, Johnson, nor Douglas ever left for Haiti, but their interest in coming to the defense of Haitians and their subsequent personal sacrifices for the Union army indicate their primary motivation for enlistment, to fight for black freedom wherever it was in jeopardy.[32]

African Americans' veneration of Haiti did not detract from their fidelity to the United States. In Philadelphia, John C. Bowers was among those who presented the regimental colors to the Sixth United States Colored Troop. The flag was six feet tall by six feet six inches wide. On one side was the Goddess of Liberty, holding the "American ensign." On the other was the United States coat of arms. Bowers addressed the men of the regiment: "The time has come when we are called upon by our countrymen to participate in this deadly strife; and, as in days of yore, our people are rushing beneath her standard with alacrity." The effort that black men made to secure victory for the Union was astonishing, Bowers asserted. "In this bloody strife," they exhibited courage similar to the world's greatest men, among them "Toussaint L'Ouverture, Cristophe and Dessalines in St. Domingo." The survival of the United States depended on black men, and Bowers implored the soldiers before him to bear proudly the flags of both their country and their regiment on every battlefield where they met the enemy. Black troops would trample the banner of slavery under their feet, "while the glorious Stars and Stripes, emblems of freedom to all mankind, irrespective of clime or complexion, will wave in graceful folds, its red, white and blue, over the land of the free and the home of the brave."[33]

One black soldier who shared Bowers's dual identification with race and nation enlisted in the Union army as a teenager to save his "beloved country" from the "cancer of slavery."[34] Decades later, he became the first chronicler of the black soldier's Civil War experience. In *A History of the Negro Troops in the War of the Rebellion*, George Washington Williams described the Civil War as a climactic battle in a war for black freedom that began in Haiti, and recognized the place of black Union soldiers alongside Louverture in the struggle to end slavery. Williams referred to Haiti as the "scene of modern Negro soldiership." Numerous black generals distinguished themselves in the Haitian Revolution, but "the most commanding character was Toussaint L'Ouverture." The great leader united blacks and whites, drafted a constitution, and created a republic without slavery. The Civil War was but a continuation of his work. Even after the Civil War, Williams remembered his debt to Louverture and bemoaned the lack of a monument of "marble or brass" to the Great Man. Still, he took solace that on Louverture's "island home the little republic he built still stands a monument to his valor as a soldier, and sagacity as a statesman; write his deeds, like stars, illumine the page of history, and his Christian character and shining example have an immortal place in the literature of the world."[35]

One Haitian shared Williams's commitment to black freedom throughout the Atlantic world. H. W. Dorsey was born in Port au Prince and traveled to the United States at age twenty-one. He landed in New Orleans and placed advertisements in local papers searching for his father, mother, and sister. Eventually word of their whereabouts came via the *New York Tribune*, and Dorsey traveled to New York City and reunited with his family. The Haitian then, according to one biographical account, "became imbued with the spirit of the war and after President Lincoln's proclamation of emancipation enlisted and served until mustered out Oct. 25, 1863."[36] This rare case of a Haitian serving in the Union army testifies to the transatlantic nature of the Civil War. When read alongside the stories of native Africans and West Indians who fought in the Civil War, and African American colonists who emigrated to a tiny island on the Haitian coast in 1862 and later served in the Union army, it confirms that the war that ended slavery in the United States transcended time, borders, and battlefields.[37]

African Americans fought to end slavery in the United States, and following heroic displays like the Fifty-Fourth Regiment's assault on Fort Wagner, the northern press quickly spread the word of the bravery of black troops. Invocation of the Haitian Revolution in these reports reinforced African Americans' identification with the black revolutionary tradition that commenced in Haiti. An Ohio newspaper, which weeks earlier had printed a narrative of the Haitian Revolution, felt its readers could "not fail to perceive the exact similarity of the stubborn heroism of the Louisiana colored guard at Port Hudson, to the desperate valor of the negro soldiers at the siege of Crete-a-Pierrot" in Haiti.[38] General William S. Smith called black soldiers the best in the army. This was no surprise based on history. "Look back a quarter of a century," Smith told a small gathering of officers and a writer for the *New York Times*, "to the heroic deliverer of St. Domingo, who made even NAPOLEON tremble at his power."[39] J. F. Cooke, a prominent member of the Relief Association for the Contrabands in the District of Columbia, commented on the significance of the Civil War while praising the heroism of black soldiers in Kansas, Florida, and Louisiana: "The conflict is not between the North and South, it is of nobler aspect, of transcendently higher nature." It was of freedom, equality, and slavery, "A strife between civilization and barbarism, truth and error, right and wrong." Cooke informed the members of the First District Columbia Volunteers who stood in front of him, "To-day we are making our own history—history that will bid defiance to prejudice and partiality." Americans no longer needed to "rake the far past" for black military heroes. Gone was the necessity to invoke foreign and dated racial paragons, like Hannibal, the "slave martyrs of 1776 and 1812," or "the soldier and the statesman of San Domingo, Toussaint L'Overture." Now the accomplishments of African American soldiers were worthy of remembrance.[40]

Tales of the heroism of militant black men prompted historical comparisons. William Tillman was among the first African Americans to receive significant attention in the northern press. A free man, Tillman became a captive of Confederate privateers. Traveling to South Carolina, he confided to a passenger, "I am not going to Charleston a live man." Around midnight on 16 July 1861, Tillman sneaked upon the ship's captain, master, and first mate as they slept, and with a hatchet took their lives. After discarding the bodies overboard, he imprisoned the two remaining white sailors and directed the boat to New York City. He was an instant celebrity. The *New York Tribune* fêted him on its front page and reported that he "created such an interest in the public mind that Mr. Barnum has induced him to receive visitors at the Museum for the next few days."[41] *Harper's Weekly* printed a number of illustrations, including one of Tillman emerging from the ship's belly, hatchet in hand, ready to attack. *Douglass' Monthly* accorded him "a degree of personal valor and presence of mind equal to those displayed by the boldest deeds recorded in history." Among the men Tillman deserved comparison was "Toussaint L'Ouverture."[42]

White abolitionists helped join African Americans' violent struggle for freedom and equality to a revolutionary black Atlantic tradition when they compared black Union soldiers to Louverture. A correspondent of the *Weekly Anglo-African* recorded the reaction of a crowd of some two thousand African Americans at Israel Church in Washington, D.C., to an address given by the well-known abolitionist Owen Lovejoy. Lovejoy predicted that when the U.S. government finally called on African Americans to fight, "there would be found many a Touissant L'Overture amongst us." The throng responded with wild shouts and applause, so much so that "the church seemed to shake."[43] A number of papers carried the story of "a new Toussaint," a Virginia contraband named Jim Lawson in northern Virginia. After separating from his master, Lawson served as a scout for the Union army and repeatedly risked both life and reenslavement to assist Union forces. The heroism demonstrated by this enslaved husband and father deserved "more honor than that accorded Touissaint L'Ouverture," one writer concluded. "He is unquestionably the hero of the Potomac, and deserves to be placed by the side of his most renowned black brethren."[44] One correspondent described the "Toussaint L'Ouverture of the 29th," Sergeant Major Horace N. Lowden of the Twenty-Ninth Regiment Connecticut Volunteers. He was "one of the noblest and finest specimens of physical development, whose princely bearing and martial tread" indicated that he was born to lead men.[45]

Prince Rivers was another soldier who gained great celebrity in the abolitionist press. Known for his dark skin, physical prowess, and natural leadership abilities, this fugitive slave from South Carolina who enlisted in the First South Carolina Volunteers and rose to the rank of sergeant drew the following remark from abolitionist Thomas Wentworth Higginson, the regiment's white commander: "He makes Toussaint perfectly intelligible; and if there should ever be a black monarchy in South Carolina, he will be its king."[46] The regiment in which Rivers served likewise inspired historical references. Scores of northern newspapers described the novelty of this early black regiment. One writer was impressed with what he saw: "a row of strong, sturdy negroes, averaging from 21 to 30 years in age, and 5 feet 8 inches in height, clad in a decent military uniform of dark blue, wearing felt hats, and armed with rifles of Belgian manufacture, and bayonets, that which they handled as promptly and dexterously in obedience to the word of command as one could wish to see—as well as any equal number of white men, not especially selected, could have done." The correspondent "noticed a look of honest endeavor in their black faces indicative of an earnest desire to learn, their docility of character rendering them apt pupils." Their success at drilling was remarkable. The spectacle reminded him of other regiments he had seen, and that "Toussaint was a negro."[47]

Abolitionists even painted white officers of black troops with Louverturian brushes. Adjutant General Lorenzo Thomas was among the army's staunchest advocates of black soldiery. A soldier of doubtful ability with a tendency to drink in excess, he was, nonetheless, John David Smith reminds us, brilliant "in recruiting freedmen, encouraging white noncommissioned officers to apply for commissions in black units, and in popularizing the employment of black soldiers."[48] In March 1863, Thomas relocated to the Lower Mississippi Valley to recruit slaves and within a year oversaw the enlistment of more than twenty thousand men.[49] The *Chicago Tribune* labeled Thomas "a champion of the black troops," a man who had "done more to raise black regiments than any one man in the country, or perhaps the world, if we except Toussaint."[50] A writer in the *New York Times* calling himself "Toussaint" interviewed Thomas and applauded him for his efforts to secure both the enlistment and education of black soldiers. Thomas saw black men as his equals and thus earned the respect of this American Toussaint.[51] David Hunter also believed in arming bondmen, and as early as 1862 began organizing black troops in defiance of official government policy. Seeking an explanation for Hunter's zealousness, a contributor to the *National Anti-Slavery Standard* insisted that it was the memory of Louverture, "one of the greatest military heroes who had ever appeared in connection with the history of this continent," which served as Hunter's inspiration.[52]

Not all military leaders were as esteemed as Thomas and Hunter. Northern abolitionists disparaged high-ranking officers for failing to live up to the military standard set by Louverture. Redpath insisted that even the Union's greatest generals were incomparable. "As a soldier, diplomatist and ruler, he [Louverture] has never been equaled either in North or South America. Grant or Sherman may possibly be his equals as mere soldiers; but they have given no indication yet, either one or them, that they could have coped with the First of the Blacks in the other fields of triumphs."[53] Massachusetts abolitionist and Union general Benjamin Franklin Butler chided Confederates who used deception, which caused Union troops to fire "upon their friends." A similar strategy was used "by Toussaint L'Ouverture toward the French forces in San Domingo," Butler wrote, "and would seem therefore to be not even original."[54]

Abolitionists saw Louverture in the clothes as well as the bodies of black soldiers and their white officers. The uniform of ordinary soldiers was enough to cause some to invoke the Haitian Revolution. Nothing better illustrates the *rage militaire* that swept the North during the Civil War than the colorful and gaudy Zouave uniforms and the eccentric Zouave drill. Thousands of black and white Union soldiers donned the baggy red trousers, fluffy white shirt, and small fez that mimicked the livery of the colonial French Army in North Africa. Martin Delany traced both the uniforms and drill to Haiti and credited Louverture with the invention of the tradition.[55] Prior to the Civil War, Delany emerged as a leading proponent of black emigration, but during the war he became an outspoken advocate of black soldiery. He pursued the organization of a regiment of black Zouaves, a "corps d'Afrique," which would wear the Algerian-style uniforms and adopt the Algerian fighting style, which he insisted the Algerian Zouaves copied from Haiti's revolutionary army.[56] Delany remarked, "It was observed years ago by persons visiting Hayti, without their comprehending it closely, perhaps, that the soldiers of that island had peculiar tactics . . . this was, doubtless, nothing but the original Zouave tactics introduced long years ago by native Africans among these people."[57] Others, like W. G. Smith of the *Pine and Palm* and abolitionist Franklin Sanborn, credited Louverture specifically with the Zouave drill.[58] Other than these reports, there is no evidence to support the claim that the Zouave tradition originated with Haitian soldiers; nevertheless, for African Americans and their white allies the distinction between myth and reality lost its significance when so much was at stake. It was enough to believe that throughout the Atlantic world, first in Africa, then in Haiti, and now in the United States, black men donned the Zouave uniform and battled for freedom.

Delany dreamed of a second Haitian Revolution in which African American men would emancipate slaves while destroying an army of slaveholders.[59] He presented such a plan to Abraham Lincoln in February 1863. "I propose, sir," Delany remembered saying, "an army of blacks, commanded entirely by black officers, except such whites as may volunteer to serve; this army to penetrate the heart of the South, and make conquests, with the banner of emancipation unfurled, proclaiming freedom as they go, sustaining and protecting it by arming the emancipated, taking them as fresh troops, and leaving a few veterans among the new freedmen, when occasion requires, keeping this banner unfurled until every slave is free, according to the letter of your proclamation."[60] Lincoln's response, according to Delany, was more than satisfactory. "This," replied the president, "is the very thing I have been looking and hoping for; but nobody offered it."[61] After agreeing to the organization of such a force, Lincoln commissioned Delany a major, making him the first commissioned black officer in the United States army. Lincoln then ordered the ranking soldier to South Carolina to begin organizing.[62]

In the last months of the war, Delany posed for a photograph in full military regalia. Given the unique opportunity of a black man posing in the uniform of an officer of the United States army, he seized the moment. The image quickly found its way onto a carte-de-viste, which abolitionists peddled for twenty-five cents apiece.[63] The similarities between this print and the most reproduced image of Louverture in the nineteenth century are unmistakable (Figure 8). Both Louverture and Delany stand erect, with their eyes focused directly on the camera. The black-and-white image accentuates their dark skin. There is no denying their blackness. Both hold a sword in their right hand that extends to the ground, touching the earth in front of their right foot; both have cockaded, black campaign hats; both wear sashes with two tassels that fall to the ground, one farther than the other. Martin's Delany's dream had come true: African Americans were fighting to end slavery, and he was an American Toussaint.

While it was one thing for northern abolitionists like Delany to draw comparisons between American and Haitian bondmen, it was another for enslaved people to do it themselves, given the widespread fears of a repetition of the "horrors of St. Domingo." There is no more telling example of the resiliency of public memory of the Haitian Revolution among African Americans during the Civil War than the evidence of fugitive slaves who, after escaping behind Union lines in interviews and conversations, invoked Louverture and the revolution. Such evidence demonstrates that bondpeople were not transparent, obtuse, and ignorant people; rather, they were informed and active participants in their own history, conscious participants in a black Atlantic revolutionary tradition.

There were two main sources of African American memory of the Haitian Revolution in the South during the Civil War. The first was print culture. Scholars note the extent to which northern periodicals found a market among southerners in spite of the war.[64] Stephanie Camp, for example, documents the case of one enslaved Mississippian who on the walls of her cabin hung a picture of Abraham Lincoln, which she had detached from a northern newspaper.[65] Black soldiers and bondmen in the South accessed northern antislavery newspapers and periodicals that discussed the Haitian Revolution at length. For evidence, we simply need to refer to the media that during the war proudly offered proof of their southern distribution. In June 1863, the *Liberator* printed a letter from a chaplain with the Thirty-Third Massachusetts Regiment, who listed the sheets he received weekly in the mail. Along with the *Liberator* and the *National Anti-Slavery Standard*, he also recorded the staunchly abolitionist *Boston Commonwealth* and *Boston Transcript*. The chaplain distributed all these papers "among the men, who read them eagerly."[66]

In the *Boston Commonwealth*, another chaplain commented on the reading habits of black soldiers in the South. "Probably there never was such an anxiety to learn to read and write as there is now in the colored regiments." The soldiers routinely requested spelling books from the chaplain. Low supplies, however, forced him to deny these requests, writing, "It mortifies me exceedingly, especially when I know how many second-hand spelling-books are lying about through the country, for which there is no use. I occasionally run off a few days, and ransack all the benevolent institutions that can spare a book or primer, besides the thousands of papers, tracts, and periodicals which I weekly procure for those who can read, and the weekly packages of [*Christian*] *Recorders* and *Anglo-Africans*." These materials did not satisfy the men, who clamored for hymn-books and Bibles. Then "*Christian Advocate, New York Independent, Boston Commonwealth, Anti-Slavery Standard,* etc.," the chaplain

Figure 8. Engraving of Major Martin R. Delany published in Joseph T. Wilson, *The Black Phalanx* (1890). The abolitionist and army recruiter became the first black field officer in the Union Army. His son, Toussaint L'Ouverture Delany, served in the famed Fifty-Fourth Massachusetts Regiment. Courtesy of the Collections of the Library of Congress.

continued, "come in a general cry from every direction, until several hundred are gone."[67] An enslaved preacher when asked about the availability of northern publications among bondpeople during the war admitted that his reading was normally limited to southern newspapers; yet, he added of these papers, "they used to have pieces taken out of Northern papers, that were friendly to us, and these I used to read and tell my friends about."[68] A southern correspondent in the *Weekly Anglo-African* asked, "Will they not send us copies of The Anglo? There are a great many colored soldiers here and they all desire to have The Anglo-African. Your humble servant gets a copy pretty regularly, but it is worn into pieces before a hundreth part of the boys get through reading it."[69]

The Confederate army failed to stop the advance of both the Union army and northern print culture. A South Carolinian named John was among the contrabands who demonstrated firsthand knowledge of Haiti. John confessed his knowledge of the political events swirling around him, admitting that, for example, he knew of John Brown and had read stories of the white martyr "to heaps of the colored people." He revealed further that he owned a "history of San Domingo," which he stored away in his trunk.[70] That a bondman counted a narrative of the Haitian Revolution among his personal possessions is notable, as historians are just beginning to understand the extent to which enslaved people's networks of communication extended beyond plantation boundaries. Through seaports and sailors, word-of-mouth communication, and hand-to-hand exchanges of printed matter, information from both the North and the greater Atlantic world penetrated America's slave society.[71] James Meriles Simms's career as a publisher provides an example. A former bondman and Union soldier, Simms published an edition of William Wells Brown's *Black Man* in Charleston, South Carolina, in 1865. It is, according to Phillip Lapsansky, "the first book written by a black, celebrating black accomplishment, published by a black in the New South—or the Old."[72] A surviving copy of this unique volume belonged to the free black merchant Anthony Desverney. That black southerners published, distributed, and read a book by a radical black abolitionist that gloried in the accomplishments of Louverture and other Haitian revolutionaries speaks to both the transforming nature of the Civil War and the reach of northern print culture. It testifies, moreover, to the resiliency of the public memory of the Haitian Revolution among African Americans.

Oral culture was the second major source of African American memory of the Haitian Revolution in the South. A Union chaplain stationed for a time at Port Royal, South Carolina, claimed an intimate knowledge of the life of bondmen, and thus felt that they had the potential to make excellent soldiers. He avowed, "From the earliest ages of the world, the people from whom the contrabands of this country originally sprang, have been a people of war." Confident in his understanding of enslaved people's oral tradition, he added, "The result of the insurrection in St. Domingo has long been known among the contrabands of the South—the name of Toussaint L'Overture has been passed from mouth to mouth until it has become a secret household word—and a love of liberty, fed by a love of arms, has been rendered universal and almost omnipotent. It has been felt that it was right for the colored Haytiens to fight to be free, it is equally right for colored Americans." This was a bold statement. For years, slaveowners had insisted that bondpeople were neither deserving of nor eager for freedom, but in his short time in South Carolina the chaplain had learned of the contrabands' "secret household word." He reasoned that if southern planters had failed to keep enslaved people ignorant of the legacy of the Haitian Revolution, then surely they had not extinguished the black man's martial spirit as well. White southerners underestimated the militancy of bondmen, the descendants of "a people of war."[73] Commenting on the patriotism of African Americans in the District of Columbia, a correspondent of the *New York Evening Post* added that black men studied the military tactics and strategies of both the present war and ancient history. "They think and speak of General Hannibal as one of their own immortal heroes. The brave deeds of Toussaint L'Ouverture, of Cristophe, Rigaud and Geffrard abroad, of Attucks and Turner at home, are as familiar to these people as household words."[74]

Further evidence of the survival of public memory of the Haitian Revolution in slaves' oral culture comes from aged contrabands who through autobiographical memory claimed to have survived the Haitian Revolution. Eyewitnesses to both the Haitian Revolution and the American Civil War, their stories emphasize the proximity of the two events. An elderly man named Launace at Port Royal, South Carolina, claimed a remarkable history. A correspondent from the *New York Tribune* called him "by far the most interesting contraband of whom any account has yet been given me, but I have been able to gather only enough to excite rather than to gratify curiosity. He is more than 75 years old, came or was brought from St. Domingo, where he was free, and where, for six years, he served in what are called the revolutionary wars." Launace's legend grew when it was revealed that "He knew Toussaint, Cristophe, and Petion, and has many interesting stories of those men still fresh in his memory."[75]

A contraband in Beaufort, North Carolina, was "said by the people who know him to be one hundred and seven years old." Lawrence Slade lived in Newbern, North Carolina, for more than seventy years. The *National Anti-Slavery Standard* reported, "He has seen his master flourish and fade down to the third and fourth generations; has lived through seven wars and scenes of bloodshed, and says he has never before seen a war like this; has never seen a sick day; was at St. Domingo, at the time of the slave insurrection and massacre."[76] The *Weekly Anglo-African* reported on a group of "colored exiles" in Charleston who planned to sail for Haiti. These were no ordinary contrabands: "There are among them descendents of exiles *from* Hayti during her Revolution of 1789!"[77] They were finally going home.

One man's story in particular highlights the survival of oral tradition of the Haitian Revolution and especially Louverture among bondpeople. A. F. Pillsbury, an abolitionist working with contrabands in South Carolina in the last year of the Civil War, interviewed Norice Wilkinson, a septuagenarian and Sea Island bondman who claimed to have fought in Louverture's army. Pillsbury forwarded excerpts of her conversation to Wendell Phillips. Anticipating a skeptical response from the renowned orator of Haitian history to such a remarkable story, Pillsbury vouched for the veracity of Wilkinson's oral testimony: "I have gathered by questions & conversation some facts from his own mouth which I forward, as you will know their reliability." Pillsbury forwarded two ambrotypes along with her letter, adding, "I take the liberty of sending you two pictures of an old man now residing on Hilton Head Island, whose life has a strange historical interest" (Figure 9). This was an understatement. Born in northeastern Saint-Domingue in 1786, slave traders sold Wilkinson to a wealthy family on Hilton Head Island, South Carolina, in the last year of the revolution. More than a half-century later, Wilkinson spoke French and Spanish fluently and recited the lines to the Marseillaise. He recalled a number of Louverture's military commands, such as "En avant!" and " 'Porter armes'— Presenter armes'," and could still perform the military exercises he learned as a teenager in Haiti's revolutionary army. He remembered Louverture vividly, remarking, the great general "occupied a splendid *tree* story house . . . rode a splendid bay horse" and "dress beautiful." Though commanding the respect of everyone around him, Louverture was physically unimpressive and melancholy, recounted Wilkinson, adding, "Neber see him smile—Always seem cross."[78]

These incredible reports require a brief comment. They share an aura of implausibility, and like many stories of the survivors of the Age of Revolution that appeared in American print culture throughout the nineteenth century seem to lack validity.[79] That veterans of the Haitian Revolution also

Figure 9. Ambrotype of South Carolina contraband Norice Wilkinson, a veteran of Louverture's army. Reprinted by permission of the Houghton Library, Harvard University.

experienced the Civil War seems improbable. That some knew Louverture personally is unlikely. Nevertheless, we must evaluate their claims carefully. Thousands of white, colored, and black Haitians migrated to the United States throughout the Haitian Revolution and after. In most cases, they traveled to southern seaports, with New Orleans, Charleston, Norfolk, and Baltimore among the common destinations.[80] Given the reported ages of these refugees, it is possible that they had seen the Haitian Revolution and lived to tell about it more than fifty years later.

Nevertheless, their authenticity is irrelevant. The veracity of each of these stories was insignificant, as long as the memory of the Haitian Revolution stayed alive. The revolution was a symbolic event—its dates and details were trivial. What mattered was that when enslaved Haitians defeated both their white masters and Europe's greatest armies they proved the capacity of the black race. That oral tradition of their accomplishments survived among enslaved African Americans is evident.

Events in a number of slave states illuminate how contrabands further contributed to the public memory of the Haitian Revolution during the Civil War. In 1863, a correspondent of the *New York Herald* noted a unique occurrence at Newbern, North Carolina, where. an estimated eight to ten thousand contrabands established a colony and gave it the name "New Hayti."[81]

In Alexandria, Virginia, freedmen likewise poured into a black settlement, which residents had for decades referred to as "Hayti." A few blocks away, they constructed a medical facility that eventually served hundreds of black soldiers and contrabands. This they named "L'Ouverture Branch Hospital."[82] Naming important spaces after the Haitian Revolution was a tradition established earlier in the century. In the South alone, there were "Haytis" in Arkansas, Maryland, Missouri, North Carolina, and Virginia.[83]

Individual naming practices provide additional evidence of the survival of the memory of the Haitian Revolution among African Americans. Naming children in honor of Haiti's founding father was a tradition. Martin Delany's son Toussaint L'Ouverture Delany is a well-known example. Toussaint L'Ouverture Lambert is less known. The son of a renowned conductor of the Underground Railroad in Detroit who assisted John Brown in planning the Harpers Ferry raid, Lambert worked as a correspondent to the *Weekly Anglo-African*. His signature or the abbreviation "T. L'O. L." appears routinely in the paper during the war.[84] Lambert was not the only black abolitionist who capitalized on Louverture's name in the northern press. The *Weekly Anglo-African* and the *New York Times* published letters of correspondents calling themselves either "Toussaint" or "L'Ouverture." It is clear that African Americans had a special place in their hearts and minds for Louverture, yet he did not have a monopoly on African American memory. John Mercer Langston, the Virginia-born abolitionist and orator who lectured on the Haitian Revolution, for example, named his eldest son Dessalines.[85]

During the Civil War, African Americans continued this naming tradition. Boston Toussaint Parsons, the noted Virginia educator, politician, and church leader, was born in Currituck, County, North Carolina six months after the firing on Fort Sumter.[86] Two years later, in Oxford, Ohio, Hezikiah and Carolina Jackson named their son, who would go on to found the first African American settlement in Colorado, Oliver Toussaint Jackson.[87] Scholars trace the centrality of African American naming practices to the naming ceremonies of West Africa. West Africans placed great importance on names, and recognized them as key indicators of one's past, kinship, and identity. Consequently, historians consider African American naming customs as essentially African, or nationalist in nature, as opposed to American, or integrationist.[88] They insist on this even when African Americans chose Anglicized instead of African names. However, the decision of African Americans to name their children after Haiti's revolutionary leaders indicates a transatlantic consciousness that defies the traditional nationalist-assimilationist paradigm of African American identity.

In the Civil War era, African Americans shared a black Atlantic consciousness, which transcended geographical, political, and temporal boundaries.

American Toussaints served as central characters in some of the most popular literature published during the Civil War, and it is perhaps in these fictional accounts that the subversiveness of the memory of Louverture among African Americans is best illuminated. In *Camps and Prisons: Twenty Months in the Department of the Gulf*, a fictional account of Union officer and prisoner of war Augustine Duganne's experiences in Louisiana during the war, a manly fugitive slave named Toussaint figured prominently. Like his namesake, this American Toussaint was "courageous and intelligent, strong and patient, who might ask only favorable surroundings to become, likewise, a chief of his enfranchised comrades." In escaping behind Union lines, Toussaint "dared to defy oppression and brave suffering, from the promptings of as generous a spirit as that which nerved his namesake in the Haytien isle."[89]

Once after being lashed by an overseer's whip, Toussaint's "manhood revolted once more," and he struck the overseer and then absconded from the plantation on a horse. This was not wanton violence. It was self-defense in the pursuit of freedom. While escaping on horseback, Toussaint was "struck by a bullet in his shoulder." Still, he did not submit. He headed for the woods and eventually found refuge in the Union army. When asked to stop working in order to let his wound heal, Toussaint responded to a white soldier, "Thank you, sah! But I reck'n it'll git along, sah! I'd rather wu'k, sah, if you please, sah!" The bondman who refused to stop working because of a bullet wound impressed Duganne. "I do not know many white soldiers who would not prefer a furlough under Toussaint's circumstances. Very few, certainly, would report for fatigue duty, with a bullet hole through the shoulder."[90]

The controversial name of an American Toussaint living in Louisiana sparked a melee that ended in murder in Stephen G. Bulfinch's historical novel, *Honor; or, The Slave-Dealer's Daughter*. In the story, a northern traveler named Frederick Bryant informs a bondman in New Orleans named Toussaint of the history behind his name. "They named you after the greatest man of your race, and one of its best men too, I fancy." Toussaint "led the slaves of St. Domingo in an insurrection against the whites; and the whites afterwards took him prisoner, and carried him to a cold country, where they kept him shut up in a very cold, damp prison, till he died." This American Toussaint knew little of the Great Man with whom he shared a name, yet the conversation led him to wonder aloud: "Maybe massa'd stand by de brack men now, if dey'd make a resurrection, jes' like in Samingo." On hearing this remark, Bryant quickly ended the conversation for fear that other whites might overhear the exchange. He understood that he was not in the North any more. Toussaint's newfound knowledge led him to broach the topics of Haiti and insurrection with other enslaved people, however, and local whites took notice. Lynch mobs formed to punish Bryant's indiscretion. Though he escaped death, the moral of the story was clear: invocation of Toussaint was a subversive act that a slave society could not tolerate.[91]

Bondmen who remembered the Haitian Revolution also had a significant role in popular wartime literature. *Among the Pines: or South in Secession Time*, a best-selling book by James Gilmore, tells the story of an enslaved man named Scipio whom the author found "in every way . . . a remarkable negro, and my three days' acquaintance with him banished from my mind all doubt as to the capacity of the black for freedom, and all questions as to the disposition of the slave to strike off his chains when the favorable moment arrives." Scipio taught Gilmore that "blacks, though pretending ignorance, are fully acquainted with the questions at issue in the pending contest." Scipio acknowledged that white southerners were fighting men, and that the North would be in for a fight, but he predicted that the Confederacy could never beat the North, "cause you see dey'll fight wid only one hand. *When dey fight de Norf wid de right hand, dey'll have to hold de nigga wid de leff.*" Taken aback, Gilmore pursued this line of thought. "But the black won't rise; most of you have kind masters and fare well." To this Scipio responded, "Dat's true, massa, but dat an't freedom, and de black lub freedom as much as de white. . . . De blacks hab strong hands, and when de day come you'll see dey hab heads, too!" Scipio described some of the events that would have to take place in order for an inevitable black rebellion in South Carolina to come about. Gilmore responded, "but you have no leaders, no one to direct the movement. Your race is not a match for the white in generalship, and without generals, whatever your number, you would fare hardly." Scipio retorted, "I knows most ob de great men, like Washington and John and James and Paul, and dem ole fellers war white, but dar was Two Sand (Toussaint L'Ouverture), de Brack Douglass, and de Nigga Demus (Nicodemus), dey war black."[92] An enslaved man in the heart of the Confederacy invoked Louverture at the same time he discussed the inevitability of an insurrection of enslaved people in the South. It is an extraordinary passage—and Americans took notice. The *North American Review* printed a twelve-page review of Gilmore's book, including the conversation with Scipio in its entirety.[93]

The veracity of Gilmore's work is disputable. Alice Fahs notes that it shared "an uncanny resemblance to the editorial pages of the [*Continental*]

Monthly," and cites one of the author's contemporaries, who called *Among the Pines* "pure fiction from beginning to end."[94] Yet Fahs cites a critic in Charleston, South Carolina, the cockpit of the Confederacy. White southerners categorically rejected northern antislavery literature like *Uncle Tom's Cabin*, which promised to tell the real story of the South and slavery. Gilmore, unlike Harriet Beecher Stowe, traveled extensively in the South and encountered enslaved people. He did this during a war that sparked an unprecedented level of slave resistance. Northerners gave Gilmore the benefit of the doubt. In praising the literary qualities of the book one reviewer insisted, "there is absolutely nothing fictitious in it."[95] Again, the authenticity of Gilmore's account matters less than its popularity. Something in the story of a militant bondman appealed to the more than 30,000 men and women who purchased the book soon after its publication and the tens of thousands of people who read excerpted passages in popular periodicals. We do not know whether Abraham Lincoln was familiar with the book; he never recorded an opinion of it. Yet it is likely he knew the piece, for during the war Gilmore interviewed the president frequently and, if Gilmore is to be believed, served as an unofficial advisor on important matters of public policy.[96]

African Americans understood that memory of the Haitian Revolution was an incendiary device that both shattered the idea of white supremacy and sent shivers up the spines of European Americans. In a "remarkable conversation" with Samuel Wilkeson of the *New York Tribune*, "an intelligent negro" named Tom, who had run away from his master in South Carolina with the hopes of enlisting in the Union army, took offense at the suggestion that bondmen were unwilling to fight for freedom. Tom declared:

> You know as well as I. We were driven from your lines and camps, and pretty plainly told that you didn't want anything to do with us; that you meant to carry on the war, and leave us in slavery at the end of the war . . . The North can't conquer the South without the help of the slaves . . . We know, too, that if the war lasts, one party or the other party will give us our freedom.

Hardly believing what he had heard, Wilkeson retorted, "What is that you say—the slaveholders free the slaves?" Tom fired back:

> They certainly will do it, if they can't whip you otherwise . . . Our position Mr. W. is like that of San Domingo blacks. They put their aid

in the market between the white and the mulattoes—put it for sale. The price was their freedom. We mean to sell ourselves for freedom . . . If your politicians and Generals kick us away, we will try to make our market with the rebels. But you had better bargain with us—had better free us, and arm us.[97]

The exchange is remarkable indeed. Tom expressed a detailed, historical consciousness of the Haitian Revolution, an awareness of the complex of race in Haiti that pitted free and enslaved black people, white planters, poor whites, and a free mulatto class against, and sometimes beside each other for thirteen years. Here is strong evidence of a black Atlantic consciousness, even if there is no way to confirm the veracity of Wilkinson's account. For African Americans who read the exchange understood that Tom placed his allegiance to freedom first and the nation second. He wanted assurances that like in "San Domingo" those in bondage would benefit from participation in the Civil War before they would cast their lot with either side. And he dared the North to try to defeat the South without them.

When African Americans put on the uniform of the United States army and went to war to be free, they and their white allies recognized the similarities of the forces aligned against them and those that confronted enslaved Haitians at the close of the eighteenth century. The transformation of the Civil War from a limited war over Union to a total war over slavery meant that the time to finish the struggle begun on the small French colony in the Caribbean had finally arrived. Heeding the clarion call to arms that had reverberated throughout the Atlantic world for decades, African Americans proved themselves worthy of the freedom they demanded by living up to the high standard of black soldiery set by Louverture and his army. Their accomplishments perhaps surpassed those of their predecessors first in Saint-Domingue and then in Haiti, for black soldiers in the Union army avoided partaking in the excesses that accompanied the earlier revolution over slavery. Armed with the symbols of Louverture and the Haitian Revolution, free and enslaved African Americans took advantage of the opportunities presented by war and continued what others like them had started more than a half-century before.

CHAPTER 7

"A Repetition of San Domingo?": Southern White Identity

IN JUNE 1863, hundreds of black Union soldiers sailed north from Beaufort, South Carolina, to the mouth of the Combahee River and disembarked amid some of the South's largest and most valuable plantations. Led by abolitionist and Kansas Jayhawker Colonel James Montgomery and accompanied by legendary Underground Railroad conductor Harriet Tubman, these former bondmen—among the first deployed in the South—were instructed to destroy the plantations that fed Confederate soldiers and in other ways continued to support the Confederate war effort. As they traveled up the river under dark of night, they proceeded to confiscate the property and burn and demolish the bridges, homes, railroads, and mills of their Confederate adversaries. Following direct orders, they also liberated the enslaved people they encountered. This was a task readily accomplished, as hundreds of bondpeople on their own initiative fled their homes and plantations and made their way to Union gunboats positioned along the beachhead. In just one night, some 750 enslaved people became free. Because of the effective use of black troops to destroy infrastructure, liberate of hundreds of bondpeople, and thus irreparably damage the Confederate war machine, the raid on the Combahee was in the words of one abolitionist, "a glorious consummation."[1]

The incursion made a different impression on a local planter who wrote of his experience in the *Charleston Mercury*. On the night of the raid, a trusted slave "rushed precipitately in my room, and informed me that two of the enemy steamers were in full sight, and would soon be opposite my landing." House servants met the planter at the portico of the house, where they "all stood around me, professing the utmost attachment, and their perfect willingness to obey my commands, but not exhibiting the slightest degree of alarm or surprise. Finding that the negroes did not come to me from the settlement, as I had ordered, I immediately went there, found them all about their houses." The planter noticed the landing of about twenty black soldiers and a white officer, and ordered his slaves to follow him into the woods. "They all professed a willingness to do so, but not one made a sign of moving. As I had not a single arm of defence about my person, I was forced to fly to the woods for protection." While he was escaping, the "enemy set house to flames, smoke rising in distance, burning simultaneously were mills, overseer's house, and barns on his property and others." Once loyal slaves "were rushing to the boat with their children, now and then greeting some one whom they recognized among the uniformed negroes, and who were probably former runaways from the various plantations in the neighborhood. The negros seemed to be utterly transformed, drunk with excitement, and capable of the wildest excesses." The horror was unimaginable. "The roaring of the flames, the barbarous howls of the negros, the blowing of horns, the harsh steam whistle, and the towering columns of smoke from every quarter, made an impression on my mind which can never be effaced. Here, I thought to myself, is a repetition of San Domingo."[2]

The planter's account reveals that while some recognized the end of slavery and the employment of some 200,000 bondmen in the United States army as singular achievements in the history of the republic, others saw in these events the opening salvo of a race war like the one in Haiti. Having demonstrated that the Haitian Revolution was a resonant symbol that southern extremists successfully exploited to convince moderates of the necessity of secession, our focus now turns toward the war years when southern speakers and writers deployed the horrific narrative of the Haitian Revolution to buttress Confederate nationalism. As white southerners would never submit to a repetition of the "horrors of St. Domingo," this fear reinforced Confederate's commitment to their nation and steeled their resolve to win the war. In addition to stoking the flames of Confederate nationalism, fear of a second Haitian Revolution also encouraged a white racial identity, which would prove even more resilient than the ties that bound the citizens of the Confederacy. For while the Civil War destroyed both the Confederate nation and the peculiar institution it was built to defend, it simultaneously bolstered the white supremacist ideology that would continue to hold this "imagined community" of white men and women together long after the war's conclusion.[3]

Scholars of southern nationhood have long debated the existence of a national identity that was capable of uniting various southern white constituencies across economic, social, and geographic boundaries. Some have gone so far as to blame the failure of southern nationalism for the defeat of the Confederacy.[4] Recent scholarship, however, swings the pendulum in a different direction. Gary Gallagher maintains that Confederate defeat came in spite of the popular will of the white population of the South to fight for national independence, concluding, "Far from being a loosely knit collection of individuals whose primary allegiance lay with their states, a substantial portion of the Confederate people identified strongly with their southern republic. Wartime writings frequently employed language that revealed a sense of national community."[5] Sara Ann Rubin suggests that the Civil War inspired such a robust and resilient national identity among white southerners that it outlived the war itself.[6] Gallagher and Rubin also agree on the importance of slavery to confederate nationhood, echoing the words of Drew Gilpin Faust, who wrote in *The Creation of Confederate Nationalism*, "the South's ideological isolation within an increasingly antislavery world was not a stigma or a source of guilt but a badge of righteousness and a foundation for national identity and pride."[7]

With slavery the cornerstone of the Confederacy, fear of a second Haitian Revolution was from the outset of the war an important touchstone of southern nationalism, as one flag presentation ceremony in Hopefield, Arkansas attests. The presentation took place on only the second day of the war, as Confederate artillery continued to reign on Fort Sumter. It culminated with the "matrons and daughters" of Crittenden County offering a flag to a cavalry unit composed of men from the local region who were known as the Crittenden Rangers. The flag was, according to one observer, "the most beautiful standard of the Southern Confederacy I have ever seen." Presenter Mollie Merriweather addressed the patriotic men who stood in front of her on the significance of the sacrifice they were about to make: "With pride and pleasure I present this banner to your gallant company—those brave spirits who have so promptly volunteered to aid the South in defending her honor and rights." As the state of Arkansas had not yet joined the Confederacy, Merriweather trusted that the rangers would cast their die with the new southern nation, entreating, "This banner is the assurance that you have our smiles and best wishes, and should the conflict come, our prayers. On its blue field are seven stars, representing the seven glorious States of the Southern Confederation. Our own state, Arkansas, may not yet claim a place among them; but with bright hope that she will ere long united her destiny with theirs, I have left a space and intrust this star to your keeping." Merriweather implored, "Will not each one pledge himself by every endeavor to place her among her sister States?" She then expressed concern that some doubted the fidelity of the men of Crittenden County to the Confederate cause, and asked, "Will brave men quietly submit to Black Republican rule? Shall our glorious South be made a second St. Domingo? Forbid it, soldiers! Forbid it, heaven!"[8]

First Lieutenant J. B. Rogers provided the company's response, revealing the gendered notion of Confederate manhood. While women had a vital part to play in the success of the Confederacy, they were not to enter the battlefield; consequently, avoiding a second Haitian Revolution depended on the heroic and manly efforts of white men.[9] After taking the stand and thanking Merriweather for the "star circled banner," he then ordered the men of Crittenden County to "unfurl to the breeze our glorious banner, and swear to defend it, come weal, come woe!" Rogers yearned for each of these men to fulfill their manly responsibilities, concluding, "Allow me to say . . . to her who gave it, long will you live in the hearts of us all; your gift we will defend till life's pulses be still, and if in death we must behold it, the last whispered prayer of the dying soldier will be for its preservation, and for the happiness of her whose fair fingers made it." To the company's flag bearer Rogers commanded, "Take it, sir, and defend it; never allow it to be polluted by an enemy's touch so long as you have strength to raise an arm to strike in its defense."[10]

In the coming months, radical changes taking place in the North suggested to many in the South that their worst fears were to be realized. A man traveling to Washington, D.C., reported on the state of mind of planters in Vicksburg, Mississippi, where he had just visited. Planters were growing increasingly concerned at the prospect of a slave uprising. Plantation laborers, who had "a very correct general idea of the condition of the country," had begun committing wanton acts of violence. In one instance, "A planter, owning several hundred negroes, ordered three of them to do some trivial work; they grumbled, and finally said they would do it, but they needn't without they wanted to, as they could be *free* whenever they liked." An instant later, "the master drew his revolver, and shot one of them dead on the spot. The next day the master met the other two negroes just as he was coming out of his house. One of them deliberately aimed an old shot-gun at him, and in an instant he was a dead man." The murderers escaped and remained at large. The incident confirmed the growing conviction that "All the 'peculiar institution' seems to want is a *leader*, when a second St. Domingo massacre will be the inevitable consequence."[11]

The Emancipation Proclamation and the employment of black troops in the Union army proved that the southern nation stood on the precipice of a terrible race war, and thus encouraged among Confederates a widespread commitment to total war. When reports surfaced that Union general John McNeil had executed ten Confederate soldiers in Palmyra, Missouri, in retaliation for the disappearance and likely murder of a well-known Union sympathizer, a writer in the *Richmond Whig* applauded the decision of the Georgia legislature to hang all "Yankees" found in the state. He encouraged the spread of the practice, offering, "Such should be the action of every southern State." Drastic times called for drastic measures; thus, he asked, "Have you reflected upon the consequences of Lincoln's proclamation, if it could be carried out? Read the history of the massacre at St. Domingo, the horrid outrages committed by mere brutes, uncivilized negroes, upon tender and defenceless women." Abolitionists were responsible for encouraging such crimes in the southern states. "They gloat in anticipation over the scenes of horror which they fancy will ensue." For the defenders of the Confederacy there was only option. "Let but one thought animate the hearts of our brave soldier, and nerve their arms—to have the heart's blood of every scoundrel who pollutes our soil, and whose soul is black with the infamy of the deeds which, fortunately, they are impotent to execute."[12]

The use of the Haitian Revolution to encourage Confederate nationalism was not a local phenomenon. In Richmond, Virginia, in 1864, members of the Senate and House of Representatives of the Confederate States of America formed a joint committee, which addressed the citizens of the Confederate States on the implications of the disturbing transformation of northern policy regarding slavery. The responsibility for drafting the text of the address fell to Jabez Lamar Monroe Curry. A native of the Deep South who studied law at Harvard University, Curry drafted a document that he intended to galvanize the men and women of the Confederacy.[13] In spite of northern aggression regarding slavery and significant military defeats of the Confederate army at Gettysburg and Vicksburg, Curry and the Confederate Congress assured the public that their cause remained just and that defeat was not an option. The desperate quality of the opening sentence of the resolution set the tone for the remainder of the text. "The present is deemed a fitting occasion to remind the people of the Confederate States that they are engaged in a struggle for the preservation both of liberty and civilization; and that no sacrifice of life or fortune can be too costly which may be requisite to secure to themselves and their posterity the enjoyment of these inappreciable blessings." Northern "Fanaticism has summoned to its aid cupidity and vengeance; and nothing short of your utter subjugation, the destruction of your State governments, the overthrow of your social and political fabric, your personal and public degradation and ruin, will satisfy the demands of the North." The days of reconciliation were past. "At one time, it was the wish and expectation of many at the South, to form a treaty of amity and friendship with the northern States." Instead, "a cruel war of invasion was commenced, which, in its progress, has been marked by a brutality and disregard of the rules of civilized warfare that stand out in un-exampled barbarity in the history of modern wars." The atrocities defied description. "Instead of a regular war, our resistance is treated as a rebellion, and the settled international rules between belligerents are ignored." During the American Revolution, the text continued, Lord Dunmore refrained from employing Americans' slaves as soldiers, rather they were considered as nothing other "than as property and plunder." The British did not arm slaves because such a policy even in times of war was "severely condemned and denounced by the most eminent publicists in Europe and the United States." Now, however, northerners ignored the rules of civilized nations. "Disregarding the teachings of the approved writers on international law, and the practice and claims of his own Government in its purer days, President Lincoln has sought to convert the South into a St. Domingo, by appealing to the cupidity, lusts, ambition, and ferocity of the slave."[14]

The fate of the southern nation rested in the hands of its men. "We combat for property, homes, the honor of our wives, the future of our children, the preservation of our fair land from pollution, and to avert a doom which we can read, both in the threats of our enemies and the acts of oppression, we have alluded to in this address." There was additionally, Curry maintained, in spite of the many obstacles now facing the Confederacy, no reason for despair. "Instead of harsh criticisms on the Government and our generals; instead of bewailing the failure to accomplish impossibilities, we should rather be grateful, humbly and profoundly, to a benignant Providence, for the results that have rewarded our labors. Remembering the disproportion in population, in military and naval resources, and the deficiency of skilled labor in the South, our accomplishments have surpassed those recorded of any people in the annals of the world." There was no reason to despair. "The fires of patriotism still burn unquenchably in the breasts of those who are subject to foreign domination. We yet have in our uninterrupted control a territory, which, according to past progress, will require the enemy ten years to overrun." The text concluded with a rousing appeal to the citizens of the southern nation. "Be of good cheer and spare no labor nor sacrifices that may be necessary to enable us to win the campaign which we have just entered. We have passed through great trials of affliction, but suffering and humiliation are the school-masters that led nations to self-reliance and independence." The trials of war were but providential measures that "mature and develop and solidify our people." What the southern states needed now was unity. "Let all spirit of faction and past party differences be forgotten in the presence of our cruel foe. . . . Moral aid has the 'power of the incommunicable,' and, by united efforts, by an all-comprehending and self-sacrificing patriotism, we can, with the blessing of God, avert the perils which environ us, and achieve for ourselves and children peace and freedom. Hitherto the Lord has interposed graciously to bring us victory, and in His hand there is present power to prevent this great multitude which come against us from casting us out of the possession which He has given us to inherit."[15]

Curry's manifesto of southern nationalism struck a chord. Curry later wrote, "The Committee approved my address. I read it to the House amid much applause; and so enthusiastic was the approbation, that every member of both Houses signed it." The more than one hundred of the South's best and brightest who affixed their names to the document represent a who's who of the southern nation. Among them were Robert Woodward Barnwell, a former United States Senator and the son of the legendary Revolutionary War soldier and Continental Congress delegate Robert Barnwell; John R. Chambliss, a prominent Virginia politician whose son, a brigadier general in the Confederate Army had recently lost his life in southern Virginia while taking part in some of the bloodiest battles of the war; Thomas Jefferson Foster, an Alabama infantryman who after the Confederate defeat at Fort Henry in Tennessee served as a representative in the First and Second Confederate Congress; and Gustavus Adolphus Henry, a grandson of revolutionary patriot Patrick Henry and the man for whom the fort along the Tennessee River was named. The "horrors of St. Domingo" resonated with all of them. Steps taken by the Confederate Congress ensured public consumption of the Joint Resolution. "Several thousand copies were ordered to be published, for circulation among the people and in the army." The address made the author somewhat of a celebrity. After stepping down from his position in the Confederate House of Representatives and enlisting in the Confederate Army, Curry on occasion encountered soldiers who, "knowing my authorship of the address, gave me the most cordial and flattering receptions."[16]

Curry's closing appeal to God, his faith in a higher power to protect the South from a second Haitian Revolution and bestow victory upon the Confederacy, reinforces the role of religion in sustaining Confederate nation-

alism. It moreover demonstrates the widely held belief among white southerners that slavery was not only a legal institution but a divinely sanctioned
one as well. Scholars of southern nationalism agree. Drew Gilpin Faust writes
that slavery was, "in both secular and religious discourse, the central com-
ponent of the mission God had designed for the South."[17] This idea is borne
out in a fiery jeremiad delivered in November 1861, deep in the heart of the
Confederacy. In observance of a national day of "Fasting, Humiliation, and
Prayer" announced by the president of the Confederacy, Jefferson Davis,
Reverend Thomas Verner Moore spoke to the First and Second Presbyterian
Churches of Richmond, with the intent of both saving the souls of Confederate Christians and strengthening their resolve to see the war through to the
bitter end. The sermon, which soon appeared in pamphlet form, contained
in the words of its publishers "such fearless, honest and forcible expression of
truths essential to our existence and success in which our Confederacy is now
engaged, that we believe its presentation to the public would be of very great
advantage." Moore encouraged the people of the Confederacy not to shrink
from the scourge of war, as their sins had helped bring the war to fruition.
Among the most evil was the lack of unity among the people. "What our
young Republic needed was a feeling of oneness, a broad, deep national unity,
binding together the separate sovereignties of the Confederacy, so that whilst,
politically, they shall be 'distinct as the billows,' yet, nationally, they shall be
'one as the sea.' Although the common of institution of domestic slavery is a
powerful bond of union, especially in view of the mighty hostility against it
that compresses its adherents together, yet even this could not have created
this national unity, as we had it, under a peaceful separation." An ever great
sin was the failure of generations of white southerners to vanquish the northern "anti-slavery Hydra," which had "Spawned in the huge Serbonian bog of
French infidelity and radicalism" during the French Revolution.[18]

Moore described the likely scenario should the Confederacy fail in its Her-
culean task and lose the war. "Let this tremendous crusade become successful,
either by mismanagement in the army, or cowardice and greediness at home,
and history furnishes no page so dark and bloody as that which would record the result." With the end of slavery, "Our best and bravest men would be
slaughtered like bullocks in the shambles; our wives and daughters dishonored
before our eyes; our cities sacked; our fields laid waste; our homes pillaged and
burned." What infuriated Moore most was that northerners encouraged slaves
to commit these barbaric acts. "Have they not kidnapped hundreds of servants
and then made them beasts of burden; and is not their mighty armada now

prowling along our coast, intending to arm the rest for another St. Domingo massacre?" Moore demanded in the third and final portion of his sermon the ultimate sacrifice of the white men of the South to resist such a threat. "WE SHOULD THEN GIRD OURSELVES FOR THIS CONFLICT IN THE HOPE THAT GOD WILL MAINTAIN OUR CAUSE." The North's effecting of total war meant that there was "nothing now left us but a death-grapple for very existence." Confederates, he vowed, would not shrink from such a challenge. Death was preferable. "If we must perish, is it not better to die the death of a man on the field of honor, than to die the death of a dog on the gibbet? Is it not better to meet this huge barbaric invasion with one flaming front of defiant resistance, than to sit hugging our treasures until the grip of the invaders is at our throats, his manacles on our wrists, and we bound helpless at his feet?" God was on the side of the Confederate States of America, Moore avowed, and "If we are worthy to take our place among the nations of the earth, no human power may hinder us; for eight millions of brave, united and determined people can never be conquered."[19]

As each of these entreaties affirms, nothing horrified Confederates more than the prospect of having to face former slaves who returned to their homes and plantations in the employ of the Union army. "Armed blacks," James McPherson writes, were "truly the bête noire of southern nightmares"[20] The employment of black soldiers marked a radical transformation in the North's military objectives, which demanded an extraordinary response. A writer in Tennessee commented, "It is announced in the Northern telegrams that one hundred thousand cavalry are soon to be armed and equipped for our destruction. Simultaneously we hear from every quarter that regiments and brigades of negroes are also to be pressed into the ranks of our foes." The reason for these movements was clear. "Enemies, despairing of conquest by armies or infantry, and unwilling to expose their own precious persons to the privation, suffering and death result and from a fair and equal conflict, are resolved to burn up our bridges, cities, depots and dwelling-houses, by raids in the interior, and to add the horrors of a St. Domingo massacre to their own plundering and brutal warfare." What did this mean for the Confederacy? There was no turning back now. "Such elements of darkness do not mean reunion; they do not even stop at the idea of conquest and subjugation; they can only portend utter desolation and extermination."[21]

As increasing numbers of black soldiers came south, the conviction grew among Confederates that they were witnessing a Second Haitian Revolution. Several Confederate newspapers reprinted an account of atrocities committed by black soldiers in an article entitled "The Horrors of St. Domingo Repeated." According to the author, black soldiers under the direction of Union general Philip Sheridan detained one white man in Virginia who "after having everything destroyed, was stripped, tied up, and given thirty-nine lashes with the cowhide." The worst was yet to come. "More horrible, but only too true, twenty or thirty ladies were violated by this party of negroes. Six negroes violated the person of Mrs. G. eleven times, she being sick at the time with an infant six months old at the breast."[22] One newspaper correspondent in Jacksonville, Florida, tried to convey the fear white southerners felt when they stood face-to-face with black soldiers. "They would not have cared if white troops had surprised them, but to wake up in the morning and find Cuffee, Dick, Bob, Sam, Hercules, Sancho—their old servants, their former riches, one million dollars of fugacious property—up in arms, with knapsack, cartridge-box and musket, was galling to human nature. The citizens, some of them talked profanely; the women went into hysterics. They were, without doubt, terribly frightened." Fear possessed them. "They had a horrid nightmare; the thought of St. Domingo; they imagined blood, outrage and death in most appalling shape!"[23]

Considering the regularity with which Confederates invoked the Haitian Revolution when contemplating the horror of black Union soldiers, it is expected that the revolution also infused the extraordinarily controversial debate over arming slaves in the Confederacy. According to Joseph Reidy, from the outbreak of war a handful of southern white men openly discussed the possibility of arming slaves, but it was not until the last year of the war after a number of important military setbacks that the Confederate government began to seriously consider the proposal.[24] Among the leading advocates of the radical measure was General Patrick Cleburne of the Army of Tennessee, who insisted that the survival of the Confederacy took precedence over the survival of the institution of slavery. "As between the loss of independence and the loss of slavery," Cleburne reasoned, "we assume that every patriot will freely give up the latter—give up the Negro slave rather than be a slave himself." In an extraordinary twist, Cleburne amplified the memories of radical abolitionists in the North who insisted that the history of the Haitian Revolution proved that given the opportunity, slaves would fight. In "Cleburne's memorial," the General and twelve signatories invoked history to answer the pressing question, "Will the slaves fight?" Spartan slaves "stood their masters good stead in battle. In the great sea fight of Lepanto where the Christians checked forever the spread of Mohammedanism over Europe, the galley slaves of portions of the fleet were promised freedom, and called on to fight at a critical moment of the battle. They fought well, and civilization owes much to those brave galley slaves. The negro slaves of Saint Domingo, fighting for freedom, defeated their white masters and the French troops sent against them." American slaves would also fight in return for freedom.[25] Cleburne's reading of Haitian history violated some of the basic tenets of the Confederate ideology, which explains why the southern republic only embraced the radical measure in the last days of the war, too late for the experiment in black Confederates to begin. Nevertheless, the decision to embrace the once unconscionable idea was not a signal of a transformation in southern racial ideology. Since the plan ultimately ignored emancipation and included no attempt to provide political and economic liberty for black Confederate soldiers after the war, it was, Bruce Levine explains, simply a desperate attempt "to salvage at least something of slavery from the Old South's wreckage."[26]

More common was the response of those who invoked the "horrors of St. Domingo" to demonstrate the insanity of any scheme that led to either slave emancipation or black soldiery. State representative Lewis Hanes warned the North Carolina General Assembly of the likely results of the presence of "200,000 negroes well-armed, with all their passions aroused." They would assuredly reenact "among us all the inexpressible horrors of the massacre of Saint Domingo."[27] Another North Carolinian echoed Hanes's belief: "The negroes are to be armed, and society is to be not merely upset, but destroyed." The events that the French Revolution stirred in Haiti "will afflict us here, if this policy be adopted. We call upon the Legislature of this State, now in session, to rise to the magnitude of the occasion, and not only to stamp this infamous proposition with the seal of its reprobation, but to adopt promptly the most vigorous measures to enact an honorable PEACE, which can alone close this Pandora's box of ills untold."[28]

Probably no other communication on black soldiery in the Confederacy reached as many readers then a speech of Mississippi State Congressman Henry Cousins Chambers, who was startled at the news that leading Confederates including President Jefferson Davis were in favor of allowing bondmen to serve in the Confederate Army.[29] Chambers acknowledged the usefulness of slaves in supplying Confederate forces on the front lines, but insisted of the southern bondman, "He cannot be made a minute man." Cousins expressed relief that the Confederacy was "not yet reduced to extremity," and he begged God that the Confederate Army "may never have to drink this cup." Chambers invoked the Haitian Revolution to suggest the futility of a Confederate policy of black soldiers. "In St. Domingo, the English, in 1792, with less than

1,000 men, captured several fortified places from the French authorities, who had over 20,000 troops, chiefly negroes and mulattoes; and finally, with less than 2,000 men, captured Port au Prince, the capital of the island. The French, in extremity, offered freedom to the slaves, more than 400,000 in number, on condition of military service; but only 6,000 accepted the boon." These were slaves "whose hands were still bloody with the massacres perpetrated in the memorable insurrection of 1790." The suggestion of arming slaves was ludicrous. Even so, Chambers asked, what would happen to the slave soldier upon completion of the war? "Will you offer him his freedom?" The North will offer him freedom. "Will you offer him the privilege of returning home to his family, a freeman, after the war? That you dare not do, remembering it was the free negroes of Saint Domingo, who had been trained to arms, that excited the insurrection of the slaves." The solution was simple. "Better far to employ mercenaries from abroad, and preserve that institution which is not only the foundation of our wealth but the palladium of our liberties." To experiment with black troops in an effort to win the war was to admit defeat. "When we shall be reduced to the extremity of exclaiming to the slaves, 'Help us, or we sink,' it will already have been quite immaterial what course we pursue!"[30]

The apocalyptical imagery of slave revolt deployed by the opponents of black Confederate soldiers calls to mind one of the most powerful symbols of the Haitian Revolution that Confederate patriots employed during the Civil War to maintain popular support of their struggle. Undoubtedly, no image evoked the horrors of a second Haitian Revolution more than that of black slaves impaling white infants on stakes and spears. First reported by white colonists from Saint-Domingue in 1791 and disseminated in speeches, newspapers, and books, the trope resonated throughout transatlantic oral and print culture for generations. In the first widely circulated account, authors described the visit of one white colonist to a plantation owned by Joseph d'Honor de Gallifet. This intrepid man, who hoped to restore law and order, was unprepared for what he encountered: "the negroes were all embodied, and attacked him. *Their standard was the body of a white infant impaled upon a stake.*"[31] Like so much of the horrific narrative of the Haitian Revolution, it remained for Bryan Edwards and Archibald Alison to instruct an expansive transatlantic reading audience of the revolting act. Edwards copied directly from the original text, going so far as to include the italics for effect, writing of the same colonist, "on approaching the estate, to his surprise and grief he found all the negroes in arms on the side of the rebels, and (horrid to tell!) *their standard was the body of a white infant, which they had recently impaled on a stake!*"[32] Alison paraphrased: "The cruelties exercised on the unhappy captives on both sides in this disastrous contest, exceeded anything recorded in history. The negroes marched with spiked infants on their spears instead of colours."[33]

There are a number of reasons to question the accuracy of these accounts. First, the propagandistic quality of the original eyewitness account is patent. In the speech before the French legislature, distressed representatives from Saint-Domingue begged military assistance from the metropole, entreating, "Our first duty is to assure you of the inviolable attachment of this important part of the empire to the mother-country, before we describe to you the terrible events which are now working its destruction, and solicit the earliest and most effectual succour, to save, if it be yet possible, its wretched remains. *Long have we foreseen the evils which afflict us*, and which, doubtless, will end in our annihilation, if the national justice and power interpose not speedily for our relief." Given Saint-Domingue's great distance from France and the potential costs of any transatlantic military expedition, only the most unspeakable atrocities would secure the intervention of the French government and army. Second, though synonymous with the Haitian Revolution in the nineteenth-century Atlantic world, descriptions of marauding armies impaling infants on their swords have a long tradition in Western literature. From Indian and colonial wars to the French Revolution, Nazi Germany in the Second World War, and most recently the Balkan Wars of the 1990s, the image has long resonated throughout western culture, serving as an antithesis of European civilization and modernity. Still, the literary imagination of European writers does not negate the authenticity of the account of the incident in Saint-Domingue. The occurrence of such an act is even likely, given both the horrors of slavery and the catalogue of atrocities recorded by black and white witnesses to the revolution.

Like so much about the Haitian Revolution, whether Haitian bondmen impaled white infants on their spears remains unknowable.[34] Even so, debate over the veracity of the descriptions of infant impalement misses the point. What matters is that the Civil War offered a tremendous opportunity for Confederates to deploy the trope with great effect. Prior to the Emancipation Proclamation, Virginia essayist T. W. MacMahon published a white supremacist harangue on the "American Crisis" that sold 5,000 copies in one month and more than 10,000 in a year. In what one historian of the Confederacy calls a "compilation of hackneyed proslavery arguments," MacMahon insisted, "In a condition of slavery, the negro may prove himself to be a most useful, interesting, and affectionate animal; but he will not work without a master." The best example of this was Haiti, "once the pride of the ocean, now a political curse and social ulcer, with the monstrous tragedy of which the reader cannot be unacquainted." In Haiti, Robespierre "and other bloodhounds and incarnate devils, of the French Revolution, calling themselves Amis des Noirs, and anticipating the Beechers, Sewards, Garrisons, Phillipses, and Parkers, of the North, stimulated the negroes of this unfortunate Island into a servile and barbarous insurrection. The atrocities which ensued are without parallel in the most diabolical annals of crime." Quoting Alison's *History of Europe*, MacMahon wrote of the victorious Haitian slaves, they "marched with spiked infants on their spears instead of colors; they sawed asunder the male prisoners, and violated the females on the dead bodies of their husbands."[35] After learning of the Emancipation Proclamation's authorization of the enlistment of black troops, one outraged writer exclaimed, 'Arming Negroes!' Why it sends a thrill of horror to every true woman's heart, that chills and freezes the soul. 'Arming Negroes!' Why, it is but another name for lust and rapine, and indiscriminate carnage. 'Arming Negroes!' Why, it means the heart of the man on a dagger, the body of the infant on a pike, and the mother strangled and dying, the victim of hellish passion."[36]

That Confederates deployed the infamous trope of infant impalement to steel the resolve of their fellow citizens is apparent, yet its frequent use by white southerners long before the war indicates that this was not the only purpose it served. That the trope appeared in one of the more memorable proslavery harangues delivered in the halls of the U.S. Congress in the antebellum period indicates that it had a much richer history. Throughout the first half of the nineteenth century, stories of Haitian slaves impaling white infants served as an explosive weapon in the arsenal of white supremacy. In January 1846, Representative William Lowndes Yancey of Alabama addressed the House of Representatives in an effort to gain Congressional support for the annexation of Texas. Yancey accused the northern opponents of annexation of conspiring in an abolitionist plot to end slavery and spread racial equality throughout the slave states. It was a horrifying possibility, the Alabama planter explained. He then, according to his biographer, proceeded to defend slavery and attack liberty, "letting loose a viciously racist salvo."[37] The precedent was set in Massachusetts, Yancey pointed out, where the legislature had recently repealed legislation outlawing interracial marriage. What was the result? "The black son of Africa, with flat nose, thick lips, protruding shin, and skin redolent of rare odors, though free to rise to the high estate of the white man—though the parlors of the proud Puritan are thrown open to him—though free to ally himself with, ay, and even invited to the arms of, the fair-skinned, cherry-lipped, and graceful daughter of that famed race, still retains his nature—rejects with scorn the tendered connection, and prefers to revel in the brothel, until imprisoned in a jail or penitentiary." Yancey warned of the dangers of abolitionism, asserting that it was imperative to remember that in Haiti "wives were violated upon the bodies of their slaughtered husbands, and the banner of the inhuman fiends was the dead body of an infant, impaled upon a spear, its golden lock dabbled in gore, and its little limbs stiffened by the last agony of suffering nature!"[38]

Years later, when writers in slave states that refused to join the Confederacy described rebel slaves impaling white youth, they, like Yancey, promoted a white racial identity that was distinct from Confederate nationalism. In the first year of the war, a Maryland writer calling himself "Harper" demanded Northerners explain how they would end slavery without inviting a race war. " 'Slavery is the cause of the war,' say you; 'let us while we are about it destroy the root of the evil.' Well, the case is ready for your surgery, how will you apply the knife? There is one way-simple, sure and deadly—the John Brown method." According to Harper, northerners would either "Establish a footing anywhere in the heart of the cotton region, or begin upon Virginia and the rebellious counties of Maryland; collect a sufficient number of blacks, free or slave; arm them with pikes, scythes, knives, pitchforks and Lucifer matches. Firearms would be rather an embarrassment." Only "a few barrels of common corn whiskey, magazines of which might be provided at different practicable points," were necessary ammunition. Starting inland the slaves would kill and burn. "The aged and feeble will perish in the flames of their homesteads, women will meet a worse fate, and infants will be carried to the next plantation impaled on pikes and pitch forks. The tossing of infants in the air to catch them on the points of bayonets was a pastime much in vogue with the liberators of St. Domingo." Once accomplished, the Union army would have little difficulty subduing southern rebels who endeavored to "check this terrible tide of 'emancipation.' "[39]

Baltimore cartoonist Adalbert Volck similarly conflated the impaling of white infants with the abolition of slavery in a popular wartime illustration (Figure 10). A German immigrant and renowned dentist, Volck was a pro-slavery zealot who produced a series of lithographs to counter the antislavery illustrations emanating from northern print culture, including those by another German-American political cartoonist, Thomas Nast. In *Writing the Emancipation Proclamation*, Volck portrays a brooding and intoxicated Abra-

Figure 10. Adalbert Volck, *The Emancipation Proclamation* (1864). The large portrait in the background labeled "St. Domingo" amplifies the widespread fear that Lincoln's proclamation would invite a second Haitian Revolution. Courtesy of the Collections of the Library of Congress.

ham Lincoln slumped at a small desk drafting the proclamation, with his left foot resting on a copy of the Constitution. A devilish figurine at the center of the desk holds an inkwell securely in place. The desk's spectral eye and cloven hooves amplify the satanic imagery. In the background, two paintings hang on the wall. Above Lincoln is a portrait of John Brown, holding a pike in his left hand. A halo floats above his head. To Lincoln's right is a portrait entitled, "St. Domingo," which depicts half-naked African slaves dancing in a wild orgy of blood and bedlam. A slave dressed in a loincloth prepares to stab a white infant he holds upside down. Other slaves impale young victims on spears and pikes in the background. One insurrectionist carries a woman into the woods where he will undoubtedly ravish the pure and innocent young captive. The message of the illustration is clear. With the writing of the Emancipation Proclamation, the Civil War had become a second Haitian Revolution. No member of the white race was safe.

Volck was not alone in carrying the mantle of white nationalism apart from that of the Confederacy. In the last months of the war, Kate Stone, a young woman from Louisiana who had fled to Texas with her family after learning of the approach of the Union army, made an entry in her diary in which she recorded her daily activities. In addition to stitching a pair of gloves and reading a biography of Stonewall Jackson, she described her having completed Harriet Martineau's lengthy fictional biography of Toussaint Louverture, *The Hour and the Man.* Though failing to comment on the author's talent as a writer, Stone had much to offer on the subject of Martineau's work. Louverture was "represented as superhumanly good and great beyond all heroes of ancient or modern times. He and Napoleon were contemporaries and comparisons are constantly drawn between them, all in favor of this darkie saint. Napoleon is completely overshadowed by Toussaint." It was, Stone concluded, "a disgusting book." Africans were "all represented as angelic beings, pure and good, while the whites are the fiends who entered in and took possession of their Eden, Haiti."[40] Stone's revulsion at the abolitionist's diminution of the white race is revealing, as it illuminates how little the war affected the strength and resiliency of her commitment to the white race.

It moreover reveals how little the demise of the Confederacy affected memory of the Haitian Revolution among white southerners. Indeed, the onset of Radical Reconstruction would only encourage the memory of the "horrors of St. Domingo" among the white residents of the former southern slave states. Eric Foner, who dates Reconstruction from the Emancipation Proclamation, has described the effort of northerners to secure both the economic and political equality of former slaves in the postwar years thusly: "The transformation of slaves into free laborers and equal citizens was the most dramatic example of the social and political changes unleashed by the Civil War and emancipation."[41] The continuance of the racial revolution launched during the war deeply disturbed white southerners who as they had done for generations continued to anticipate Armageddon.

In *De Bow's Review,* University of Virginia history professor George Frederick Holmes and racial theorist George Fitzhugh contemplated the future of civilization in a rapidly devolving world. "The most remarkable characteristics of the current generation," Holmes wrote after the war, "appears to be the fever of anarchy and revolution which rages in the veins of society." Scripture offered a clue as to what was now in store. "The earth shall be destroyed by fire, and consumed 'with fervent heat.' The destruction of Sodom and Gomorroh by the sulphurous storm of flame has long been regarded as typical of the destiny which awaits a guilty world when its sins become incurable and unendurable by either man or heaven." The bloodshed and slaughter of the Civil War, along with "the devastation of the lands of the lately Confederated States; the agony and anguish and destitution which have been left behind; the oppression and anarchy which are menaced," all combined to prepare the way for the impending storm. "For good or evil a new birth of time is at hand; a new cycle of the ages is preparing to unroll itself; a new revolution of fate is in prospect." Fitzhugh added that soon the entire South would be engulfed in a tidal wave of slave insurrection, leaving white southerners at the mercy of "savage tribes of negroes." The consequences were difficult to imagine. "After the proposed reconstruction, the federal troops will be withdrawn, and the negroes, trained at the polls to hostility towards the white, and outnumbering them greatly in all the fertile parts of the South, with arms in their hand, gaffed and pitted for the fight, will be turned loose upon the feeble remnant of unarmed whites, to celebrate another greater than St. Domingo tragedy." The dark forecast was a sign of things to come. Though allusions to the Haitian Revolution would decline in the postbellum period, memory of the revolution among white southerners endured.[42]

The Civil War ignited an explosion of popular memory of the "horrors of St. Domingo," which Confederate speakers and writers exploited throughout the Civil War to reinforce the public's commitment to the new nation that had been built to defend both slavery and white supremacy. In speeches, pamphlets, articles, and tracts, they used the fear of a second Haitian Revolution to steel the resolve of the men and women of the Confederacy to wage war. When General Lee surrendered to the Union Army at Appomattox, Virginia, in April 1865 and the Confederate States of America collapsed, many in the North hoped that the social and political revolution regarding race that had taken place above the Mason-Dixon Line would have had a similar impact beneath it; this, however, was not the case. It would be more accurate to say that the war had the opposite effect. While the abolition of slavery and employment of tens of thousands of former slaves in the Union army helped topple the Confederacy, the revolutionary measures simultaneously encouraged a strong racial identification among white southerners who joined arms at the outset of the war and following its conclusion stubbornly refused to let go. Confederate's wartime references to the "horrors of St. Domingo" furthered a drive for white nationalism that predated the birth of the Confederacy and survived long after its death. In the next chapter, we see just how successful the movement to build and maintain a white nation was by turning our attention to the North.

CHAPTER 8

"Do we want another San Domingo to be repeated in the South?" Northern White Identity

IN DECEMBER 1859, Edward Everett, the celebrated politician, educator, and orator, emerged from retirement to deliver an address in support of the Union at Boston's historic Faneuil Hall. At the institutional epicenter of American abolitionism, the septuagenarian explained to his audience the motivation behind his return to public life: "The war of words—of the press, of the platform, of the State legislatures, and, must I add, the pulpit," had brought the nation to the brink of disaster. Everett saw on the horizon a "convulsion, which will shake the Union to its foundation; and that a few more steps forward in the direction in which affairs have moved for a few years past, will bring us to the catastrophe." Northern sympathy for John Brown infuriated Everett, who urged those listening to empathize with the intended victims of Brown's attack. "Suppose a party of desperate, misguided men, under a resolved and fearless leader, had been organized in Virginia, to come and establish themselves by stealth in Springfield in this State . . . to stir up a social revolution." What if "pikes and rifles to arm twenty-five hundred men had been procured by funds raised by extensive subscriptions throughout the South?" Everett vilified those in the North who celebrated a deranged man who spent years plotting a southern slave insurrection. "To talk of the pikes and rifles not being intended for offensive purposes" was contemptible. Everett explained that there was historical precedent for what Brown hoped to accomplish. The attack on Harpers Ferry was nothing less "to do on a vast scale what was done in St. Domingo in 1791." Hoping to convey the horrors of slave revolt, he invoked Bryan Edwards's account of infant impalement. Words were unable to describe accurately what took place in Haiti. "The conflagrations, which were visible in a thousand different quarters, furnished a prospect more shocking, and reflections more dismal than fancy can paint, or the powers of man describe." Everett depicted the people for whom Brown intended to "extend the awful calamity, which turned St. Domingo into a heap of bloody ashes." They were good Americans, "of education and culture—of moral and religious lives and characters—virtuous fathers, mothers, sons, and daughters, persons who would adorn any station of society, in any country— men who read the same Bible that we do, and in the name of the same master, kneel at the throne of the same God—forming a class of men from which have gone forth some of the greatest and purest characters which adorn our history—Washington, Jefferson, Madison, Monroe, Marshall." These were the men and women "for whose bosoms pikes and rifles are manufactured in New England, to be placed in the hands of an ignorant and subject race, supposed, most wrongfully, as recent events have shown, to be waiting only for an opportunity to use them!"[1]

Everett was a prominent New Englander, a northerner staunchly in support of the Union. But when pondering the horrors of a second Haitian Revolution, his sympathies lay southward with Brown's intended victims. The extraordinary public reception of the speech demonstrates the popularity of this sentiment. According to one observer the day after the lecture, "The strength of the galleries of Faneuil Hall was terribly tested by the crowds of people who, from an hour long proceeded the time fixed for the meeting, continued to pour in to the large building upon a never-falling stream." Though the famed hall when at full capacity held as many as six thousand people, "Yesterday there was no chance of speaking of capacity at all. The place was so crammed that it was fairly impossible to accommodate anybody else, even beyond the portals of the hall." Edward took the stage to "loud and laud applause, followed by nine cheers." Upon concluding, "the immense assembly broke forth into the most rapturous and vehement applause. Nine vociferous cheers were given for the honorable gentleman, followed by the clapping of hands, waving of hats and handkerchiefs, and every demonstration of satisfaction and delight."[2] While pamphlets and newspapers that carried the speech soon flowed from northern presses, perhaps the greatest significance of the speech was its warm reception hundreds of miles south of New England. Everett's biographer writes that the speech "circulated widely, especially in the South."[3] We know moreover that copies of the speech surfaced in Memphis,

Richmond, and New Orleans.[4] Everett's speech and the ebullient response from readers across the continent testified to the bonds that remained strong between northerners and southerners on the eve of war.

After seeing how both Brown's raid and the Civil War triggered an explosion of popular memory in the South of the horrific narrative of the Haitian Revolution, we now turn to a similar phenomenon that took place in the North. An analysis of northern popular culture reveals that white northerners often shared the same fear of a second Haitian Revolution as their counterparts in the Confederacy. This collective fear and the alacrity with which both northerners and southerners exploited it illuminate the existence of a trans-sectional and transatlantic white identity that the war proved incapable of eradicating. Indeed, the revolutionary nature of the Civil War—the abolition of slavery and the employment of black troops in the Union army—reinforced white nationalism across sectional lines. Northerners who were committed to the Union but opposed to both the abolition of slavery and civil rights for African Americans showed racial solidarity with Confederates and generations of slaveowners throughout the Atlantic world when they exploited racially inspired fears of a second Haitian Revolution. During the war, they launched a verbal and textual war against the abolition movement in an effort to both keep the Union intact and maintain the status quo antebellum regarding slavery. Whether they won this war would remain to be seen long after the war's conclusion. For while the Civil War ended slavery, it did not end resistance to the social and political revolution the conflict wrought.

In the first half of the nineteenth century, the American people forged a nation out of a multitude of racial and ethnic groups. It was a new republic in which both political rights and the benefits and responsibilities of citizenship were reserved for white men.[5] The hegemony of this ethnocracy prevailed throughout the antebellum period, but when the Civil War came, the destruction of slavery, the employment of black soldiers in the Union army, and the promise of equal rights for the freedmen "thoroughly fractured this white republic." Edward Blum maintains that by the end of the war "the antebellum white republic lay in shambles." The citizens of the Confederacy had forfeited their right to membership in the new nation in which "northern whites sought to include African Americans as full citizens." The egalitarian dreams of both freedmen and abolitionists were short-lived, however; while the war over slavery had reached a decisive climax, the battle over racial equality persisted. In the end, white nationalists in the northern United States, in the process of "reforging the white republic," delivered a crushing blow to African Americans and their white allies.[6]

While the role of northerners in the restoration of the white republic has recently fallen under the microscope of historians of both Reconstruction and postbellum America, the extent to which northern white nationalism transcended sectional and national boundaries remains largely unexplored.[7] The quest of white northerners to keep the United States a republic of white men suggests the existence of a white Atlantic, a transatlantic white racial identity that united proslavery white northerners in common cause with generations of Europeans who peopled the slave societies of the Atlantic world.[8] Evidence is the extent to which, throughout the Civil War, northern opponents of abolition relied heavily on the horrific narrative of the Haitian Revolution to build a racial consensus. Labeled variously Copperheads, Democrats, and Unionists, they were in the most general sense anti-abolitionists. Jennifer Weber explains: "Their combination of fundamentalist constitutional interpretation and deeply held racism was like dry timber and a fat log. When Lincoln turned the war from one whose only goal was saving the Union to one that also sought to free the slaves, he struck the match."[9] To illuminate how the fear of a second Haitian Revolution buttressed a transcendent white nationalism throughout the Civil War, we turn now to northerners' reactions to the secession crisis, the Emancipation Proclamation, the employment of black troops, and the presidential election and ensuing miscegenation scare of 1864.

Edward Everett inspired others in the North to deploy the "horrors of St. Domingo" in the aftermath of John Brown's raid. Louis Schade produced one of the remarkable documents of the Civil War era to win support for the Union. In the first book-length proslavery narrative of the Haitian Revolution published in North America in more than half a century, the German immigrant and veteran of the European Revolutions of 1848 narrated the "horrors of St. Domingo" so that northerners would learn from history. He began by reprinting portions of Everett's speech, and throughout the text, like Everett, quoted Bryan Edwards at length, including his most explicit descriptions of black atrocities, such as the following: "Young women of all ranks were first violated by a whole troop of barbarians, and then generally put to death. Some of them were indeed reserved for the further gratification of the lust of the savages, and others had their eyes scooped out with a knife." One white woman was far advanced in pregnancy, Schade continued, and "The monsters, whose prisoner she was, having first murdered her husband in her presence, ripped her up alive, and threw the infant to the hogs. They then (how shall I relate it?) sewed up the head of the murdered husband in—!!!" Schade promised a repetition of these horrors in the South if the Union collapsed, asking rhetorically, "Are the people of the United States prepared for such horrid scenes of devastation, atrocities, and bloodshed, in their midst?" Like a southern secessionists he found obvious parallels between abolitionists in the North and those in France in the eighteenth century. "The rebellion of the negroes in St. Domingo, and the insurrection of the mulattoes, were caused by the very same means and agencies which are now employed by our Northern fanatics, and the Republican party in general, against the Southern States." Schade insisted Americans read "the bloody history" of the Haitian Revolution. Men such as John Brown and Wendell Phillips preached treason, and they "would glory, if they could incite slaughter, rapine, and destruction, as occurred in St. Domingo." It was up to those who did not subscribe to these fanatical ideas, "the honest, patriotic masses," to save both the Union and the race.[10]

Others joined Schade in amplifying the secessionist argument that an abolitionist conspiracy existed to prompt a second Haitian Revolution. One New Yorker avowed that the philosophies and teachings of northern abolitionists were "identical with those of the infamous 'friends of the blacks' in the French National Assembly in 1790," who instigated the slaves of "St. Domingo to the revolution, massacre and ruin that swept that fair island from the family of civilized nations." The threat was real, and "Against such a fate the South must unite."[11] In Princeton, New Jersey, the venerable Commodore Stockton, scion of one of the nation's most prominent and influential families and a grandson to one of the signers of the Declaration of Independence, in a public letter condemned the radicalism of what he termed the political party of John Brown, the Republican Party. The party was, he asserted, at the mercy of a radical faction, which pulled members "from one stage of excitement to another, 'until it has reached that point in which a further advance must be over the broken and dismembered fragments of a once glorious Union.'" Pondering what a shattered Union might look like if abolitionism triumphed, the ex-soldier and war hero drew a picture of the evils that endangered the South. "The horrors of a St. Domingo tragedy threaten to make desolate their homes; to drench their peaceful plains with blood—to light up their midnight skies with the conflagration of their cities and plantation villages, and to convert their faithful and contented domestics into incarnate fiends, inviting (after rivers of blood have flowed) their own extermination."

Wanting none of this, Stockton testified to his solidarity with the white men and women of the South, declaring, "I, for one, will stand by them as a friend . . . *I will stand by them because they are right.*"[12]

New York's fiery mayor Fernando Wood received great approbation from a crowd at a Democratic National Committee convention in Syracuse after delivering a rousing Union speech in which he described the current state of affairs in the South. "A spirit of armed resistance which but yesterday was confined to the adventurous and the reckless now exists in every household and actuates every inhabitant. There is but one feeling, but one determination. The whole country is a military camp, and every woman prepared to defend herself against negro insurrection at home, and against white aggression from abroad." Like Stockton, Wood left no doubt as to the people he held responsible for the sectional crisis. Abolition, he maintained, was the uncompromisable position of the "Black Republican Party," and there was no limit to what the party would do to reach their wicked objectives. Republicans threatened "to hang those who dissent at the North, and to compel the South to submit by force." When this happened, "The horrors of St. Domingo are to be reenacted. Rapine and massacre incited, encouraged and protected by Northern fanaticism, are to be the instruments by which these *philanthropic* results are to be obtained." Wood drew comparisons between French and American abolitionists. "How singularly the present attitude of this question and of this country rehearses what existed in the latter part of the Eighteenth Century between the Island of St. Domingo and its Home Government of France. For ten years preceding the massacre at St. Domingo, in 1790, an Abolitionist Party existed in France, based upon the same principles, advocating the same doctrines, as applied to negro servitude in the French Colonies, including St. Domingo, maintaining the same theories as those enunciated by the Black Republican Party of to-day." Wood invoked Wendell Phillips's oration on Louverture as proof of abolitionists' intention of bringing an apocalyptical race war down upon the South. He demanded that Democrats reinvent themselves as a party that was committed wholly to maintaining the white republic at all cost. On the issue of Union there was no compromise.[13]

Northerners' appropriation of public memory of the horrific narrative of the Haitian Revolution in the wake of the Harpers Ferry raid culminated in a lengthy piece in the *New York Herald* devoted to the horrors of slave insurrection. The author explained that if abolitionists eventually succeed where John Brown had failed the result "would be but blood, blood, blood, and the utter annihilation of that very race for whose freedom they are for a variety of motives contending." As can be expected, the paper devoted much of its discussion to the Haitian Revolution. Shortly after the initial outbreak of slaves in August 1791, "the country was wrapped in flames and every white person, without distinction of sex or age, was brutally massacred. Prisoners taken in battle were put to death with such studied tortures as cannot be named without a thrill of horror. They tore them with red hot pincers—sawed them asunder between planks—roasted them by a slow fire, or tore out their eyes with red hot cork screws." The paper illuminated the Haitian Revolution's impact on American slave resistance and reviewed the case of Denmark Vesey as evidence of the capability of southern slaves to produce a second Haitian Revolution. Citing published documents familiar to historians today, the paper remarked that Vesey was the mastermind behind the planned insurrection. He was "a free negro of superior abilities, who had stated to another negro that they (the blacks) *were fully able to conquer the whites if they were only unanimous and courageous as the St. Domingo people were.*" Vesey planned to set mills and houses on fire and murder the white men who ran to safety. "When he was told that it was cruel to kill the women and children, he answered that it was for their own safety to do so, and *not to spare one white skin, for this was they plan they pursued in St. Domingo.* In fact they seemed to have decided on adopting the same fiendish and bloody course that marked the progress of the revolution in that island." The connections between the black republic and the southern slave plot did not end there. "The design of Vesey was to induce the slaves in the country parts to co-operate with those in the city, and *then, after a general massacre of the unsuspecting inhabitants, to take possession of the forts and ships, to kill all on board of the latter except the captains, and then, having plundered the banks and the stores, to set sail for St. Domingo.*" The obvious conclusion to be drawn was that if abolitionism prevailed, the result would be "a war of annihilation, which would present scenes the most revolting and terrific that the imagination can picture." White Americans in the South were to be subjected to a second Haitian Revolution if abolitionists had their way.[14]

During the Civil War northern print culture remained fertile ground for the anti-abolitionist propaganda deployed in these antebellum polemics. Nothing, however, encouraged public discourse on the Haitian Revolution more than the prospect of emancipation. As the mind of Abraham Lincoln and the policy of the United States Government began to evolve over the issue of slavery, anti-abolitionists went on the attack. Filling the pages of popular newspapers and pamphlets with the "horrors of St. Domingo," they strove to stop the momentum generated by the abolitionist movement, which was rapidly pushing the federal government towards the adoption of a policy of both widespread and immediate emancipation. Amplifying the argument set forth by Confederates that emancipation was tantamount to a second Haitian Revolution, a writer in the *New York Herald* asked whether abolitionists "ever seriously considered the effect of their insane proposition?" Throughout the South, slaves commonly outnumbered whites. Once free, they would feel "entitled to be members of Congress and Governors of States." In a short time, then, whites could "reasonably expect to see some hundred Negroes in the House of Representatives, if not even in the Senate Chamber." Black political rule in the South meant that America was destined to become a laughing stock in the "eyes of wondering nations." Yet, this was only a secondary concern. "As the Negroes in a Southern climate increase more rapidly than white men, it would not be long till they would have a preponderance in numbers, and then perhaps the idea would occur to Sambo that he ought to have the entire South to himself, and that it would be well to get rid of the whites, after the fashion of St. Domingo, so earnestly recommended by the abolition tribe."[15]

Northerners who lashed out at abolitionists for destroying the United States underscore how the transformation of the war for Union into a war over slavery left many Americans unconverted to the racial egalitarianism that abolitionists intended to accompany emancipation. One writer made the comparison between northern abolitionists and the French radicals who ignited the Haitian Revolution and ultimately bore responsibility for the subsequent "horrors heaped on horrors," which he considered "unfit for publication." Haitian slaves would not have revolted if not for instigation by abolitionists. "Were it not for fiendish white incendiaries the negroes would have remained peaceful and happy, and the fruitful island would have continued to prosper, instead of becoming a desolate wilderness, the abode of savages." There was only one way to ensure that "such horrors are not to be repeated in out own day." The army must prohibit the radical ideas of the abolitionists to infiltrate slaves' quarters. "The bloodthirsty Jacobins of the abolition school will move Heaven and earth to propagate their diabolical ideas among the negroes, and, if permitted, will sow the seeds of future massacres on a scale of magnitude far exceeding the tragedy of St. Domingo."[16]

Two anti-abolitionist pamphlets published under the same title, "Emancipation and Its Result," confirm the existence of what Larry Tise calls a "conservative counterrevolution," an ideological movement that during the Civil War brought white northerners "ever closer to a complete identification with the thinking and interests of the South."[17] The first pamphlet transmitted a speech delivered before the United States House of Representatives by Congressman Samuel Sullivan Cox, who insisted that southern slaves would if emancipated "re-enanct the scenes of Hayti," bringing on "a war of extermination between black and white." Cox entreated, "Let us heed the lesson which history has given in other times, as to what is convenient and advantageous under similar circumstances." France abolished slavery, and "In less than a half century, the industry and commerce of Hayti were annihilated; the Sabbath, the family and the school became obsolete; the missionaries were more in danger—as the historian of the West Indies, Mr. Edwards, says—of being eaten than of being heard." At this, Cox's congressional audience erupted in laughter. He continued, "Haiti was free! But her freedom was the freedom of fiends. Unschooled and undisciplined, she ran riot in her liberty." There was only one advantage to the career of the Haitian Revolution: "It admonishes us of what our fate shall be, if we are launched on the same stormful sea."[18]

In the second pamphlet, published by a northern proslavery group calling itself the Society for the Diffusion of Political Knowledge, an anonymous writer fumed at the disruption of the racial status quo promised by emancipation. "GIGANTIC efforts are now being made to convince the people of the North that the overthrow of the present relations of the black and white races in the South, or what is mistakingly called 'the Abolition of Slavery,' would be a great benefit to all concerned—a benefit to the white race, to the negro race, and a grand step in the progress of civilization and Christianity. Now the simple TRUTH is the exact opposite of this." The accomplishment of "free negroism" would produce a convulsion between the races "to which even civil war, with all its horrors, will be but a faint parallel." There was only one precedent available for the American people to draw from. "Robespierre and Brissot, in 1791, tried the 'impartial freedom' of Sumner and Greeley, in St. Domingo, and Alison has vividly painted the result. Speaking of the Haytien tragedy, he says: 'That negroes *marched with spiked infants on their spears, instead of colors; then sawed asunder the male prisoners, and violated the females on the dead bodies of their husbands.'*" These were crimes that white Americans could scarcely conceive, "yet they are common to negroes, when perverted into what is called freedom."[19]

Lincoln's announcement of the preliminary Emancipation Proclamation prompted a vigorous anti-abolitionist response. In the *Monthly Law Reporter*, the well-known New York City patent lawyer Charles Frederick Blake refuted the claim made by William Whiting in his widely read *War Powers of the President* that the wartime powers of the commander in chief included the authority to legislate slavery. Blake tackled Whiting's reading of the Haitian Revolution head on, avowing that what took place in Saint-Domingue at the close of the eighteenth century was "not warfare, but indiscriminate massacre of every age, sex and condition." Slaves burned every house and murdered every white man, woman, and child. They "garnished their fortifications with rows of the heads of their victims." Bound by the rules of civilization, the U.S. government had no authority to encourage slaves to commit such heinous acts. This was the opinion of America's founding fathers in the Declaration of Independence, when they complained that George III incited slave insurrections in the colonies, endeavoring "to bring on the inhabitants of our frontiers the merciless Indian savages, whose known rule of warfare is an undistinguished destruction of all ages, sexes and conditions." Returning to the Haitian Revolution, Blake affirmed that in Haiti slaves revolted before emancipation. "At the time of the arrival of the French commissioners a vast servile war was in progress, which had baffled the power of the government for more than two years." It was only in desperation that the French Commissioners "opened the prisons, armed the slaves, and called in to their aid a band of insurgent negroes who were ravaging the surrounding country." Revolting slaves forced abolition upon the French commissioners, who surrounded by uncontrollable black savages had no choice. "They in vain sought by promises of freedom to win to their side the great army of blacks which so long had defied their power." Only after learning that a black leader ordered the colony's slaves to murder their masters did both the French commissioners and terrified planters sign the dreaded proclamation. It was thus impossible to conclude "from these events that France had by her conduct afforded a precedent for the emancipation of enemy's slaves as a belligerent right." Blake concluded speciously, "In point of fact the negroes wrested their freedom from the commissioners by force. It was wholly unauthorized by the French government, and it was not until several months afterwards that the abolition of slavery in the colonies was voted by the convention." Whiting was wrong, Blake asserted; neither the president nor the U.S. government had the authority to end slavery.[20]

Despite the incredible efforts of anti-abolitionists, Lincoln issued the Emancipation Proclamation on 1 January 1863, thus freeing slaves in the rebellious southern states. Though the historic document had little real impact on the liberation of enslaved people, it nevertheless represents a significant moment in the history of the republic. The president of the United States, using the Civil War as a pretext, took an official stance against slavery and claimed the Constitutional authority to abolish the institution. Like fuel to a fire, the landmark declaration fed the flames of anti-abolitionism. A popular musical score published in the widely distributed songbook *Copperhead Minstrel* illuminates. Entitled "De Serenade," it deserves quotation in its entirety:

> Get de bones and get de banjo, get de soundin' tamborine
> When de 'casion calls for moosic, you can count dis nigger in;
> And I feels de glow inspirin', as de instruments I take,
> For de 'casion is a serenade for Massa Linkin's sake!
>> Oh, limber up de fingers,
>> Let the Serenade begin!
>> When de 'casion calls for moosic,
>> You can count dis nigger in.
> Oh, de Sangomingo darkeys had a standard which dey bore;
> 'Twas a pretty little baby's head, all dripping in its gore!
> And if we undahstand aright de President's Proclaim,
> He tells de Dixie niggers day may go and do de same!
>> Oh, limber up de fingers,
>> Let de serenade begin!
>> When de 'casion calls for moosic,
>> You can count dis nigger in!
> Oh, de Sangomingo darkies, dare old Massas took and tied,
> And den dey got de handsaw and sawed 'em till dey died!
> And after dey had sawed 'em till dey sawed away dare lives,
> You may bet dey had a good time a kissin' ob dare wives!
>> And if we undahstand him,
>> Massa Linkin makes proclaim,
>> Dat de niggers down in Dixie
>> Have a right to do de same!
> Massa Beecher! Massa Cheever! you must set apart a day,
> And get your Congo-rations for the handsaws for to pay,
> De little baby's curly head, ourselves can easy get,
> And spike it do de standard while it's dripping warm and wet!

On the old plantation homestead,
Waits de woe widout a name,
If darkies undahstand aright
The President's proclaim!
Oh, wake up Massa Linkin! for the night is not far spent,
And hear de free Americans ob African descent,
Wid de bones and wid de banjo, and de soundin' tamborine,
We have come to serenade you ere de sawin' we begin.
We have come to serenade you,
Ere we raise, with life-blood red,
De Sangomingo standard
Of de little baby's head![21]

The lyrics underscore both the resiliency of the memory of the horrific narrative of the Haitian Revolution among northerners during the Civil War and the virulent racism of northern popular culture that the revolutionary character of the war encouraged.

Given the tenor of anti-abolitionists' response to the Emancipation Proclamation, it is expected that the issue of black soldiery was as maddening to them as it was to white southerners. Again, the Democratic press led the way. A writer in the *Boston Pilot* justified the secession of the Confederate states on the ground that northerners suffered from an illness he labeled "nigger on the brain." The disease led to the Emancipation Proclamation, and it "would be immediately followed by a universal massacre of the planters and their families. . . . Union men, anti-union men, boys, girls, women, children, and all." Such an outcome was unavoidable. "Are the blacks of the South more humane than those of the San Domingo? They are not?" There was, consequently, "no reasonable doubt, but a very legitimate and pressing dread that the fate of the whites of San Domingo is hanging over the whites of the Southern plantations." Lincoln's proclamation was "a *Constitutional* torch to a magazine of savagery." The enrollment of black regiments increased the likelihood of a Second Haitian Revolution. Black troops would "propagate among the slaves the sentiment of bold rebellion to their masters. Every black soldier will put, if he can, a weapon of murder into the hands of every slave he meets; his words will be the words of revolt; and his military appearance in itself, and military example in shooting down rebels, will serve as excitements to horrid violence, which the slave will not pause to resist." The author asked, "Do we want another San Domingo to be repeated in the South? Have we no horror at seeing the females of the South treated in a manner and in circumstances too shocking to name, by the slaves of the plantations? Are we to save the history of the Republic from the broad, indelible disfigurement of the massacre, lust, conflagration and sacrilege on a white minority, committed by four millions of Africans in wild, unbridled license from every law?" Confederates committed treason. But surely they were not deserving of this. "The proclamation is a fearful violation of its order. The enrollment of black soldiers is the same. Both have the sanguinary insurrection of four millions of slaves for their direct, for their first, and for their final consequence." There was only one hope for the white republic now. "The permanent character of nations is in the hands of God; and there is nothing He chastises so heavily as fanaticism. May His mercy save the country from the scenes of San Domingo!"[22]

Anti-abolitionists maintained that in an Atlantic world filled with slavery the employment of black soldiers in the military violated the boundaries of warfare, and accordingly brought down on the United States the opprobrium of every other civilized white nation. A pamphlet published by the Democratic State Central Committee in Philadelphia expressed outrage at the employment of black soldiers. Aiming its venom at the abolitionists who advocated the revolutionary plan, the authors of the text avowed that slaves were inherently unable to endure the hardships of war, the musketry, the artillery fire, and especially the bayonet charge. "The history of negro wars and insurrection in St. Domingo, and other West Indian Islands, is replete with the barbarities of rapine and slaughter of helpless women and infants, that shock the sensibilities." Should slaves be allowed to fight for the Union army and against the South, "then the atrocities of the West India Islands we may naturally expect to be repeated here on a vastly more extended scale. Against such a fiendish policy would not only the moral sensibilities of all the whites of the Northern States who have not become brutalized by the devilishness of Abolitionism, be more painfully shocked, but the whole civilized world would condemn us, and probably, in the cause of humanity, rise to stay atrocities so disgraceful."[23]

The Harvard-educated lawyer, constitutional historian, and noted Unionist George Ticknor Curtis argued that the decision to arm black men would destroy the public's widespread support for the Union army both in the North and internationally. "What we are doing now—organizing and arming negroes, forming negro Battalions, Regiments, and Brigades—is but outraging public sentiment. All Europe is crying out against it. The whole civilized world shrinks from and abhors any prospect of the repetition of the bloody scenes of Hayti and St. Domingo." For years, Europeans considered the United States the model republic. They now "turned with horror from white men cooperating with African slaves to shed fraternal blood." Having lost the world's hope, "we can have no hope in ourselves, until we retreat from this disgraceful exhibition of twenty millions of white men calling on four millions of negroes to fight eight millions, at the most, of white fellow-men."[24]

Congressional representatives who invoked the Haitian Revolution in the chambers of Congress to warn of the horrors of black soldiers illuminated the transcendent fear of black men. In the House of Representatives, Charles Biddle of Pennsylvania, who had only recently returned from the front lines, was outraged at the spread of abolitionism throughout the North. Alluding to the prominent abolitionist volume by Moncure Daniel Conway *The Golden Hour*, Biddle retorted, "I differ wholly from those who look upon the present as a 'golden hour;' who regard it with exultation as the dawn of a black millennium. In me, their hopes and schemes inspire disgust and horror." The idea of slaves proving valiant soldiers was preposterous, Biddle explained. "Of the slave you cannot make a soldier; you may make an assassin. But the shrieks of white households murdered, and worse than murdered, by the negro, would appall the hearts and palsy the arms of more of the supporters of this war than all the race of Ham could take the place of." Northerners must reject a "black alliance," for such an enterprise "offers to northern white men a fellowship that most of them abhor; it proffers to the southern white man no terms that he prefers to extermination—it proffers negro equality or negro domination; it drives the Union men of the South into the ranks of the enemy." Arming slaves opened the door to "a dreary prospect of a protracted, devastating, ruinous guerilla warfare; it shocks the sentiment of the white race throughout the world." Biddle concluded his diatribe, offering a hint as to where his loyalties lie: "Born and bred on the soil of the State, whose proudest title is to be 'the Keystone of the Federal arch,' I do not wish to see a new St Domingo on her southern border. These are my sentiments as a Pennsylvanian and a white man."[25]

John Law was indignant at the likelihood of Congress passing legislation, which permitted the confiscation of Confederate's property. The Indiana Representative clung to the argument that the Civil War was not about abolition but Union. "This is the object for which your soldiers rallied around the flag of the Union when it was thrown to the 'battle and the breeze.' It is the one, and the sole one, for which they are shedding their blood like water on every battle-field of your country. It is for this, and this alone, they lay dead and buried in your fields and forests far from their homes filling a soldier's grave, or are now maimed and wounded laying in your hospitals by thousands." Slavery was sacrosanct, and any desire of the federal government to confiscate slaves, Law insisted, represented "the most shocking proposition ever submitted to a deliberative assembly since the world began." Law imagined a nightmare scenario: "pass these acts; confiscate, under these bills, the property of these men; emancipate their negroes; place arms in the hands of these human guerillas to murder their masters and violate their wives and daughters, and you will have a war such as was never witnessed in the worst days of the French Revolution, and horrors never exceeded in St. Domingo, for the balance of this century, at least."[26]

As Law's alarm attests, fears of sexual encounters between black men and white women were part and parcel of the northern anti-abolitionist argument. Indeed, northern white men's racial solidarity with southern white men is most evident in the "miscegenation" scare of 1864. The episode took place when anti-abolitionist in an effort to in the words of Jennifer Weber, "mock the abolitionist community," published anonymously a radical pamphlet that zealously promoted race mixing and ascribed its authorship to the Republican Party.[27] The controversial pamphlet and the literary dialogue it opened demonstrate the conviction among northerners that the greatest fear of the abolition of slavery lay perhaps not in the loss of white lives, but in both the legalization of racial equality and the elimination of racial distinctions. It was no coincidence that the so-called miscegenation scare coincided with the presidential election of 1864; to the contrary, it was the prospect of four more years of executive rule by a man who had come to see the Civil War as an opportunity to finish a revolution that was more than half a century in the making, which compelled anti-abolitionists to embrace a strategy of both fear mongering and race baiting.[28]

The authors of *Miscegenation: The Theory of the Blending of the Races, Applied to the American White Man and Negro* mockingly celebrated the Emancipation Proclamation as they pondered the future of the white and black races in America. They then turned their attention to black soldiers. Emancipation was only "the first step towards the redemption of the black and his absorption with the white. The second step is in making him a soldier of the United States. If he has fought beside the white, if he has spilled his blood for the common country, the most ordinary sense of justice will revolt at the idea of remanding him back to slavery, or of denying him any opportunity or right accorded to his white comrade." The authors insisted that even un-skilled slaves would perform adequately as soldiers. Still, the army needed black officers: "It will be a sad misfortune if this war should end without a battle being fought by a black general in command of a white or mixed body of troops. We want an American Toussaint L'Ouverture, to give the black his proper position on this continent, and the day is coming." The war's end was not as close as people presumed. The Confederacy would continue to resist until at last black soldiers forced them to submit. Backed by the government the former slaves would rule the South. "The slave of yesterday not only is the soldier of to-day, but is destined to be the conqueror of to-morrow."[29]

In a more direct attack, the notorious white supremacist John H. Van Evrie blamed abolitionists for promoting miscegenation when, in fact, the re-moval of enslaved women from the clutches of their masters and overseers would have undoubtedly decreased sexual contact between white and black southerners. "No matron in the South ever heard the names of Garrison or John Brown uttered without clasping more closely the child on her bosom, not from any personal fear of these men, but from that instinct of self-preservation God has endowed her with, and which taught her that the 'idea' connected with these names involved the extinction of her blood." The Haitian Revo-lution portended indescribable horrors for white citizens. The decree of the French National Convention of 1792 resulted in the "impartial freedom" of the island's slaves, "but the twenty-five thousand whites of that island re-sisted this monstrous crime to the uttermost. The result was that the negroes, stimulated by British and outside agents, and led on by mongrel chiefs, exter-minated the whites, not one man, woman, or child being left on that island to tell the tale of their destruction." Everywhere emancipation meant the same, even in Jamaica where the end of slavery came peacefully. White Jamaicans "were overcome, not by physical force, but by the corrupt and perverse opin-ions of England embodied in the Parliament." The result was "social equal-ity, amalgamation, mongrelism, and rapidly approaching extinction of the white blood. A few years hence this hideous process must complete itself, and the white element as utterly disappear from Jamaica as it has from Hayti." The only difference was the method of extinction. The threat of miscegena-tion throughout the United States was just as real. What was the solution? It was the destiny of white Americans to extend the existing boundaries of the United States "to the equator, and, perhaps, over the whole continent, and with a government of white men we shall preserve the purity of our blood, the unity of our nationality with the integrity of our Republican system, and save American civilization from the blight and desolation now resting on the *mongrel* Republics South of us, and which God has decreed forever, as the penalty for disregarding the distinctions and natural relations of races."[30]

The conclusion of the Civil War failed to discourage anti-abolitionists' racist diatribes, even after southern bondpeople responded to freedom peaceably and with great dignity. As anticipated, the horrific narrative of the Haitian Revolution infused anti-abolitionists' reaction to Reconstruction just as it had their reaction to the government's decision to abolish slavery and enlist of black men in the Union army previously. Two documents published by Van Evrie shortly after the war, illuminate this trajectory. In the *Democratic Almanac*, Van Evrie took readers back to the turn of the century by devoting nearly twenty pages to reprinting Bryan Edwards's narrative of the Haitian Revolution, in an effort to prove that *"the rebellion of the negroes in St. Domingo, and the insurrection of the mulattoes, were caused by the very same means and agencies which are now employed by our Northern fanatics, and the Republican party in general, against the Southern States."* It was a clear sign that some were not going to let the public memory of the "horrors of St. Domingo" die along with the antebellum white republic. Van Evrie resented abolitionists for promoting both emancipation and the equality of all men and thus deployed the Haitian Revolution as evidence of the inevitable result of such extreme measures. According to Van Evrie, Edwards offered a valuable account, "but no European writer can grasp the fullness, or depth, and breadth, of that monstrous and unspeakable crime of the French Convention which *forced* the hapless negroes to exterminate the white people of that unfortunate island. An outside power—the will of a distant people—those who had no negroes among them, decreed that THEIR idea should be applied to St. Domingo, and those whom God made unequal *forced* into unnatural equality, and thus *compelled by nature herself to exterminate each other!* But this monstrous and wholesale murder was committed by the French Convention in utter ignorance of what they were dealing with, and therefore, when contrasted with what the people of the Northern States have done and are now striving to do at the South, seems almost forgivable by future generations, though every drop of blood shed, every life destroyed, and every hour of torture and horror suffered in that awful catastrophe, *must* cling to their skirts forever." There were no words to express "the unalterable and unfathomable crime of those who, having seen negroes all their lives, and with the transcendent horror of St. Domingo straight before them, are now striving to force the same doom on the South, and compel eight millions of their own race, and four millions of negroes, to *exterminate* each other!"[31]

The author elaborated on his fear of miscegenation and race war in *Abolition Is National Death,* a postbellum revision of his earlier invective *Abolition and Secession.* Describing what a racial holocaust might look like, Van Evrie explained that the revolutionary transformation of slaves into citizens—the social and political equal of whites—signaled the end of both the nation and the white race. Equality meant miscegenation, but since white southerners, the "descendents of the men of 1776," refused to "amalgamate" with their former slaves, he predicted a conflict of the races, "as in San Domingo." In the regions of the South where whites were in the majority, the black race would vanish. Where blacks were in the majority the opposite would occur. The great republican experiment would draw to a close: "all the country south of 36.30 substantially will become and must become what Hayti is now, and as utterly lost to American civilization as if swallowed up by an earthquake." This was the "final end, the unavoidable result, the inexorable necessity, the unescapable doom of the American people." Every man and women who accepted either the abolition of slavery or the equality of the races invited these consequences. The choice was simple: "*amalgamation or extermination.*"[32]

Alice Fahs in her examination of Civil War literature describes a "shared public culture" of newspapers, books, pamphlets, and songs that the war failed to eliminate.[33] Her findings are significant, for it was in this popular trans-sectional print culture that writers and publishers supplied northern and southern audience with an abundance of radical proslavery and anti-abolitionist literature, which both warned of the dangers and perpetuated the fear of a second Haitian Revolution. The widespread dissemination of this literature on both sides of the Mason-Dixon line suggests a shared racial consciousness among white Americans that neither secession nor rebellion could eradicate. While white northerners may have rejected the legitimacy of both sectionalism and secession, many wholeheartedly agreed with white southerners on the issue of slavery and shared their belief in the superiority of the white race. Expressing racial solidarity with the men and women of the Confederacy, they likewise invoked the "horrors of St. Domingo" to ensure that abolitionists would fail in their efforts to end slavery, establish racial equality, and shatter the white republic. Anti-abolitionists who deployed the horrific narrative of the Haitian Revolution in their public speeches and printed texts bolstered a cross-sectional and transatlantic racial alliance that outlived both the Confederacy and the war.

The resonance of the "horrors of St. Domingo" in both northern and southern popular culture throughout the Civil War era testifies to the depth of the shadow the Haitian Revolution cast over the United States and Atlantic world. Generations of European Americans throughout the western hemisphere feared a second Haitian Revolution, and it was this fear that provided committed speakers and writers with a resonant and polarizing symbol to assist them in winning the hearts and minds of men and women during the second war over slavery in the Americas. Though southern secessionists seized upon the memory of the Haitian Revolution in order to build a new nation and northern anti-abolitionists appropriated it to keep an existing one from falling apart, the gulf separating these two constituencies was negligible. White Americans in both sections shared a commitment to white nationalism that the Civil War not only failed to eliminate but in fact reinforced. Though the war ended slavery, it failed to complete the revolutionary transformation of the United States into a truly free and equal society. When viewed from a distance, the Civil War was not a grand finale. It was, in spite of its magnitude, merely another important battle in the great war over slavery and freedom that had raged throughout the Atlantic world for centuries.

CONCLUSION

In 1893, MORE than twenty-seven million people from the United States and around the world traveled to Chicago to attend the World's Columbian Exposition. The World's Fair, which organizers intended to mark the four-hundredth anniversary of Columbus's arrival in the Americas, came a year late; it was, nevertheless, a phenomenal success. With the construction of hundreds of buildings and the staging of concerts, plays, and more than 250,000 exhibitions, the event was a testament to American ingenuity, technology, and wealth.[1] It was, moreover, an affirmation of the reconstructed republic. The fair symbolized the sectional reconciliation that had taken place in the three decades since the Civil War. On the eve of a new century, some maintained that the future had never been as bright for the United States of America.

One speaker who attended the exposition refused to share in the spirit of optimism and amusement that pervaded Chicago. Frederick Douglass traveled to the "windy city" to open old wounds. The former bondman came to discuss the painful issues of race, slavery, and war. In front of an estimated 1,500 spectators at Quinn Chapel, home to the oldest African American congregation in the city, Douglass conjured some of the old memories of his listeners by reminding them of the impact of the Haitian Revolution on the United States. "From the beginning of our century until now," Douglass pronounced, "Haiti and its inhabitants under one aspect or another, have, for various reasons, been very much in the thoughts of the American people. While slavery existed amongst us, her example was a sharp thorn in our side and a source of alarm and terror." Born in blood, Americans thought of Haiti as a hell of unthinkable horror. "Her very name was pronounced with a shudder. She was a startling and frightful surprise and a threat to all slave-holders throughout the world, and the slave-holding world has had its questioning eye upon her career ever since." Douglass reminded his audience of the special importance of the revolution. "We should not forget that the freedom you and I enjoy to-day . . . is largely due to the brave stand taken by the black sons of Haiti ninety years ago." Haitian slaves fought not only for themselves. "They were linked and interlinked with their race, and striking for their freedom, they struck for the freedom of every black man in the world." Haiti taught the entire world a valuable lesson, of "the danger of slavery and the value of liberty."[2]

More than a century removed from the first outbreak of rebellion in the northern plains of Saint-Domingue, this onetime abolitionist, army recruiter, and ambassador to Haiti did not forget the Haitian Revolution. And he was not alone. Decades after the Civil War, African Americans fought desperately to keep the memory of the Haitian Revolution alive. Robert Charles O'Hara Benjamin, Charles W. Mossell, and Theophilus Gould Steward are among those who at the turn of the twentieth century published new biographies of Louverture and histories of the Haitian Revolution, while Williams Wells Brown's antebellum lecture on "St. Domingo" and his more famous anthology of great black men reappeared in a revised collection entitled, *Rising Son; or, The Antecedents and Advancement of the Colored Race.*[3] W. E. B. Du Bois also made Louverture and the revolution a central theme in his pioneering work, famously writing of the former's influence on the early American republic, "The role which the great Negro Toussaint, called L'Ouverture, played in the history of the United States has seldom been fully appreciated. Representing the age of revolution in America, he rose to leadership through a bloody terror, which contrived a Negro 'problem' for the Western Hemisphere, intensified and defined the anti-slavery movement, became one of the causes, and probably the prime one, which led Napoleon to sell Louisiana for a song, and finally, through the interworking of all these effects, rendered more certain the final prohibition of the slave-trade by the United States in 1807."[4]

Decades after the Civil War, black writers in an effort to prove the equality of the race continued to publish short biographies of prominent African Americans throughout history and especially Louverture.[5] His memory proved extraordinarily resilient, serving as the synecdoche of the Haitian Revolution. In the words of the lawyer, political activist, and author David Augustus Straker, African Americans were committed to "perpetuate the memory" of Louverture and the Haitian Revolution, because they understood that as the distance between themselves and the war that ended slavery increased, and the issue of black civil rights faded from the national spotlight, "the negro must be himself his own historian."[6] African Americans' effort to remember the Haitian Revolution had changed little since the middle of the nineteenth century when the prominent black abolitionist James Theodore Holly implored, "never let the self emancipating deeds of the Haytian people be effaced; never let her heroically achieved nationality be brought low; no, never let the names of her Toussaint, her Dessalines, her Rigaud, her Cristophe, and her Petion be forgotten, or blotted out from the historic pages of the world's history."[7]

Also unchanged was that African Americans, though isolated, were not alone in waging this losing battle in a longstanding history war over the most successful slave revolt in history. A small contingent of sympathetic white editors and writers continued to insist upon its relevance. Though many of the radical white abolitionists who served as architects of the public memory of the Haitian Revolution during the Civil War had passed, their words continued to reverberate in American print culture more than a half-century later. Publishers and editors continued to publish Wendell Phillips's sensational oration, and in 1905, a revised version of Charles Wyllys Elliott's antebellum lecture appeared in a popular collection of essays entitled, *The Great Events by Famous Historians*.[8] Compiled by the prolific New York writer and editor Rossiter Johnson the volume promised "a comprehensive and readable account of the world's history, emphasizing the more important events, and presenting these as complete narratives in the master-words of the most eminent historians." The introduction to Elliott's essay testified to the resiliency of Louverture's reputation among European Americans as one of the world's Great Men. "This black hero, of whose origin and personality information is given below, has been made the subject of a noble sonnet by Wordsworth, of an equally fine eulogy by Wendell Phillips, of a tragedy by Lamartine, and of a romance, *The Hour and the Man*, by Harriet Martineau. The renowned French philosopher Auguste Comte, the founder of positivism, placed Louverture in his new calendar among the great modern liberators—Hampden, Cromwell, Algernon Sidney, Washington, and Bolivar."[9]

Most significant among white authors who remembered the Haitian Revolution decades after the Civil War was the renowned historian Henry Adams, who descended from a long line of anti-slavery activists. Adams's grandfather and great grandfather were both Presidents who opposed slavery. They had also expressed public sympathy with the rebellious Haitian slaves who demonstrated an indomitable quest for freedom that rivaled that of the most patriotic Americans during their own violent struggle for individual freedom and political independence. During the Civil War, Adams's brother, Charles Francis, Jr., ended the Adams tradition of speaking out against slavery and instead did something about it: like so many white abolitionists, he served during the war as an officer of a black military unit, in his case, the Fifth Massachusetts Cavalry. The family was, Henry Adams remembered proudly, as "anti-slavery by birth, as their name was Adams and their home was Quincy."[10] In his chronicle of the United States published in 1890, the historian remarked on the national forgetting that had taken place regarding the Haitian Revolution. He was particularly vexed at the loss of memory of Haiti's preeminent founding father. "The story of Toussaint Louverture," Adams lamented, "has been told almost as often as that of Napoleon, but not in connection with the history of the United States, although Toussaint exercised on their history as decisive as that of any European ruler."[11]

At the turn of the twentieth century, the memory of the Haitian Revolution survived among various publics. Yet most Americans had forgotten. Since the Civil War, public memory of the Haitian Revolution had dissipated along with that of the Civil War itself. While the wounds of the war remained fresh in the minds of veterans and their families, for most it had like the Haitian Revolution, become a distant memory. As David Blight has pointed out, the painful recollections of four years of both private and public suffering and sacrifice resulted in a widespread epidemic of historical amnesia. Northerners and southerners agreed on little else in the years following the Civil War besides the importance of forgetting both the causes and the terrible costs of the war. As the close of the nineteenth century approached and the war disappeared into the horizon, however, the American people embarked upon a massive collective remembering. Centering their memories on the sentimental and romantic aspects of the war—the myths and legends as opposed to its ideological causes and profound social effects—they remembered a Civil War that was devoid of the issues of slavery and emancipation. In an effort to build a powerful national consensus, northerners and southerners sacrificed their memory of slavery as the root cause of the Civil War on the altar of a cross-sectional alliance. Though sectional reconciliation had its benefits, it also, writes Blight, "had its costs."[12]

While today the Civil War occupies a conspicuous place in American memory, there is a void where the Haitian Revolution once resided. After the abolition of slavery, as the issues of sectionalism and black freedom faded into the past, the national forgetting of the Haitian Revolution began apace. The removal of both slavery and the concomitant threat of slave revolt, along with the political redemption of the white South, meant a dramatic decline of the viability of the memory of an extraordinary slave revolt that took place a century earlier. In an era of consensus and compromise, there was little need for the divisive symbols provided by the Haitian Revolution. Public amnesia of this iconic event developed quickly. Whereas the national trauma of sectional violence once sparked the remembrance of the Haitian Revolution, the arrival of peace and reunion spelled the end of the need for those memories. More than a decade of extralegal violence and racial unrest encouraged by the Federal Government's effort to both reconstruct the South and promote racial egalitarianism among an overwhelmingly resistant white population, proved the death knell of American memory of the Haitian Revolution. It also delayed for nearly a century the climactic battle for black freedom and equality that began unexpectedly in a small yet extraordinary French colony in the Caribbean at the close of the eighteenth century and continued in the United States.

In the middle of the nineteenth century, Americans fought a war to determine the fate of slavery in the republic once and for all. Lacking a deep reservoir of national memory of slave revolt and racial revolution from which to draw on, they remembered the only other war over slavery that matched the Civil War in both intensity and violence. Throughout the war, citizens and slaves alike recalled the Haitian Revolution to help them cope with the crisis that confronted them. Ironically, in spite of the bifurcated and hotly contested narrative of the Haitian Revolution, the various constituencies who fought over the memory of the most successful slave revolt in history shared something in common. Abolitionists and anti-abolitionists, slaves and secessionists, in spite of their divergent views on such important issues as race, slavery, and abolition, all used the symbols of the Haitian Revolution as a touchstone of both their causes and their crusades. Though never reaching a consensus, they all drank from the same historical cup. While disagreeing on the legacy of the Haitian Revolution and the various lessons it taught, all agreed that in the case of the sectional war over slavery, the past was prologue.

NOTES

INTRODUCTION

Epigraph: W. E. B. Du Bois, *The Suppression of the African Slave Trade to the United States of America, 1638–1870* (1896; Mineola, N.Y.: Dover, 1999), 70.

1. Nineteenth-century Americans often referred to the colony that would become the nation of Haiti as St. Domingo, San Domingo, or St. Domingue; however, the spelling used in contemporary French- and Haitian-language newspapers, books, and pamphlets was Saint-Domingue. This is the spelling employed throughout, unless quoting original text. Various spellings of Haiti will also be used within quotations.

2. Louverture did not spell his name with an apostrophe, though abolitionists often did. I have left the various spellings of his name unchanged when quoting.

3. Though versions of the oration appeared in books, newspapers, and periodicals throughout the Civil War era, all are similar. There are no extant copies of the speech delivered in Washington; I have used this version, which Phillips delivered in both New York and Boston just three months before the Smithsonian address and which is reprinted in Wendell Phillips, "Toussaint L'Ouverture," *Speeches, Lectures, and Letters* (Boston: Lee & Shepard, 1872), 468–94.

4. Phillips, "Toussaint L'Ouverture," 493–94.

5. "Wendell Phillips in Washington," *National Anti-Slavery Standard*, 22 March 1862.

6. "Wendell Phillips," *Christian Recorder*, 29 March 1862.

7. "Wendell Phillips in Washington," *Liberator*, 21 March 1862.

8. William Lloyd Garrison, Garrett Davis, and Alexander Stephens, *Three Unlike Speeches, by William Lloyd Garrison, of Massachusetts, Garrett Davis, of Kentucky, Alexander H. Stephens, of Georgia. The Abolitionists, and their Relations to the War. The War not for Emancipation. African Slavery, the Corner-stone of the Southern Confederacy* (New York: E.D. Barker, 1862), 34.

9. "The Rights of Minorities," *Crisis*, 29 April 1863.

10. "Political Blasphemy," *Daily Picayune*, 19 March 1863.

11. Herbert Aptheker, *American Negro Slave Revolts* (New York: International Pub-

lishers, 1993); Ira Berlin, *Generations of Captivity: A History of North American Slaves* (Cambridge, Mass.: Belknap Press of Harvard University Press, 2003); David Brion Davis, *Inhuman Bondage: The Rise and Fall of Slavery in the New World* (New York: Oxford University Press, 2006); Eric Foner, *Reconstruction, 1863–1877* (New York: Harper & Row, 1988); Winthrop Jordan, *White Over Black: American Attitudes Toward the Negro, 1550–1812* (Chapel Hill: University of North Carolina Press, 1968); Leon Litwack, *Been in the Storm So Long: The Aftermath of Slavery* (New York: Knopf, 1980); James McPherson, *Battle Cry of Freedom: The Civil War Era* (New York: Oxford University Press, 1988).

12. Laurent Dubois, *Avengers of the New World: The Story of the Haitian Revolution* (Cambridge, Mass.: Belknap Press of Harvard University Press, 2004); Dubois, *A Colony of Citizens: Revolution & Slave Emancipation in the French Caribbean, 1787–1804* (Chapel Hill: University of North Carolina Press, 2004); David Barry Gaspar and David Patrick Geggus, eds., *A Turbulent Time: The French Revolution and the Greater Caribbean* (Bloomington: Indiana University Press, 1997); David Patrick Geggus, *Haitian Revolutionary Studies* (Bloomington: Indiana University Press, 2002); Geggus, ed., *The Impact of the Haitian Revolution in the Atlantic World* (Columbia: University of South Carolina Press, 2001); Alfred N. Hunt, *Haiti's Influence on Antebellum America: Slumbering Volcano in the Caribbean* (Baton Rouge: Louisiana State University Press, 1988).; Lester D. Langley, *The Americas in the Age of Revolution, 1750–1850* (New Haven, Conn.: Yale University Press, 1996).

13. Davis, *Inhuman Bondage*, 173–74; David Patrick Geggus, "Epilogue," in *The Impact of the Haitian Revolution in the Atlantic World*, 247–50; Seymour Drescher, *Capitalism and Slavery* (New York: Oxford University Press, 1987), 98; Drescher, *The Mighty Experiment: Free Labor Versus Slavery in British Emancipation* (Oxford: Oxford University Press, 2002), 100–105; Drescher, "The Limits of Example," in Geggus, *The Impact of the Haitian Revolution in the Atlantic World*, 10. See also Robin Blackburn, "Haiti, Slavery, and the Age of Democratic Revolution," *William and Mary Quarterly* 3rd ser. 63, 4 (October 2006): 673–74

14. Dubois, *Avengers of the New World*, 30, 39.

15. *A Particular Account of the Insurrection of the Negroes of St. Domingo, Begun in August, 1791: Translated From the French*, 4th ed. (London: s.n., 1792), 2.

16. The name most likely derives from his ability to find openings in enemy lines, though the possibility remains that it was a reference to a natural gap in his teeth or to the fact that a battlefield injury resulted in the loss of his front teeth and part of his jaw. Fritz Daguillard, *Enigmatic in His Glory: An Exhibit Commemorating the Bicentennial of the Death of Toussaint Louverture* (Washington, D.C.: Fritz Daguillard, 2003), 15, 26; C. L. R. James, *Black Jacobins: Toussaint L'Ouverture and the San Domingo Revolution*, 2nd ed. (New York: Vintage, 1989), 126; Geggus, *Haitian Revolutionary Studies*, 22; Madison Smartt Bell proposes yet another explanation: "The name Louverture has a Vodouisant resonance: a reference to Legba, the spirit of gates and of crossroads, a rough equivalent of Hermes in the Greek pantheon. . . . The association of his surname with Legba lent a spiritual power to the essential message of the proclamation from Camp Turel: that

Toussaint Louverture alone was master of the crossroads of liberty for the former slaves of Saint Domingue," Madison Smartt Bell, *Toussaint Louverture: A Biography* (New York: Vintage, 2007), 56.

17. Geggus, *Haitian Revolutionary Studies*; Dubois, *Avengers of the New World*, 171; Stewart King, "Toussaint L'Ouverture Before 1791: Free Planter and Slave-Holder," *Journal of Haitian Studies* 3 and 4 (1997–98): 68; Gabriel Debien, Jean Fouchard, and Marie Antoinette Menier, "Toussaint Louverture avant 1789: légendes et réalités," *Conjonction* 134 (June–July 1997): 65–80.

18. Guillaume Thomas François Raynal, *Histoire philosophique et politique des établissements et du commerce des européens dans les deux Indes*, vol. 3 (Genève: Jean-Leonard Pellet, 1780), 204–5. It is likely that Dénis Diderot authored this famous quotation: Michèle Duchet, *Diderot et l'histoire des deux Indes; ou, l'Écriture fragmentaire* (Paris: Nizet, 1978). C. L. R. James wrote of Raynal's work, "It was a book famous in its time and it came into the hands of the slave most fitted to make use of it, Toussaint L'Ouverture," who read the famous passage, "Over and over again." James, *Black Jacobins*, 24–25; Dubois illuminates the pervasiveness of French political tracts among Caribbean bondpeople: *Avengers of the New World*, 102–6, and Dubois, *A Colony of Citizens*, 105–7.

19. Bell provides evidence to suggest Louverture may have obfuscated his participation in the revolt from its inception. Bell, *Toussaint Louverture*, 43.

20. Dubois, *Avengers of the New World*, 170.

21. George Tyson, ed., *Toussaint L'Ouverture* (Englewood Cliffs, N.J.: Prentice-Hall, 1973), 28.

22. Geggus, *Haitian Revolutionary Studies*, 20.

23. Dubois, *Avengers of the New World*, 251.

24. James, *Black Jacobins*, 274.

25. Dubois, *Avengers of the New World*, 102, 124, 286; Theophilus Gould Steward, *The Haitian Revolution, 1791–1804: Or, Side Lights on the French Revolution* (New York: T.W. Crowell, 1914), 198.

26. P. L. Roederer, *Oeuvres du Comte P. L. Roederer, ed. Antoine M. Roederer, vol. 3* (Paris: Firmin Didot, 1853–59), 461.

27. Douglas R. Egerton, "The Empire of Liberty Reconsidered," in *The Revolution of 1800: Democracy, Race, and the New Republic*, ed. James Horn, Jan Ellen Lewis, and Peter Onuf (Charlottesville: University of Virginia Press, 2002), 309–30; Adam Rothman, *Slave Country: American Expansion and the Origins of the Deep South* (Cambridge, Mass.: Harvard University Press, 2005), 15–19.

28. Bell, *Toussaint Louverture*; Bell, *All Souls' Rising: A Novel* (New York: Random House, 1995); Bell, *Master of the Crossroads: A Novel* (New York: Pantheon, 2000); Bell, *The Stone That the Builder Refused: A Novel* (New York: Pantheon, 2004); Gordon S. Brown, *Toussaint's Clause: The Founding Fathers and the Haitian Revolution* (Jackson: University Press of Mississippi, 2005); Dubois, *Avengers of the New World* and *A Colony of Citizens*; Gaspar and Geggus, *A Turbulent Time*; Geggus, *Haitian Revolutionary Studies* and *The Impact of the Haitian Revolution on the Atlantic World*; Langley, *The Americas in*

the Age of Revolution; Michel-Rolph Trouillot, *Silencing the Past: Power and the Production of History* (Boston: Beacon Press, 1995).

29. Bell, *Toussaint Louverture*, 3.

30. Hunt, *Haiti's Influence on Antebellum America*, 146.

31. Elizabeth Rauh Bethel, "Images of Hayti: The Construction of an Afro-American Lieu de Memoire," *Callaloo* 15, 3 (Summer 1992): 827–41; Chris Dixon, *African Americans and Haiti: Emigration and Black Nationalism in the Nineteenth Century* (Westport, Conn.: Greenwood Press, 2000); Sara C. Fanning, "The Roots of Early Black Nationalism: Northern African Americans' Invocations of Haiti in the Early Nineteenth Century," *Slavery & Abolition* 28, 1 (April 2007): 61–85; Maurice Jackson, "'Friends of the Negro! Fly with me, The path is open to the sea': Remembering the Haitian Revolution in the History, Music, and Culture of the African American People," *Early American Studies* 6, 1 (Spring 2008): 59–103; Léon Dénius Pamphile, *Haitians and African Americans: A Heritage of Tragedy and Hope* (Gainesville: University Press of Florida, 2001).

32. Brown, *Toussaint's Clause; Tim Matthewson, A Proslavery Foreign Policy: Haitian-American Relations During the Early Republic (Westport, Conn.: Praeger, 2003); Nathalie Dessens, From Saint-Domingue to New Orleans: Migration and Influences (Gainesville: University of Florida Press, 2007); Ashli White, "'A Flood of Impure Lava': Saint Dominguan Refugees* in the United States, 1791–1820" (Ph.D. dissertation, Columbia University, 2003).

33. Peter Linebaugh and Marcus Rediker, *The Many-Headed Hydra: Sailors, Slaves, Commoners, and the Hidden History of the Revolutionary Atlantic* (Boston: Beacon Press, 2000), 7.

CHAPTER 1. "THE INSURRECTION OF THE BLACKS IN ST. DOMINGO": REMEMBERING TOUSSAINT LOUVERTURE AND THE HAITIAN REVOLUTION

1. Bryan Edwards, *An Historical Survey of the French Colony in the Island of St. Domingo* (Philadelphia: James Humphreys, 1806), 68–69; Larry Tise writes, "Having spent much of his career as a West Indian merchant and planter with vast estates in Jamaica, Edwards had long been critical of British emancipators and served as one of their chief antagonists in Parliament in the early 1790s. It was, therefore, understandable that his mammoth History should reflect his intense proslavery sentiments and that his heavy anti-French pen, particularly in his treatment of St. Domingo, should continue to feed the ideological fires of British and American proslavery thought until the end of the Civil War," in *Proslavery: A History of the Defense of Slavery in America, 1701–1840* (Athens: University of Georgia Press, 1987), 84.

2. Marcus Rainsford, *An Historical Account of the Black Empire of Hayti* (London: James Cundee, 1805), x–xi, xvi, 249.

3. "St. Domingo," *Monthly Register and Encyclopedia Magazine* 2, 11 (March 1803): 440.

4. "French West-Indies," *Courier of New Hampshire*, 16 December 1802.

5. Rainsford, *Historical Account*, xviii, 250.

6. David Brion Davis, *Inhuman Bondage: The Rise and Fall of Slavery in the New World* (New York: Oxford University Press, 2006), 7.

7. Herbert Aptheker, *American Negro Slave Revolts* (New York: International Publishers, 1993).

8. Winthrop Jordan, *White over Black: American Attitudes Toward the Negro, 1550–1812* (Chapel Hill: University of North Carolina Press, 1968), 114.

9. Scot French, *The Rebellious Slave: Nat Turner in American Memory* (Boston: Houghton Mifflin, 2004), Epilogue.

10. John W. Cromwell, "The Aftermath of Nat Turner's Insurrection," *Journal of Negro History* 5, 2 (April 1920): 208–34.

11. Thomas R. Gray, *The Confessions of Nat Turner: The Leaders of the Late Insurrection in Southampton, Va.* (Baltimore: Thomas Gray, 1831); Samuel Warner, *Authentic and Impartial Narrative of the Tragical Scene Which Was Witnessed in Southampton County (Virginia) on Monday the 22d of August Last. When Fifty-Five of its Inhabitants (mostly women and children) were inhumanly MASSACRED BY THE BLACKS! Communicated by those who were eye witnesses of the bloody scene, and confirmed by the confessions of several of the Blacks while under Sentence of Death* (New York: Warner & West, 1831), 5.

12. Herbert Aptheker writes, "This pamphlet is almost wholly inaccurate but rumors are often quite as important as facts." Henry Irving Tragle notes that Warner obtained a copyright for his pamphlet in New York nine days before Turner's capture, and finds the work "quite obviously culled largely from newspaper accounts. . . . No sources are identified. Presumably Warner worked primarily from news accounts, although he probably had reports sent north by letter." Herbert Aptheker, *Nat Turner's Slave Rebellion* (New York: Humanities Press, 1966), 116; Henry Irving Tragle, *The Southampton Slave Revolt of 1831: A Compilation of Source Material* (Amherst: University of Massachusetts Press, 1971), 279–80.

13. Warner, *Authentic and Impartial Narrative*, 6, 18, 30–31.

14. Ira Berlin, "After Nat Turner: A Letter from the North," *Journal of Negro History* 55, 2 (April 1970): 144–151.

15. Elizabeth Rauh Bethel first applied the notion "lieu de memoire" to African American memory of the Haitian Revolution in "Images of Hayti: The Construction of an Afro-American Lieu de Memoire," *Callaloo* 15, 3 (Summer 1992): 827–28, 830, 839; Pierre Nora, "Between Memory and History: Les Lieux de Mémoire," in *History and Memory in African-American Culture*, ed. Geneviève Fabre and Robert O'Meally (New York: Oxford University Press, 1994), 284.

16. Douglas R. Egerton, *Gabriel's Rebellion: The Virginia Slave Conspiracies of 1800 and 1802* (Chapel Hill: University of North Carolina Press, 1993), 43–45, 51, 102, 182–85; Jordan, *White over Black*, 395–96; James Sidbury, "Saint Domingue in Virginia: Ideology, Local Meanings, and Resistance to Slavery, 1790–1800," *Journal of Southern History* 63, 3 (August 1997): 531–52.

17. Adam Rothman, *Slave Country: American Expansion and the Origins of the Deep*

South (Cambridge, Mass.: Harvard University Press, 2005), 255; Aptheker, *American Negro Slave Revolts*, 249.

18. Junius Rodriguez, "Rebellion on the River Road: The Ideology and Influence of Louisiana's German Coast Slave Insurrection of 1811," in *Antislavery Violence: Sectional, Racial, and Cultural Conflict in Antebellum America*, ed. John R. McKivigan and Stanley Harrold (Knoxville: University of Tennessee Press, 1999), 71.

19. James Lofton, *Denmark Vesey's Revolt: The Slave Plot That Lit a Fuse to Fort Sumter* (Kent, Ohio: Kent State University Press, 1983), 214, 271; James Hamilton, *Negro Plot: An Account of the Late Intended Insurrection Among a Portion of the Blacks of the City of Charleston, South Carolina* (Boston: Joseph W. Ingraham, 1822).

20. Eugene Genovese, *From Rebellion to Revolution: Afro-American Slave Revolts in the Making of the New World* (Baton Rouge: Louisiana State University Press, 1979), 50.

21. Acclaimed southern historian Ulrich B. Phillips argued that plantations were "schools" that aided African American "pupils" in their transition for barbarism to civility. He wrote, "the slaves were negroes, who for the most part were by racial quality submissive rather than defiant, light-hearted instead of gloomy, amiable and ingratiating instead of sullen, and whose very defects invited paternalism rather than repression," in *American Negro Slavery: A Survey of the Supply, Employment and Control of Negro Labor Determined by the Plantation Regime* (Baton Rouge: Louisiana State University Press, 1918), 341–42; Ironically, Genovese in his discussion of paternalism rejected Phillips's racism but also found strong evidence of slave acquiescence. Genovese considered slave assent a form of resistance, writing, "Accommodation itself breathed a critical spirit and disguised subversive actions and often embraced its apparent opposite—resistance." Eugene D. Genovse, *Roll, Jordan, Roll: The World the Slaves Made* (New York: Random House, 1974), 596.

22. For some of the varieties of slave resistance, see John W. Blassingame, *The Slave Community: Plantation Life in the Antebellum South*, rev. enl. ed. (New York: Oxford University Press, 1979); W. Jeffrey Bolster, *Black Jacks: African American Seamen in the Age of Sail* (Cambridge, Mass.: Harvard University Press, 1997); Albert J. Raboteau, *Slave Religion: The "Invisible Institution" in the Antebellum South* (Oxford: Oxford University Press, 1980); Kenneth M. Stampp, *The Peculiar Institution: Slavery in the Ante-Bellum South* (New York: Vintage, 1956).

23. Stephanie M. H. Camp, *Closer to Freedom: Enslaved Women and Everyday Resistance in the Plantation South* (Chapel Hill: University of North Carolina Press, 2004); Walter Johnson, *Soul by Soul: Life Inside the Antebellum Slave Market* (Cambridge, Mass.: Harvard University Press, 2000); Anthony E. Kaye, *Joining Places: Slave Communities in the Old South* (Chapel Hill: University of North Carolina Press, 2007). The search for alternative forms of resistance came only after the successful quest of historians in the twentieth century to unearth evidence of slave revolts in early America. Classic accounts include Aptheker, *American Negro Slave Revolts*; Sylvia Frey, *Water from the Rock: Black Resistance in a Revolutionary Age* (Princeton, N.J.: Princeton University Press, 1991); Peter

H. Wood, *Black Majority: Negroes in Colonial South Carolina from 1670 Through the Stono Rebellion* (New York: Norton, 1975).

24. Thomas O. Ott, *Haitian Revolution, 1789-1804* (Knoxville: University of Tennessee Press, 1973), 53.

25. Edward Stevens to Brigadier-General Sir Thomas Maitland, May 3, 1799, in "Letters of Toussaint Louverture and Edward Stevens, 1798-1800," *American Historical Review* 16, 1 (October 1910): 64-101.

26. This convinced Stevens of the goodness of Louverture, and may have also encouraged U.S. support for Louverture's cause in subsequent years. Ott, *Haitian Revolution*, 108.

27. According to C. L. R. James, Louverture planned to end the Atlantic slave trade by sailing to Africa, and "had sent millions of francs to American to wait for the day when he would be ready." While an invasion of the American South by a foreign black army was unlikely, the threat was arguably quite real. C. L. R. James, *Black Jacobins: Toussaint L'Ouverture and the San Domingo Revolution*, 2nd ed. (New York: Vintage, 1989), 265; Douglas R. Egerton, "The Empire of Liberty Reconsidered," in *The Revolution of 1800: Democracy, Race, and the New Republic*, ed. James Horn, Jan Ellen Lewis, and Peter Onuf (Charlottesville: University of Virginia Press, 2002), 313-14.

28. In Martinique in December 1800, Jean Kina, a former Haitian bondman, led a "strange variety of rebellion" that officials quickly suppressed. A decade later, officials thwarted a slave conspiracy led by Edmond Thétis, a six-year veteran of the Haitian army. In Spanish Florida, a veteran named George Biassou wandered the embattled colony at the head of a Spanish army. Years earlier Louverture had taken orders from him. David Geggus, "The Slaves and Free Coloreds of Martinique During the Age of the French and Haitian Revolutions: Three Moments of Resistance," in *The Lesser Antilles in the Age of European Expansion*, ed. Robert L. Paquette and Stanley L. Engerman (Gainesville: University Press of Florida, 1996), 289-95; Jane G. Landers, "Rebellion and Royalism in Spanish Florida: The French Revolution on Spain's Northern Colonial Frontier," in *A Turbulent Time: The French Revolution and the Greater Caribbean*, ed. David Barry Gaspar and David Patrick Geggus (Bloomington: Indiana University Press), 157-77.

29. Defiant Jamaican slaves sang songs about the Haitian Revolution and celebrated Haitian independence. Black rebels in Rio de Janeiro wore necklaces bearing the image of Louverture's successor, Dessalines. Cuban officials found the portrait of Louverture and other leading Haitian revolutionaries in a book, "a blueprint for revolution," which the notorious black rebel José Antonio Aponte showed to free blacks and slaves to enlist their support. African Americans also sang songs about the Haitian Revolution and named their children after Haiti's founding fathers. Most symbolic of blacks' racial identification with Haiti are the numbers of African Americans who emigrated there. Elizabeth Rauh estimates that as many as 20 percent of all free blacks in the northern United States emigrated to Haiti in the early nineteenth century. Even so, Christopher Dixon asserts, "historians have understated African Americans' relationship with the island republic of Haiti." David P. Geggus, "The Enigma of Jamaica in the 1790s: New Light on the Causes

of Slave Rebellions," *William and Mary Quarterly* 3rd ser. 44, 2 (April 1987): 276; David P. Geggus, *The Impact of the Haitian Revolution in the Atlantic World* (Columbia: University of South Carolina Press, 2001), x; Christopher Dixon, *African Americans and Haiti: Emigration and Black Nationalism in the Nineteenth Century* (Westport, Conn.: Greenwood Press, 2000), 2, 27; João José Reis, *Slave Rebellion in Brazil: The Muslim Uprising of 1835 in Bahia* (Baltimore: Johns Hopkins University Press, 1993), 48; Matt D. Childs, "A Black French General Arrived to Conquer the Island: Images of the Haitian Revolution in Cuba's Aponte Rebellion," in Geggus, *Impact of the Haitian Revolution*, 136–37; James T. Holly, "A Vindication of the Capacity of the Negro Race for Self-Government and Civilized Progress," in *Black Separatism and the Caribbean 1860*, ed. Howard H. Bell (Ann Arbor: University of Michigan Press, 1970), 39; Paul N. Thornell, "The Absent Ones and the Providers: A Biography of the Vashons," *Journal of Negro History* 83, 4 (Autumn 1998): 284–301; Genovese, *From Rebellion to Revolution*, 96–97; Elizabeth Rauh Bethel, *The Roots of African-American Identity: Memory and History in Free Antebellum Communities* (New York: St. Martin's, 1997), 145.

30. Bolster, *Black Jacks*; David Cecelski, *The Waterman's Song: Slavery and Freedom in Maritime North Carolina* (Chapel Hill: University of North Carolina Press, 2000), chaps 5, 6; Julius Sherrod Scott, III, "The Common Wind: Currents of Afro-American Communication in the Era of the Haitian Revolution" (Ph.D. dissertation, Duke University, 1986).

31. In the aftermath of Denmark Vesey's trial and execution, South Carolina and other slave states began to restrict the entry of black sailors into their ports. Douglas R. Egerton, *He Shall Go Out Free: The Lives of Denmark Vesey* (Lanham, Md.: Rowman & Littlefield, 2004), 217–18; Robert Pierce Forbes, *The Missouri Compromise and Its Aftermath: Slavery and the Meaning of America* (Chapel Hill: University of North Carolina Press, 2007), 156–57.

32. James Alexander Robertson, *Louisiana Under the Rule of Spain, France, and the United States*, vol. 2 (Cleveland: Arthur H. Clark, 1911), 300–301.

33. Joseph X. Pontalba to his wife, 6 March 1796, in *The Letters of Baron Joseph X. Pontalba to His Wife* (Baton Rouge: Works Progress Administration of Louisiana, Survey of Federal Archives in Louisiana, 1939).

34. Mary Boykin Chesnut, *A Diary from Dixie*, ed. Ben Ames Williams (Cambridge, Mass.: Harvard University Press, 1980), 147.

35. "Hayti and the Haytiens," *De Bow's Review* 16, 1 (January 1854): 35–36.

36. Louis Moreau Gottschalk, *Notes of a Pianist*, ed. Jeanne Behrend (New York: Knopf, 1964), 10.

37. Gilbert Moxley Sorrel, *Recollections of a Confederate Staff Officer* (New York: Neale, 1905), 17, 19.

38. John Gordon Freymann, *The Sorrel Family in Saint-Domingue (Haiti): 1763–1813* (Avon, Conn.: Freymann, 2000), 24.

39. Prince Hall, *A Charge Delivered to the African Lodge, June 24, 1797, at Menotomy* (Boston: Benjamin Edes, 1797), 11–12.

40. "John Browne Russwurm: A Document," *Journal of Negro History* 54, 4 (October 1969): 393–95.

41. James McCune Smith, *A Lecture on the Haytien Revolutions; With a Sketch of the Character of Toussaint L'Ouverture* (New York: Daniel Fanshaw, 1841), 5, 15, 28.

42. J. P. Martin [Abraham Bishop], "Rights of Black Men," *American Museum* 12, 5 (November 1792): 299–300; Tim Matthewson, "Abraham Bishop, 'The Rights of Black Men,' and the American Reaction to the Haitian Revolution," *Journal of Negro History* 67, 2 (Summer 1982): 148–54.

43. Theodore Dwight, "An Oration, Spoken Before the Connecticut Society, for the Promotion of Freedom and the Relief of Persons Unlawfully Holden in Bondage," in *American Political Writing During the Founding Era 1760–1805*, ed. Charles S. Hyneman and Donald S. Lutz, vol. 2 (Indianapolis: Liberty Press, 1983), 894–99.

44. Garry Wills, *"Negro President": Jefferson and the Slave Power* (Boston: Houghton Mifflin, 2003), 41.

45. Paul Goodman and Charles Sellers, *Of One Blood: Abolitionism and the Origins of Racial Equality* (Berkeley: University of California Press, 2000); John McKivigan, *Forgotten Firebrand: James Redpath and the Making of Nineteenth-Century America* (Ithaca, N.Y.: Cornell University Press, 2008); McKivigan and Harrold, eds., *Antislavery Violence*; David Reynolds, *John Brown, Abolitionist: The Man Who Killed Slavery, Sparked the Civil War, and Seeded Civil Rights* (New York: Knopf, 2005); John Stauffer, *The Black Hearts of Men: Radical Abolitionists and the Transformation of Race* (Cambridge, Mass.: Harvard University Press, 2002).

46. Sarah J. Purcell, *Sealed with Blood: War, Sacrifice, and Memory in Revolutionary America* (Philadelphia: University of Pennsylvania Press, 2002).

47. François Furstenberg, "Beyond Freedom and Slavery: Autonomy, Virtue, and Resistance in Early American Political Discourse," *Journal of American History* 89, 4 (March 2003): 1295–1330.

48. Madison Smartt Bell details Louverture's effort to reconcile his status as an "ancient libre" with the black masses of Haitian freedmen who became known as "nouveaux libres," while Carolyn Fick decenters Louverture from the leadership of the revolution. Madison Smartt Bell, *Toussaint Louverture: A Biography* (New York: Vintage, 2007), 56; Carolyn Fick, *The Making of Haiti: The Saint Domingue Revolution from Below* (Knoxville: University of Tennessee Press, 1990); French officer Pamphile Lacroix captured the mythology surrounding the memory of Louverture, writing, "Judged by the interest of the moment, through the prism of passions, Toussaint Louverture has been represented in turn as a ferocious brute, or as the most surprising and the best of men, more often as an execrable monster or saintly martyr: he was none of these," in *La Révolution de Haiti: édition présentée et annotée par Pierre Pluchon* (Paris: Pillet aîné, 1819; reprint Paris: Karthala, 1995), 244.

49. Allen D. Candler, *The Confederate Records of the State of Georgia* (Atlanta: Chas. P. Ryrd, 1909), 833.

50. The words of Winthrop D. Jordan regarding slavery in the colonial period are

helpful here: "Indeed if there was one thing about which Americans of the eighteenth century were certain (in fact there were a great many) it was that men everywhere yearned for freedom. Nothing would have surprised them more than to learn that later generations spoke knowingly of the contented slave," in *White over Black*, 388.

51. Aptheker, *American Negro Slave Revolts*, 369–70.

52. Edmund Ruffin, *The Political Economy of Slavery; or, The Institution Considered in Regard to Its Influence on Public Wealth and the General Welfare* (Washington, D.C.: Lemuel Towers, 1857), 17.

53. Significant is the degree to which Louverture's enemies contributed to the emerging heroic legend. A supplement to Bryan Edwards's *Historical Survey of St. Domingo* included a biographical sketch of Louverture, which described him as "a man worthy to be held in honourable remembrance for his courage, his talents, and his virtues, and especially for those virtues which are least often found in persons holding authority, namely, forgiveness of injuries, a strict adherence to his word and to truth, and a temperate exercise of power." The French historian Jean-Louis Dubroca produced what must be considered among the most acidulous biographies of Louverture ever published. This hired literary gun of the French Consul accused Louverture of treason and murder; still, he quoted the Spanish marquis who remarked that, "if God were to come down on this earth, he could not inhabit a heart, to all appearance, more worthy of him than that of Toussaint." The quotation would become standard in abolitionists' accounts of the revolution. Dubroca's biography did something else noteworthy. The frontispiece included a portrait of Louverture's head drawn from profile. The nonracialized image of a uniformed and dignified black soldier contrasts sharply with the fiend described by Dubroca in the accompanying text. Bryan Edwards, *The History, Civil and Commercial, of the British West Indies, With a Continuation to the Present Time* (London: T. Miller, 1819), 112, 147; Jean-Louis Dubroca, *The Life of Toussaint Louverture, Late General in Chief and Governor of the Island of Saint Domingo* (Charleston, S.C.: T.B. Bowen, 1802), 14, 43; discussed below, this image is considered along with the frontispiece of Cousin D'Avallon's biography, one of the first visual representations of Louverture. Its accuracy is along with every extant image, uncertain, though it is likely, in the words of Fritz Daguillard, "the result of pure fantasy." Cousin d'Avallon, *Histoire de Toussaint-Louverture, chef des noirs insurgés de Saint-Domingue* (Paris: Pillot, 1802); Fritz Daguillard, *Enigmatic in His Glory: An Exhibit Commemorating the Bicentennial of the Death of Toussaint Louverture* (Washington, D.C.: Fritz Daguillard, 2003), 9.

54. Adam Hochschild, *Bury the Chains: Prophets and Rebels in the Fight to Free an Empire's Slaves* (Boston: Houghton Mifflin, 2005), 294.

55. "History of Europe," *Annual Register* 44 (London: R. Wilks, 1803): 211.

56. James Stephen, *The History of Toussaint Louverture: A New Edition* (London: J. Butterworth and Son, 1814), iii–iv, 2; see also James Stephen, *Buonaparte in the West Indies: or, the History of Toussaint Louverture, the African Hero* (London: J. Hatchard, 1803), 7–8.

57. Joseph François Michaud, *Biographie universelle ancienne et moderne* (1843; reprint Graz, Akademische Druck- u. Verlagsanstalt, 1966), 399–400.

58. "A Sketch of the Life of Toussaint L'Ouverture, the Haytian Patriot," *Oriental Herald* 60, 19 (December 1828): 404, 419.

59. Rainsford, *Black Empire of Hayti*, xix.

60. William Jackson published Charles Knight's *Penny Magazine* in New York. The magazine was England's most widely read periodical, known especially for its illustrations. Scott Bennett calls the magazine "the first mass-market periodical published in Britain" and records its average annual circulation at 187,000, in "The Editorial Character and Readership of *The Penny Magazine*: An Analysis," *Victorian Periodical Review* 17 (1984): 127–28.

61. "To the Editor of the Christian Recorder," *Christian Reflector*, 15 February 1839.

62. [Harriet Martineau], "Account of Toussaint L'Ouverture," *Monthly Supplement of the Penny Magazine of the Society for the Diffusion of Useful Knowledge* 385, 7 (28 February–1 March 1838): 128.

63. Samuel Goodrich, *Lights and Shadows of American History: by the Author of Peter Parley's Tales* (Boston: Bradbury, Soden & Co., 1844), 183.

64. Felix Huston, *Address of Gen. Felix Huston, to the Members of the Southern Convention, to be Held at Nashville, on the Third June, 1850* (Natchez, Miss.: Free Trade Office, 1850), 12.

CHAPTER 2. "HE PATTERNED HIS LIFE AFTER THE SAN DOMINGAN":
JOHN BROWN, TOUSSAINT LOUVERTURE, AND THE TRIUMPH OF VIOLENT
ABOLITIONISM

1. The literature on the conspiracy is extensive. Reliable accounts include William Freehling, *Prelude to Civil War: The Nullification Controversy in South Carolina, 1816–1836* (New York: Oxford University Press, 1965), 53–61; Douglas R. Egerton, *He Shall Go Out Free: The Lives of Denmark Vesey* (Madison: Madison House, 1999); Walter C. Rucker, "'I Will Gather All Nations': Resistance, Culture, and Pan-African Collaboration in Denmark Vesey's South Carolina," *Journal of Negro History* 86, 2 (Spring 2001): 132–47. See note 7 below.

2. Lionel H. Kennedy and Thomas Parker, *An official report of the trials of sundry Negroes, charged with an attempt to raise an insurrection in the state of South-Carolina: preceded by an introduction and narrative: and, in an appendix, a report of the trials of four white persons on indictments for attempting to excite the slaves to insurrection* (Charleston, S.C.: James R. Schenck, 1822), 40–42, 68, 82–83, 96–98, 118.

3. Kennedy and Parker, *An official report of the trials of sundry* Negroes, 75, 98, 112–14, 126–27, 145; For a discussion of free and enslaved refugees in Charleston, see David Geggus, "The Caradeux and Colonial Memory," in Geggus, ed., *The Impact of the Haitian Revolution in the Atlantic World* (Columbia: University of South Carolina Press, 2001), 231–47; Alfred Hunt, *Haiti's Influence on Antebellum America: Slumbering Volcano in the Caribbean* (Baton Rouge: Louisiana State University Press, 1988), 110–11.

4. Robert L. Paquette, "Jacobins of the Lowcountry: The Vesey Plot on Trial," in "Forum: The Making of Slave Conspiracy, part 2," *William and Mary Quarterly* 3rd ser. 59, 1 (January 2002): 185.

5. This may be the most important lesson learned from the plot. James Sidbury writes, regarding the knowledge that bondmen mailed a letter requesting Haitian assistance, "it is almost as interesting to know that black Charlestonians imagining a conspiracy to overthrow slavery would include a letter to the president of Haiti, as it is to know whether such a letter was sent." James Sidbury, "Plausible stories and Varnished Truths," in "Forum: The Making of Slave Conspiracy, part 2," 183.

6. Peter Hinks, *To Awaken My Afflicted Brethren: David Walker and the Problem of Antebellum Social Reform* (University Park: Pennsylvania State University Press, 1997), 30, 39–40.

7. David Walker, *David Walker's Appeal to the Coloured Citizens of the World, but in Particular, and very expressly, to those of the United States of America*, ed. James Turner (Boston, 1830; reprint Baltimore: Black Classic Press, 1993), 40, 75.

8. Daniel Alexander Payne, *Recollections of Seventy Years* (Nashville: A.M.E. Sunday School Union, 1888), 15–16.

9. David Brion Davis has for now provided the last word in the debate over the existence of a conspiracy, asserting, "I am now convinced that Denmark Vesey and a significant number of slaves were in all probability involved in a plot to rise in insurrection on the night of Sunday, July 14—Bastille Day—1822," in *Inhuman Bondage: The Rise and Fall of Slavery in the New World* (New York; Oxford University Press, 2006), 222. The debate over the legitimacy of the plot began with Richard Wade, *Slavery in the Cities: The South, 1820–1860* (New York: Oxford University Press, 1964), 228–29, 237; "The Vesey Plot: A Reconsideration," *Journal of Southern History* 30, 2 (1964): 413–61; Michael P. Johnson took up the mantle of skepticism in "Denmark Vesey and His Co-Conspirators," *William and Mary Quarterly* 3rd ser. 58, 4 (October 2001): 915–76; For extensive commentary on Johnson's piece, see "Forum: The Making of a Slave Conspiracy, part 2," 135–202; and Robert L. Paquette, "From Rebellion to Revisionism: The Continuing Debate About the Denmark Vesey Affair," *Journal of the Historical Society* 6, 3 (Fall 2004): 291–334.

10. Martin Duberman, *The Antislavery Vanguard: New Essays on the Abolitionists* (Princeton, N.J.: Princeton University Press, 1965). Other works that root the movement in the Second Great Awakening are James Brewer Stewart, *Holy Warriors: The Abolitionists and American Slavery*, rev. ed. (New York: Hill and Wang, 1997); Ronald Walters, *The Antislavery Appeal: American Abolitionism After 1830* (Baltimore: Johns Hopkins University Press, 1976).

11. Important works that date American abolitionism prior to the 1830s include Richard S. Newman, *The Transformation of American Abolitionism: Fighting Slavery in the Early Republic* (Chapel Hill: University of North Carolina Press, 2002); Paul Goodman and Charles Sellers, *Of One Blood: Abolitionism and the Origins of Racial Equality* (Berkeley: University of California Press, 2000); Stanley Harrold, *American Abolitionists*

(New York: Longman, 2001); Richard Newman, Patrick Rael, and Phillip Lapsansky, *Pamphlets of Protest: An Anthology of Early African-American Protest Literature, 1790–1860* (New York: Routledge, 2001).

12. John R. McKivigan and Stanley Harrold, eds., *Antislavery Violence: Sectional, Racial, and Cultural Conflict in Antebellum America* (Knoxville: University of Tennessee Press, 1999); John Stauffer, *The Black Hearts of Men: Radical Abolitionists and the Transformation of Race* (Cambridge, Mass.: Harvard University Press, 2002).

13. William H. Pease and Jane H. Pease, "Antislavery Ambivalence: Immediatism, Expediency, Race," *American Quarterly* 17, 4 (Winter 1965): 682–95.

14. Stauffer, *The Black Hearts of Men*; David S. Reynolds, *John Brown, Abolitionist: The Man Who Killed Slavery, Sparked the Civil War, and Seeded Civil Rights* (New York: Knopf, 2005), 450; Goodman and Sellers, *Of One Blood: Abolitionism and the Origins of Racial Equality*.

15. R. J. M. Blackett, *Building an Antislavery Wall: Black Americans in the Atlantic Abolitionist Movement, 1830–1860* (Baton Rouge: Louisiana State University Press, 1983); Audrey A. Fisch, *American Slaves in Victorian England: Abolitionist Politics in Popular Literature and Culture* (Cambridge: Cambridge University Press, 2000); Jeffrey R. Kerr-Ritchie, *Rites of August First: Emancipation Day in the Black Atlantic World* (Baton Rouge: Louisiana State University Press, 2007); Alan J. Rice, *Liberating Sojourn: Frederick Douglass & Transatlantic Reform* (Athens: University of Georgia Press, 1999); Clare Taylor, *British and American Abolitionists: An Episode in Transatlantic Understanding* (Edinburgh: Edinburgh University Press, 1974).

16. Davis, *Inhuman Bondage*, 259–60.

17. Van Gosse, " 'As a Nation, the English Are Our Friends': The Emergence of African American Politics in the British Atlantic World, 1772–1861," *American Historical Review* 113, 4 (October 2008): 1003–28.

18. William Leonard Joyce, et al., eds., *Printing and Society in Early America* (Worcester, Mass.: American Antiquarian Society, 1983).

19. "Haytien Revolution," *Freedom's Journal*, 6 April 1827; "Hayti," *Freedom's Journal*, 20 April, 27 April 27, 4 May, 15 June, 29 June, 12 October 1827; "Theresa, A Haytien Tale," *Freedom's Journal*, 18 January, 25 January, 8 February, 15 February 1828; "Toussaint L'Ouverture," *Freedom's Journal*, 4, 11, 18 May 1827; "Mémoires pour servir à l'histoire de la Révolution de Saint Domingue," *Quarterly Review* 21 (April 1819): 430–60.

20. James McCune Smith, *A Lecture on the Haytien Revolutions; With a Sketch of the Character of Toussaint L'Ouverture* (New York: Daniel Fanshaw, 1841), 18–19, 25.

21. Other accounts of the Haitian Revolution by antebellum African Americans include Prince Saunders, *Haytian Papers* (1816; reprint Westport, Conn.: Negro Universities Press, 1969); Philip S. Foner, "John Browne Russwurm, A Document," *Journal of Negro History* 54, 4 (October 1969): 393–95. We should also consider the narratives published by the American Anti-Slavery Society, given the organization's African American membership and readership: "Toussaint L'Ouverture," *Anti-Slavery Record* 1 (April 1835): 37–40; *St. Domingo* (New York: American Anti-Slavery Society, 1839); Elizur Wright,

"The Horrors of St. Domingo," *Quarterly Anti-Slavery Magazine* 1 (April 1836). For why African Americans may have refrained from publicly celebrating the Haitian Revolution, see Bruce Dain, "Haiti and Egypt in Early Black Radical Discourse in the United States," *Slavery and Abolition* 14 (December 1993): 139–61; Mitch Kachun, *Festivals of Freedom: Memory and Meaning in African American Emancipation Celebrations, 1808–1915* (Amherst: University of Massachusetts Press, 2003), 57, 272; "Antebellum African Americans, Public Commemoration, and the Haitian Revolution: A Problem of Historical Mythmaking," *Journal of the Early Republic* 26, 2 (2006): 249–73.

22. John R. Beard, *The Life of Toussaint L'Ouverture: The Negro Patriot of Hayti: Comprising an Account of the Struggle for Liberty in the Island, and a Sketch of Its History to the Present Period* (London: Ingram, Cooke, 1853), 279.

23. Wilson Armistead, *A Tribute for the Negro: Being a Vindication of the Moral, Intellectual, and Religious Capabilities of the Coloured Portion of Mankind. Illustrated by Numerous Biographical Sketches, Facts, Anecdotes, etc. and Many Superior Portraits and Engravings* (Manchester: William Irwin; New York: William Harned, 1848), 299.

24. Henry Gardiner Adams, *God's Image in Ebony: Being a Series of Biographical Sketches, Facts, Anecdotes, etc. Demonstrative of the Mental Powers and Intellectual Capacities of the Negro Race* (London: Partridge and Oakey, 1854), i.

25. Beard, *Life of Toussaint L'Ouverture*, 1.

26. Armistead, *Tribute for the Negro*, 5.

27. Armistead, *Tribute for the Negro*, 286.

28. Bruce Dorsey writes of the sentimentalization of slaves in antebellum reform culture, "By sentimentalizing slaves, anti-slavery writers depicted all enslaved people with characteristics that were clearly understood in that culture to be feminine," in *Reforming Men and Women: Gender in the Antebellum City* (Ithaca, N.Y.: Cornell University Press, 2002): 187.

29. Adams, *God's Image in Ebony*, 15.

30. Martineau, *The Hour and the Man: An Historical Romance in Two Volumes* (New York: Harper, 1841), 26. For the popularity of the book both in England and the United States, see Susan Belasco, "Harriet Martineau's Black Hero and the American Antislavery Movement," *Nineteenth Century Literature* 55 (2000): 157–94.

31. George Fredrickson, *Black Image in the White Mind: The Debate on Afro-American Character and Destiny, 1817–1914* (New York: Harper & Row, 1971), 97–129; Ronald G. Walters, *The Antislavery Appeal: American Abolitionism After 1830* (New York: Norton, 1984), 54–69; François Furstenberg, "Beyond Freedom and Slavery: Autonomy, Virtue, and Resistance in Early American Political Discourse," *Journal of American History* 89, 4 (March 2003): 1295–1330.

32. William Wells Brown, *St. Domingo: its Revolutions and its Patriots. A Lecture, Delivered Before the Metropolitan Athenæum, London, May 16, and at St. Thomas' Church, Philadelphia, December 20, 1854* (Boston: Bela Marsh, 1855); James Theodore Holly, "A Vindication of the Capacity of the Negro Race for Self-Government, and Civilized Progress, as Demonstrated by Historical Events of the Haytian Revolution; and the Subsequent Acts

of That People Since Their National Independence," in Howard H. Bell, ed., *Black Separatism and the Caribbean 1860* (Ann Arbor: University of Michigan Press, 1970); John Mercer Langston, "The World's Anti-Slavery Movement, its Heroes and its Triumphs: a Lecture Delivered at Xenia, O., Aug. 2, and Cleveland, O., Aug. 3, 1858," in Langston, *Freedom and Citizenship. Selected Lectures and Addresses of Hon. John Mercer Langston, LL.D., U.S. Minister Resident at Haiti. With an Introductory Sketch By Rev. J.E. Rankin, D.D., of Washington* (Miami: Mnemosyne, 1969), 41–67; Charles Wyllys Elliott, *Heroes Are Historic Men. St. Domingo, its Revolution and its Hero, Toussaint Louverture: An Historical Discourse Condensed for the New York Library Association. February 26, 1855.* (New York: J.A. Dix, 1855).

33. Observers noted the peripatetic Phillips normally carried a copy of Martineau's biography of Louverture with him to lectures. Vera Wheatley, *The Life and Work of Harriet Martineau* (Fair Lawn, N.J.: Essential Books, 1957), 218.

34. The journal of Charlotte Forten on December 16, 1857 provides the earliest mention of Phillips's "Toussaint L'Ouverture" that I have found. *The Journal of Charlotte Forten, With an Introduction and Notes by Ray Allen Billington* (New York: Dryden Press, 1953), 97. Another early account comes from the Wendell Phillips Papers at the Houghton Library, Harvard University, in which the writer remarked, "Rarely has a Boston audience enjoyed an opportunity of listening to an address, fulfilling the requirements of a popular lecture to a greater degree, than last evening." *Boston Early Evening Transcript*, 28 January 1858,

35. Both black and white abolitionists had lectured on the Haitian Revolution before. Among them were Orville Luther Holley, John Jay, James McCune Smith, and John Brown Russwurm. "Extract of an Oration, Delivered on the 4th of July, 1822, by O. L. Holly Esq.," *Genius of Universal Emancipation* 2 (December 1822): 93; "Public Lectures of the New York Phoenixonian Literary Society," *Colored American*, 6 February 1841; "Lecture on the Haytien Revolutions," *Colored American*, 5 June 1841; Foner, "John Brown Russwurm, a Document," 393–95. On the conservative nature of American oratory and the potential for subversion, see Sandra Marie Gustafson, *Oratory & Performance in Early America* (Chapel Hill: University of North Carolina Press, 2000); Gustafson, "Performing the Word: American Oratory, 1630–1860" (Ph.D. dissertation, University of California at Berkeley, 1993); Cristopher Looby, *Voicing America: Language, Literary Form, and the Origins of the United States* (Chicago: University of Chicago Press, 1996).

36. Forten, *Journal of Charlotte Forten*, 97.

37. "White People Allowed," *New York Times*, 26 February 1855.

38. "Toussaint L'Ouverture—Lecture by C. W. Elliott, *New York Times*, 27 February 1855.

39. "Toussaint L'Ouverture," *New York Times*, 28 February 1855.

40. "St. Domingo, Its Revolution and Its Hero," *Putnam's Monthly Magazine of American Literature, Science, and Art* 5, 29 (May 1855): 552.

41. "The Danger to the South," *New York Times*, 9 May 1855.

42. "Public Lectures of the New York Phoenixonian Literary Society," *Colored American*, 6 February 1841.

43. Helpful here is David Leverenz's notion of a "battlefield code," in *Manhood and the American Renaissance* (Ithaca, N.Y.: Cornell University Press, 1989), 73; Also helpful are Amy S. Greenberg, *Manifest Manhood and the Antebellum American Empire* (Cambridge: Cambridge University Press, 2005); Anthony Rotundo, *American Manhood: Transformations in Masculinity from the Revolution to the Modern Era* (New York: Basic Books, 1993); Stauffer, *The Black Hearts of Men*, 200–207.

44. Brown, *St. Domingo*, 36.

45. Elliott, *Heroes Are Historic Men*, 38, 70.

46. Holly, "Vindication of the Capacity of the Negro Race," 49, 54.

47. Langston, "World's Anti-Slavery Movement," 56. A clear indication of Langston's militancy was the naming of his son, Arthur Dessalines Langston. *From the Virginia Plantation* (Hartford, Conn.: American Publishing, 1894), 157.

48. Brown, *St. Domingo*, 37.

49. Holly, "Vindication of the Capacity of the *Negro Race*," 24–25.

50. Langston, "World's Anti-Slavery Movement," 57.

51. Kachun, *Festivals of Freedom*; Bruce Dain, "Haiti and Egypt in Early Black Radical Discourse in the United States."

52. "Our Cleveland Letter," *Weekly Anglo-African*, 6 August 1859.

53. "The Black Man," *Weekly Anglo-African*, 28 March 1863.

54. James Redpath, ed., *A Guide to Hayti* (New York: Haytian Bureau of Migration, 1861), 9.

55. "Toussaint L'Ouverture," *Boston Commonwealth*, 9 June 1866.

56. The image first appeared on the frontispiece of a caustic biography of Louverture published in Paris and Charleston, South Carolina in 1802: Louis Dubroca, *The Life of Toussaint Louverture: Late General in Chief and Governor of the Island of Saint Domingo: With Many Particulars Never Before Published: to which is Subjoined, an Account of the First Operations of the French Army under General Leclerc* (Charleston: T.W. Bowen, 1802); Fritz Daguillard, *Enigmatic in His Glory: An Exhibit Commemorating the Bicentennial of the Death of Toussaint Louverture* (Port-au-Prince: Musée du Panthéon National Haïtien, 2003), 7–8.

57. Phillips acquired the painting from Thomas Madiou, the renowned Haitian historian and author of the multivolume *Histoire d'Haiti*, 3 vols. (Port-au-Prince: J. Courtois, 1847–48).

58. Benjamin Quarles, *Allies for Freedom: Blacks and John Brown* (New York: Oxford University Press, 1974), 60–61.

59. *Pine and Palm*, 18 May 1861.

60. [William J. Wilson], "Afric-American Picture Gallery-Second Paper," *Anglo-African Magazine* 1 (March 1859): 87; For further discussion see John Stauffer, "Creating an Image in Black: The Power of Abolition Pictures," in *Prophets of Protest: Reconsidering the History of American Abolitionism*, ed. Patrick McCarthy and John Stauffer (New York: New Press, 2006), 264.

61. [Wilson], "Afric-American Picture Gallery-Second Paper," 87.

62. Stephen B. Oates, *To Purge This Land with Blood: A Biography of John Brown* (New York: Harper Torchbooks, 1970), 223.

63. "The Haytians and John Brown," *New York Times*, 8 August 1860.

64. Gerrit Smith, *Speech of Gerrit Smith, in Congress, on the Reference of the President's Message* (Washington, D.C.: Buell & Blanchard, 1853), 10–11.

65. Toussaint Louverture, *Mémoires du Général Toussaint-L'Ouverture: Écrits par lui-méme, pouvant servir à l'histoire de sa vie*, ed. Joseph Saint-Rémy (Paris: Pagnerre, 1853).

66. "Emancipation: A Sermon Preached at Music Hall," *Supplement to the Weekly Anglo-African*, 20 April 1861.

67. Reynolds, *John Brown, Abolitionist*, 450.

68. Thomas Wentworth Higginson, "Denmark Vesey," *Atlantic Monthly* 7 (June 1861): 728–44; *Travellers and Outlaws: Episodes in American History* (Boston: Lee and Shepard, 1889).

69. Thomas Wentworth Higginson, *Army Life in a Black Regiment* (New York: Norton, 1984), 74.

70. Jeffrey Rossbach, *Ambivalent Conspirators: John Brown, the Secret Six, and a Theory of Slave Violence* (Philadelphia: University of Pennsylvania Press, 1982), 154–55.

71. John Weiss, *Life and Correspondence of Theodore Parker, Minister of the Twenty-Eighth Congregational Society, Boston*, vol. 2 (New York: Appleton & Co., 1864), 174–75.

72. James Redpath, *The Roving Editor; or, Talks with Slaves in the Southern States* (New York: A.B. Burdick, 1859), 129; Albert J. von Frank, "John Brown, James Redpath, and the Idea of Revolution," *Civil War History* 52, 2 (2006): 142–60.

73. Oates, *To Purge This Land with Blood*, 149–51, 253–54, 284.

74. James Redpath, *A Guide to Hayti*, 13

75. Undated letter, Wendell Phillips Papers, Houghton Library, Harvard University.

76. "Toussaint L'Ouverture," *Boston Commonwealth*.

77. James Redpath, *Life of Toussaint L'Ouverture*, Preface.

78. John R. McKivigan considers Redpath among Brown's greatest influences, writing, "It does not appear to be a coincidence that during their Kansas years both Redpath and Brown shifted from advocating small-scale projects for assisting slaves to escape to plans for a massive slave insurrection," in "James Redpath, John Brown, and Abolitionist Advocacy of Slave Insurrection," *Civil War History* 37, 4 (1991): 313.

79. John McKivigan, *Forgotten Firebrand: James Redpath and the Making of Nineteenth-Century America* (Ithaca, N.Y.: Cornell University Press, 2008).

80. For the reaction of local free blacks and slaves to the incursion see Hannah Geffert, "They Heard His Call: The Local Black Community's Involvement in the Raid on Harpers Ferry," in *Terrible Swift Sword: The Legacy of John Brown*, ed. Peggy A. Russo and Paul Finkelman (Columbus: Ohio University Press, 2005), 23–45.

81. Oates, *To Purge This Land with Blood*, 288–301; Potter, *The Impending Crisis*, 369–71; Oswald Garrison Villard, *John Brown: A Biography 1800–1859* (Boston: Houghton Mifflin, 1910), 426–55.

82. Reynolds, *John Brown, Abolitionist*, 9.

83. Brown's father subscribed to the *Liberator* and other anti-slavery papers. Oswald Garrison Villard, *John Brown 1800–1859, A Biography Fifty Years After* (Gloucester, Mass.: Peter Smith, 1965), 49.

84. Richard J. Hinton, *John Brown and His Men: With Some Account of the Roads They Traveled to Reach Harpers Ferry* (New York: Funk & Wagnall, 1968), 66.

85. *Report [of] the Select Committee of the Senate Appointed to Inquire into the Late Invasion and Seizure of the Public Property at Harpers Ferry* (Washington, D.C., s.n., 1860), 96. The decision to invade Harpers Ferry, as opposed to alternative locations, is further proof of Brown's faith in the Haitian insurrectionary model. Brown considered at least ten other locales as potential points of invasion. What these places shared in common was the location of federal forts or arsenals. What distinguished Harpers Ferry were mountains. Students of the Haitian Revolution like Brown were aware of the tradition of slave marronage in Haiti, as detailed in various abolitionist publications. They knew of Louverture's use of the mountains to successfully wage guerilla warfare against Europe's best armies. It is likely for this reason that Brown considered the mountains of western Virginia and Maryland the key to a successful American slave insurrection. Oates, *To Purge This Land with Blood*, 213–14; Holly, "Vindication of the Capacity of the Negro Race," 29–30.

86. James Cleland Hamilton, "John Brown in Canada," *Canadian Magazine of Politics, Science, Art & Literature* 4 (December 1894): 132.

87. Franklin B. Sanborn, ed., *The Life and Letters of John Brown, Liberator of Kansas, and Martyr of Virginia* (Boston: Roberts Brothers, 1891), v, 122.

88. "Saw John Brown Hanged," *New York Sun*, 13 February 1898.

89. Stauffer, *Black Hearts of Men*.

90. "Charged With Inciting Rebellion," *New York Times*, 6 November 1860.

91. James Sidbury notes both the large number of black Haitian refugees to Norfolk at the opening of the century and the insurrectionary conspiracies they advanced, while David S. Cecelski documents the deep penetration of black sailors and their revolutionary Atlantic consciousness along the Virginia and North Carolina border. James Sidbury, "Saint Domingue in Virginia: Ideology, Local Meanings, and Resistance to Slavery, 1790–1800," *Journal of Southern History* 63, 3 (August 1997): 531–52; David S. Cecelski, *The Waterman's Song: Slavery and Freedom in Maritime North Carolina* (Chapel Hill: University of North Carolina Press, 2001); Also helpful in this regard is Julius Sherrard Scott, III, "The Common Wind: Currents of Afro-American Communication in the Era of the Haitian Revolution" (Ph.D. dissertation, Duke University, 1986).

92. "Hayti and the Martyrs of Harpers Ferry," *Boston Commonwealth*, 9 October 1863; Elizabeth Rauh Bethel, "Images of Hayti: The Construction of an Afro-American Lieu de Memoire," *Callaloo* 15, 3 (Summer 1992): 839.

93. "John Brown in Hayti," *National Anti-Slavery Standard*, 24 March 1860.

94. American Anti-Slavery Society, *Annual Report of the American Anti-Slavery So-*

ciety, by the Executive Committee, for the Year Ending May 1, 1860 (New York: American Anti-Slavery Society, 1861), 165.

CHAPTER 3. "CONTEMPLATE, I BESEECH YOU, FELLOW-CITIZENS, THE EXAMPLE OF ST. DOMINGO": ABOLITIONIST DREAMS, CONFEDERATE NIGHTMARES, AND THE COUNTERREVOLUTION OF SECESSION

1. Villard, *John Brown, 1800–1859: A Biography Fifty Years After* (Boston: Houghton Mifflin, 1910), 527.

2. Robert M. DeWitt, *The Life, Trial, and Execution of Captain John Brown Known as "Old Brown of Ossawatomie," With a Full Account of the Attempted Insurrection at Harpers Ferry* (New York, 1859; reprint New York: Da Capo, 1969), 92–93.

3. Murat Haltstead, "The Tragedy of John Brown," *The Independent . . . Devoted to the Consideration of Politics, Social and Economic Tendencies, History, Literature, and the Arts* 50 (1 December 1898): 1543–48.

4. "The Harper's Ferry Criminals," *Richmond Daily Dispatch*, 17 March 1860.

5. The transcendent fear of a second Haitian Revolution affirms the work of historians who find the North and South to be quite similar at mid-century: Edward L. Ayers, *In the Presence of Mine Enemies: War in the Heart of America, 1859–1863* (New York: Norton, 2003); Alice Fahs, *The Imagined Civil War: Popular Literature of the North and South, 1861–1865* (Chapel Hill: University of North Carolina Press, 2001); Edward Pessen, "How Different From Each Other Where the Antebellum North and South?" *American Historical Review* 85 (December 1980): 1119–49.

6. Charles Dew, *Apostles of Disunion: Southern Secession Commissioners and the Causes of the Civil War* (Charlottesville: University Press of Virginia, 2001); Jon L. Wakelyn, ed., *Southern Pamphlets on Secession, November 1860–April 1861* (Chapel Hill: University of North Carolina Press, 1996).

7. James M. McPherson in his chapter on the secession winter of 1860–61, "The Counterrevolution of 1861," describes the manufacturing of secessionist support in response to Abraham Lincoln's election as a "pre-emptive counterrevolution" in the defense of slavery and white supremacy, in *Battle Cry of Freedom: The Civil War Era* (Oxford: Oxford University Press, 1988), 245.

8. James Henley Thornwell, *Our Danger and Our Duty* (Columbia, S.C.: Southern Guardian Steam-Power Press, 1862), 5.

9. George Fitzhugh, "Revolutions of '76 and '61 Contrasted," *De Bow's Review* 4, 2 (August 1867): 42, 45.

10. The author adds with a bit of irony, "One might also point out that the true inheritors of the revolutionary fervor of this era were not slaveholders but the slaves of the New World." Manisha Sinha, *The Counter-Revolution of Slavery: Politics and Ideology in Antebellum South Carolina* (Chapel Hill: University of North Carolina Press, 2000), 7.

11. William Freehling, *The Road to Disunion: Secessionists Triumphant*, vol. 2 (Oxford: Oxford University Press, 2007), 205–21, 369–71.

12. Bryan Edwards, *The History, Civil and Commercial, of the British Colonies in the West Indies*, vol. 4, *An Historical Survey of the French Colony in the Island of St. Domingo: Comprehending an Account of the Revolt of the Negroes in the Year 1791, and a Detail of the Military Transactions of the British Army in that Island, in the Years 1793 & 1794* (Philadelphia: James Humphreys, 1806), 68, 74–80.

13. Archibald Alison, *History of Europe, from the Commencement of the French Revolution in 1789, to the Restoration of the Bourbons in 1815*, vol. 2 (New York: Harper, 1850–52), 243. An example of Alison invoking Edwards more explicitly is "The cruelties exercised on the unhappy captives on both sides, in this disastrous contest, exceeded anything recorded in history. The negroes marched with spiked infants on their spears instead of colors; they sawed asunder the male prisoners, and violated the females on the dead bodies of their husbands" (241).

14. John C. Calhoun, *Report and Public Letters of John C. Calhoun*, ed. Richard K. Crallé, vol. 5 (New York: D. Appleton and Company, 1855), 388–89.

15. Clement Eaton, *A History of the Southern Confederacy* (New York: Macmillan, 1954), 3.

16. "The Secession of the South," *De Bow's Review* 28, 4 (April 1860): 378–79; The magazine claimed 4,600 subscribers in 1855. "James Dunwoody Brownson De Bow," *American National Biography* (New York: Oxford University Press, 1999), 313.

17. "The Secession of the South," 380.

18. Freehling, *The Road to Disunion*, 390.

19. John Townsend, *The South Alone, Should Govern the South: And African Slavery Should be Controlled by Those Only, Who Are Friendly to It*, 3rd ed. (Charleston, S.C.: Steam-Power presses of Evans & Cogswell, 1860), 12–13.

20. Albert Taylor Bledsoe, "Liberty and Slavery," in E. N. Elliott, ed., *Cotton Is King, and Pro-Slavery Arguments Comprising the Writings of Hammon, Harper, Christy, Stringfellow, Hodge, Bledsoe, and Cartwright on this Important Subject* (Augusta, Ga., 1860; reprint New York: Negro Universities Press, 1969), 404–5, 412–13.

21. Bledsoe, "Liberty and Slavery," 405, 412–13.

22. John B. Thrasher, *Slavery, A Divine Institution. By. J.B. Thrasher, of Port Gibson. A Speech, Made Before the Breckinridge and Lane Club, November 5th, 1860* (Port Gibson, Miss.: Southern Reveille Book and Job Office, 1861), 5.

23. "A Voice from Georgia," *Charleston Mercury*, 3 November 1860.

24. Benjamin Morgan Palmer, *The South, Her Peril, and her Duty; a Discourse, Delivered in the First Presbyterian Church, New Orleans, on Thursday, November 29, 1860* (New Orleans: True Witness and Sentinel, 1860), 8–9, 11, 13–14.; For Palmer's role in the aftermath of the Vesey conspiracy, see: Douglas R. Egerton, "Forgetting Denmark Vesey; Or, Oliver Stone Meets Richard Wade," Forum: The Making of a Slave Conspiracy, part 2, *William and Mary Quarterly* 3rd ser. 59, 1 (January 2002): 148–49; Egerton, *He Shall Go Out Free: The Lives of Denmark Vesey, Revised and Updated Edition*

(Lanham, Md.: Rowman and Littlefield, 2004), 246–47; Robert L. Paquette, "Jacobins of the Lowcountry: The Vesey Plot on Trial," *William and Mary Quarterly* 3rd ser. 59, 1 (January 2002): 189–90; Paquette, "From Rebellion to Revisionism: The Continuing Debate About the Denmark Vesey Affair," *Journal of the Historical Society* 4, 3 (Fall 2004): 302–3.

25. The figures are provided by Wayne C. Eubank, who adds, "No other southern sermon on slavery and secession received greater acclaim or wider attention," in "Benjamin Morgan Palmer's Thanksgiving Sermon, 1860," in *Antislavery and Disunion, 1858–1861: Studies in the Rhetoric of Compromise and Conflict*, ed. John Jeffery Auer (Gloucester, Mass.: P. Smith, 1968), 308–9.

26. Wakelyn, *Southern Pamphlets on Secession*, 63.

27. Freehling, *The Road to Disunion*, 461.

28. "From the Montgomery Advertiser," *Douglass' Monthly*, December 1860.

29. "Letters to Secretary Chase from the South," *American Historical Review* 4, 2 (January 1899): 335–36.

30. Mary Howard Schoolcraft, *The Black Gauntlet: A Tale of Plantation Life in South Carolina* (Philadelphia: J.P. Lippincott & Co., 1860), 563–64.

31. "Annual Address of President A. P. Calhoun, delivered in the State House, before the State Agricultural Society, on Tuesday Evening, November 13, 1860," *Daily South Carolinian*, 14 November 1860.

32. The proslavery press dismissed the Haitian Revolution as the product of radical abolitionism before. In 1855, for example, *De Bow's Review* offered the following, in response to the popularity of *Uncle Tom's Cabin*: "Any one familiar with the history of Commissioner Santhonase, Abbe' Gregore', and Toussaint l'Ouverture, knows that the insurrection of St. Domingo is not to be attributed to the negroes, but to the instigation of French devils and mad republicans sent among them; and the Oge' drama was got up then, as that of Uncle Tom now, to excite and heighten the prejudice of classes and sections, and to set all France against her colonies, and the north now against her *southern colonies*; but poor Oge', a man of life, fell, finally, the tool and victim of his own friends, while Uncle Tom, a mere creature of imagination, enjoys a sort of apotheosis. The instigators and authors, however, in both instances made money by the calamity." "Practical Effects of Emancipation, Part II," *De Bow's Review* 18, 5 (May 1855): 595.

33. "Slaveholders and Non-Slaveholders of the South," *Charleston Mercury*, 1 November 1860.

34. Bledsoe, "Liberty and Slavery," 409–12.

35. Charles P. Roland, *An American Iliad: The Story of the Civil War*, 2nd ed. (Boston: McGraw-Hill, 2002), 38.

36. The novel imagines a failed slave insurrection ignited by one of John Brown's sons, and describes slaves' yearning to remain on the plantations of their white masters. Edmund Ruffin, *Anticipations of the Future, to Serve as Lessons for the Present Time: in the Form of Extracts of Letters From an English Resident in the United States, to the London Times, From 1864 to 1870* (Richmond: J.W. Randolph, 1860), 395–96.

37. Jefferson Davis, "Remarks on the Special Message on Affairs in South Carolina," in Wakelyn, *Southern Pamphlets on Secession*, 138–39.

38. Richard K. Call, *Union—Slavery—Secession: Letter from Governor R. K. Call, of Florida, to John S. Littell, of Germantown, Pennsylvania* (Philadelphia: Sherman and Son, 1861), 5, 12–13, 27.

39. Stephanie McCurry, *Masters of Small Worlds: Yeoman Households, Gender Relations, and the Political Culture of the Antebellum South Carolina Low Country* (New York: Oxford University Press, 1995), 304.

40. "Slaveholders and Non-Slaveholders of the South."

41. Allen D. Candler, ed., *The Confederate Records of the State of Georgia* (Atlanta: Chas. P. Byrd, State printer, 1909), 133.

42. Dew, *Apostles of Disunion*, 66–67.

43. Dew, *Apostles of Disunion*, 55.

44. Dew, *Apostles of Disunion*, 54–55, 66–67; S. F. Hale to B. Magoffin, December 12, 1860, in *The War of the Rebellion: A Compilation of the Official Records of the Union and Confederate Armies in the War of the Rebellion* (Washington, D.C.: Government Printing Office, 1880–1901), Ser. IV, Vol. I, 8 (hereafter O.R.).

45. "The Border Slave States and Their Slaves," *Daily Delta*, in Dwight Lowell Dumond, ed., *Southern Editorials on Secession* (Gloucester, Mass.: P. Smith, 1964), 432

46. "The Position of the Cotton States," *Daily Courier*, in Dumond, *Southern Editorials on Secession*, 360.

47. "The Commissioner of Alabama in Jefferson City," *St. Louis Democrat*, 1 January 1861.

48. James D. B. De Bow, *The Interest in Slavery of the Southern Non-Slaveholder. The Right of Peaceful Secession. The Character and Influence of Abolitionism* (Charleston, S.C.: Presses of Evans & Cogswell, 1860), 10, 12.

49. Avery Craven, "Coming of the War Between the States, an Interpretation," *Journal of Southern History* 2, 3 (August 1936): 322.

50. "Slaveholders and Non-Slaveholders of the South."

51. Michael P. Johnson, *Toward a Patriarchal Republic: The Secession of Georgia* (Baton Rouge: Louisiana State University Press, 1977), 48.

52. McPherson, *Battle Cry of Freedom*, 245.

53. "The Secession of the South," 368, 381.

54. William Henry Holcombe, "The Alternative: A Separate Nationality, or the Africanization of the South," *Southern Literary Messenger* 32 (February 1861): 81–82, 85, 88.

55. William Watson Davis, *The Civil War and Reconstruction in Florida* (Gainesville: University Presses of Florida, 1964), 48.

56. Palmer, *The South: Her Peril, and her Duty*, 16.

57. "Annual Address of President A. P. Calhoun."

58. John Townsend, *The Doom of Slavery in the Union: Its Safety Out of It*, 2nd ed. (Charleston, S.C.: Evans & Cogswell, 1860), 4; Freehling, *The Road to Disunion*, 394.

59. Townsend, *The South Alone, Should Govern the South*, 12.

60. "The Designs of Redpath, John Brown , Jr., Fred. Douglass, & c.," *Liberator*, 15 March 1861; one writer added the possible involvement of the British. "Negro Movement," *Boston Herald*, 14 May 1861.

61. Still, the possibility that such a plot existed is something that scholars are beginning to take seriously: Albert J. Von Frank, "John Brown, James Redpath, and the Idea of Revolution," *Civil War History* 52 (June 2006): 158–60.

62. "Negro Movement."

63. Alfred N. Hunt, *Haiti's Influence on Antebellum America: Slumbering Volcano in the Caribbean* (Baton Rouge: Louisiana State University Press, 1988), 141.

CHAPTER 4. "LIBERTY ON THE BATTLE-FIELD": HAITI AND THE MOVEMENT TO ARM BLACK SOLDIERS

1. Wendell Phillips, "Toussaint L'Ouverture," in Phillips, *Speeches, Lectures, and Letters* (Boston: Lee & Shepard, 1872), 492.

2. George Lowell Austin, *The Life and Times of Wendell Phillips* (Boston: Lee & Shephard, 1884), 226.

3. James M. McPherson, *Battle Cry of Freedom: The Civil War Era* (New York: Oxford University Press, 1988), 563–64.

4. John David Smith, "Let Us Be Grateful That We Have Colored Troops That Will Fight," in Smith, ed., *Black Soldiers in Blue: African American Troops in the Civil War Era* (Chapel Hill: University of North Carolina Press, 2004), 3, 9.

5. William E. Alt and Betty L. Alt, *Black Soldiers, White Wars: Black Warriors from Antiquity to the Present* (Westport, Conn.: Praeger, 2002), 33.

6. Elizur Wright, *The Lesson of St. Domingo: How to Make the War Short and the Peace Righteous* (Boston: Williams and Co., 1861), 3–4, 18. The text was reprinted in the following: *New York Tribune*, 27 May 1861; *Douglass' Monthly*, August 1861; and *Liberator*, 19 July 1863.

7. "The Lesson of St. Domingo," *Douglass' Monthly*, August 1861.

8. John Weiss, "The Horrors of San Domingo," *Atlantic Monthly* 9, 56 (June 1862): 732–54; 10, 58 (August 1862): 212–28; 10, 59 (September 1862): 347–59; 11, 65 (March 1863): 289–306; 11, 68 (June 1863): 768–86.

9. James Redpath, *Toussaint L'Ouverture: Biography and Autobiography* (Boston: James Redpath, 1863), vi.

10. "A Book to be Read and Circulated," *Liberator*, 23 October 1863.

11. "Literary Review," *Boston Commonwealth*, 30 November 1863.

12. "Will the Blacks Fight?" *New York Evening Post*, 10 July 1862. Though it is impossible to determine the number of people who read Weiss's letter, its reprinting in newspapers across the North suggests its reach; another indication of the letter's impact is that copies are found today in the manuscript collections of Wendell Phillips and Abraham Lincoln. Wendell Phillips Papers, Harvard University; Abraham Lincoln Papers, Library

of Congress. Weiss continued his argument in the *Atlantic Monthly* piece, writing, "Will the Negro fight as well, if the motive and the exigency are inferior? We make a present to the Southern negro of an excellent chance for fighting, with our compliments. Some of us do it with our curses." Weiss warned those in the South who thought that bondmen were unwilling to both fight and kill for freedom. Such an assumption was, he insisted, "a great mistake." "The Horrors of San Domingo," 11, 68 (June 1863): 785.

13. "Negroes for Soldiers," *Burlington (Vermont) Times*, in *Liberator*, 24 January 1862.

14. Redpath, *Toussaint L'Ouverture*, 151.

15. "The Freed Blacks of South Carolina," *National Anti-Slavery Standard*, 2 August 1862; the best source on the Port Royal Relief Committee remains Willie Lee Rose, *Rehearsal for Reconstruction: The Port Royal Experiment* (London: Oxford University Press, 1964).

16. Jonathan C. Gibbs, "Freedom's Joyful Day," in Philip Foner, ed., *The Voice of Black America: Major Speeches by Negroes in the United States, 1797–1973* (New York: Capricorn, 1975): 263–65.

17. William Wells Brown, *The Black Man, His Antecedents, His Genius, and His Achievements*, Second Edition (New York: Thomas Hamilton, 1863), 6, 96, 101, 104–5, 110–17.

18. "The Black Man in the Army," *Salem Observer*, in *Liberator*, 8 August 1862.

19. "Capacity of Blacks," *Providence Journal*, in *National Anti-Slavery Standard*, 20 September 1862.

20. "Negro-Regiments," *Weekly Anglo-African*, 23 May 1863.

21. Brown, *Black Man*, 99.

22. Phillips, *Toussaint L'Ouverture*, 478–79.

23. Brown, *Black Man*, 97.

24. Redpath, *Toussaint L'Ouverture*, 48.

25. "Negroes for Soldiers."

26. Weiss, "Horrors of San Domingo," 780.

27. "Will the Blacks Fight."

28. "Review of the Week," *Boston Commonwealth*, 20 March 1863.

29. "Wendell Phillips' Greatest Speech," *Weekly Anglo-African*, 4 May 1861.

30. "Wendell Phillips," *New York Daily Tribune*, 11 March 1863.

31. "Special Notice," *New York Daily Tribune*, 11 March 1863.

32. "Wendell Phillips's Oration on Toussaint L'Ouverture," *New York Daily Tribune*, 12 and 13 March 1863.

33. "Mr. Editor," *Christian Recorder*, 28 March 1863.

34. C. Peter Ripley estimates that without the support of African Americans, the "*Liberator* would not have survived its crucial early years." A grateful Garrison acknowledged this when writing, the *Liberator* 'belongs especially to the people of color—it is their organ'." C. Peter Ripley, ed., *Witness for Freedom: African American Voices on Race, Slavery, and Emancipation* (Chapel Hill: University of North Carolina Press, 1993), 4–5;

See also Henry Mayer, *All on Fire: William Lloyd Garrison and the Abolition of Slavery* (1998), 116; Peter P. Hinks, *To Awaken My Inflicted Brethren: David Walker and the Problem of Antebellum Slave Resistance* (University Park: Pennsylvania State University Press, 1997), 112–13; Jane J. Pease and William H. Pease, *They Who Would Be Free: Blacks' Search for Freedom, 1830–1861* (New York: Atheneum, 1974), 113; James Oliver Horton and Lois E. Horton, *Black Bostonians: Family Life and Community Struggle in the Antebellum North*, rev. ed. (New York: Holmes & Meier, 1999), 85.

35. Robert Spiller, *Literary History of the United States*, 3rd ed. rev., vol. 1 (London: Macmillan, 1969), 558; Paul Lauter, ed., *Heath Anthology of American Literature*, 4th ed. (Boston: Houghton Mifflin, 2002), 1997.

36. James M. McPherson, *The Struggle for Equality: Abolitionists and the Negro in the Civil War and Reconstruction* (Princeton, N.J.: Princeton University Press, 1964), 142.

37. There are no extant copies of the printed address; however, the paper reads, "We will publish, week after next, the masterpiece of Wendell Phillips—his oration on Toussaint L'Ouverture and the Revolution of Hayti which swept the whites from the Island." "Wendell Phillips' Greatest Speech," *Weekly Anglo-African*, 4 May 1861.

38. "Toussaint L'Ouverture: An Oration, by Wendell Phillips," *Pine and Palm*, 18 May 1861.

39. *Pine and Palm*, 3 November 1861.

40. "Wendell Phillips, on Toussaint L'Ouverture," *Boston Commonwealth*, 3 April 1863; *National Anti-Slavery Standard*, 11 May 1863; "Toussaint L'Ouverture: An Address by Wendell Phillips, Esq. Delivered at New York March 11, 1863," *Liberator*, 3 March 1863.

41. "Wendell Phillips's Oration on Toussaint L'Ouverture," *New York Daily Tribune*, 13 March 1863. For circulation information of the *Tribune*, see "The New York Tribune," *Frank Leslie's Illustrated Monthly*, 20 June 1861.

42. "Wendell Phillips's Speech on Toussaint L'Ouverture," *Liberator*, 3 April 1863; "Toussaint L'Ouverture," *Liberator*, 24 March 1863.

43. "Wendell Phillips's Oration on Toussaint L'Ouverture," *New York Daily Tribune*, 14 March 1863; *New York Weekly Tribune*, 19 March 1863.

44. "Toussaint L'Ouverture an Address by Wendell Phillips," *Boston Commonwealth*, 20 March 1863; "Wendell Phillips, on Toussaint L'Ouverture," *Boston Commonwealth*, 3 April 1863.

45. "Great Oration of Wendell Phillips on Toussaint L'Ouverture, Price 10 cents," *Weekly Anglo-African*, 30 October 1863.

46. There is another source to consider for the popularity of Phillips's "Toussaint L'Ouverture." Early in 1863, James Redpath placed advertisements in multiple Northern newspapers for *Speeches, Lectures, and Letters*, a book-length edition of Phillips's lectures that was "in preparation," and included "Toussaint L'Ouverture" among twenty-four popular orations. Three months later Redpath published the book. The first edition sold out in three days. The *National Anti-Slavery Standard* reported that consumers purchased the volume "as rapidly as it could be bound—while the second was covered by orders

received before it was out of press." A third edition quickly followed. Literary plaudits came in from across the Northeast and as far West as Kansas. One New England paper considered its success evidence of "a marvelous revolution in political sentiment, and it is one that will not go backward." Newspapers reported the sale of nearly one thousand copies a week between September and October. The book was reprinted in multiple editions, including a "people's edition," which appeared on "common paper, in boards, and without portrait," and a more expensive and "sumptuous style of book-making" known as a "Library Edition." The *Christian Recorder* referred to the latter as "one of the finest specimens of book manufacture ever produced in the United States." The editors of the *Boston Commonwealth* sought agents to sell the anthology "in every county of the Loyal States" with "Liberal Commissions allowed." The paper reported the sale of seven thousand copies by September, and two thousand more the following month. "Speeches and Lectures by Wendell Phillips," *Liberator*, 31 July 1863; "Speeches of Wendell Phillips," *Liberator*, 1 September 1863; See "Just Published: Toussaint L'Ouverture: A Biography and Autobiography," *Boston Commonwealth*, 11 September–9 October 1863, and "James Redpath, Boston," *American Publisher's Circular and Literary Gazette*, 13 September 1863; "Nearly Ready. Speeches, Lectures, and Letters," *Boston Commonwealth*, 28 August 1863; "Books for Our Times," *Christian Recorder*, 2 January 1864; "Just Published. Speeches, Lectures, and Letters," *Boston Commonwealth*, 17 July 1863; "Speeches, Lectures, and Letters, by Wendell Phillips: Seventh Thousand," *Boston Commonwealth*, 18 September, 9 October 1863; "New Publications," *National Anti-Slavery Standard*, 1 August 1863.

47. Michael F. Conlin, "The Smithsonian Abolition Lecture Controversy: The Clash of Antislavery Politics with American Science in Wartime Washington," *Civil War History* 46, 4 (2000): 314.

48. "Wendell Phillips in Washington," *Liberator*, 21 March 1862.

49. "Wendell Phillips," *New York Tribune*, 19 March 1862; "Wendell Phillips in Washington," *National Anti-Slavery Standard*, 22 March 1862; James Brewer Stewart, *Wendell Phillips: Liberty's Hero* (Baton Rouge: Louisiana State University Press, 1986), 236.

50. John Hay, "Inklings of Idleness," *Washington Sunday Morning Chronicle*, 23 March 1862, in Hay, *An Idler: John Hay's Social and Aesthetic Commentaries for the Press During the Civil War, 1861–1865*, ed. Douglas Warren Hill (Bethesda, Md.: Academica Press, 2006), 3–4, 44.

51. Stewart, *Wendell Phillips*, 184, 1991; Irving H. Bartlett, *Wendell Phillips, Brahmin Radical* (Boston: Beacon, 1961; reprint, Westport, Conn.: Greenwood Press, 1973), 86, 246, 248.

52. "Wendell Phillips's Lecture on 'Toussaint L'Ouverture,'" *Roxbury Journal*, in *Liberator*, 27 March 1863.

53. Lorenzo Sears, *Wendell Phillips: Orator and Agitator* (New York: Doubleday, Page & Co., 1909), 244.

54. George Edward Woodberry, *Wendell Phillips: The Faith of an American* (Boston: D.B. Updike, 1912), 35.

55. Benjamin N. Martin, *Classics of American Literature: Choice Specimens of American Literature, and Literary Reader, Being Selections from the Chief American Writers* (New York: Sheldon & Company, 1871), 208; Bartlett, *Wendell Phillips, Brahmin Radical*, 247. Bartlett cites estimates that between 1861 and 1862 more than 50,000 people heard Phillips lecture on various topics, while as many as five million read his speeches.

56. Carlos Martyn, *Wendell Phillips: The Agitator* (New York: Funk & Wagnalls, 1890), 446.

57. Bartlett, *Wendell Phillips, Brahmin Radical*, 247.

58. "Wendell Phillips," *Boston Commonwealth*, 4 September 1863.

59. The best review of Phillips's lifelong commitment to social change remains Stewart, *Wendell Phillips*.

60. Chauncey Mitchell Depew, *Orations, Addresses and Speeches of Chauncey M. Depew*, vol. 3 (New York: privately printed, 1910), 14.

61. Richard Wheatley, "Wendell Phillips," *Methodist Review* 74, 5th ser. 8 (July 1892): 552.

62. "Lecture on Toussaint L'Ouverture," *Weekly Anglo-African*, 21 February 1863.

63. "Mr. Editor," *Weekly Anglo-African*, 4 April 1863.

64. "Letter from Denver City, Col.," *Christian Recorder*, 10 December 1864.

65. "A Colored Female Lecturer," *Liberator*, 8 April 1864.

66. "Baltimore, MD," *Weekly Anglo-African*, 14 January 1863.

67. "A Colored Female Lecturer."

68. "Miss DeBois's Lecture," *Bethlehem (Pennsylvania) Moravian*, in *Liberator* 8 April 1864.

69. "Alexandria Correspondent," *Christian Recorder*, 25 April 1863.

70. "Literary Taste of the Colored People," *Weekly Anglo-African*, 12 April 1862.

71. "Speech of Benjamin Butler," *Douglass' Monthly*, June 1863; *Character and Results of the War. How to Prosecute and How to End It: A Thrilling and Eloquent Speech by Major-General B. F. Butler* (Philadelphia: s.n., 1863), 18.

72. *Proceeding at the Mass Meeting of Loyal Citizens, on Union Square, New York. 15th day of July, 1862* (New York: Nesbitt, 1862), 111–13.

73. "Wendell Phillips and His Gods," *New York Herald*, 3 February 1860.

74. *Mass Convention of the Democracy and Conservative Citizens of Indiana, Held at Indianapolis, July 30th, 1862* (Indianapolis: Sentinel office, 1862), 13.

75. Allen C. Guelzo, *Lincoln's Emancipation Proclamation: The End of Slavery in America* (New York: Simon and Schuster, 2006).

76. "Emancipation Proclamation," in Leslie E. Fishel, Jr., and Benjamin Quarles, eds., *The Negro American: A Documentary History* (Glenview, Ill.: Scott, Foresman, 1967), 226.

77. McPherson, *Battle Cry of Freedom*, 565.

78. The official number of United States Colored Troops is 186,097, including 178,975 enlisted men and 7,122 officers. Some 94,000 came from the seceded states and 44,000 from border states that allowed slavery. The U.S. Navy employed an additional

29,511 African Americans. *O.R.* ser. 3, vol. 5, 132, 138, 662. Benjamin Quarles, *The Negro in the Civil War* (New York: Da Capo, 1989), xiv, 230.

CHAPTER 5. "EMANCIPATION OR INSURRECTION": HAITI AND THE END OF SLAVERY IN AMERICA

1. William Whiting, *The War Powers of the President, and the Legislative Powers of Congress in Relation to Rebellion, Treason and Slavery* (Boston: John L. Shorey, 1862).

2. "The Washington *Republican*," *Liberator*, 24 April 1863.

3. Lincoln biographer Mark Neely speculates that Whiting's book helped convince the president he had the constitutional power to end slavery, though Lincoln's familiarity with John Quincy Adams's argument that the war powers of the commander in chief included the authority to emancipate slaves is well known. Mark Neely, Jr., *The Fate of Liberty: Abraham Lincoln and Civil Liberties* (New York: Oxford University Press, 1991), 220 ; Allen C. Guelzo, *Lincoln's Emancipation Proclamation: The End of Slavery in America* (New York: Simon and Schuster, 2005), 118, 120; David Brion Davis, *Inhuman Bondage: The Rise and Fall of Slavery in the New World* (New York: Oxford University Press, 2006), 313; David Herbert Donald, *Lincoln Reconsidered: Essays on the Civil War Era* (New York: Random House, 1961), 204–5; *Charles Sumner and the Coming of the Civil War* (New York: Knopf, 1960), 388.

4. Francis B. Carpenter, *Six Months at the White House with Abraham Lincoln: The Story of a Picture* (New York: Hurd and Houghton, 1866), 353.

5. Seymour Drescher, *Capitalism and Slavery* (New York: Oxford University Press, 1987), 98; *The Mighty Experiment: Free Labor Versus Slavery in British Emancipation* (Oxford: Oxford University Press, 2002), 100–105. Though he underscores the limits of the influence of the Haitian Revolution, Drescher leaves room for further investigation: "how much of a turning point for Atlantic slavery was the revolution, beyond the boundaries of Hispaniola? Much of the answer to this question depends upon the geographical and temporal scope of one's analysis." "The Limits of Example," in David P. Geggus, *The Impact of the Haitian Revolution in the Atlantic World* (Columbia: University of South Carolina Press, 2001), 10.

6. Geggus, "Epilogue," in *Impact of the Haitian Revolution*, 247; Davis, *Inhuman Bondage*, 173–74.

7. Franklin B. Sanborn, ed., *The Life and Letters of John Brown, Liberator of Kansas, and Martyr of Virginia* (Boston: Roberts Brothers, 1891), v.

8. Jeffrey Rossbach, *Ambivalent Conspirators: John Brown, the Secret Six, and a Theory of Slave Violence* (Philadelphia: University of Pennsylvania Press, 1982), 220–23, 228–32, 237–42.

9. "Emancipation. A Sermon Preached at Music Hall, Boston. Supplement to the Weekly Anglo-African," *Weekly Anglo-African*, 20 April 1861.

10. For an overview of the nation's capital as a battleground for the fight over slavery,

see Stanley Harrold, *Subversives: Antislavery Community in Washington, D.C., 1828–1865* (Baton Rouge: Louisiana State University Press, 2003).

11. Conway distributed the book liberally to subscribers of the *Boston Commonwealth* and among the soldiers of the Union Army. Years later he remembered, "The response to my book was astonishing." The book went through three editions within a year of publication. Charles Sumner reportedly sent a copy to Lincoln "who told him soon after that he was reading it with interest." Conway also published *The Golden Hour* in 1862, which was based on a series of lectures he gave in Washington, D.C., after which he had a private meeting with Lincoln regarding emancipation. Conway reported in his autobiography that Lincoln ended the conversation gravely with the following, "When the hour comes for dealing with slavery I trust I will be willing to do my duty though it cost my life. And, gentlemen, lives will be lost." *Golden Hour* was less successful commercially than *Rejected Stone*, though the two works bore obvious similarities. Moncure Daniel Conway, *The Rejected Stone: or Insurrection vs. Resurrection in America. By a Native of Virginia* (Boston: Walker, Wise, 1861), 43, 97, 124, 127; Conway, *The Golden Hour* (Boston: Ticknor and Fields, 1862), 346, 366; Conway, *Autobiography, Memories and Experiences of Moncure Daniel Conway*, vol. 1 (Boston: Houghton, Mifflin, 1904), 341, 346, 366.

12. George Boutwell, "Emancipation: Its Justice, Expediency and Necessity, as the Means of Securing a Speedy and Permanent Peace," *Liberator*, 20 December 1861.

13. Sara G. Stanley, "TOUSSAINT L'OVERTURE," *Weekly Anglo-African*, 27 July 1861.

14. "Horrors of St. Domingo," *Weekly Anglo-African*, 16 November 1861.

15. James Brewer Stewart, *William Lloyd Garrison and the Challenge of Emancipation*; *Holy Warriors: the Abolitionists and American Slavery* (New York: Hill and Wang, 1976), 44, 54, 169–74; John L. Thomas, *The Liberator: William Lloyd Garrison, a Biography* (Boston: Little, Brown, 1963), 381–82, 397–98, 402–5. David Reynolds accentuates Garrison's pacifism vis-à-vis John Brown, *John Brown Abolitionist: The Man Who Killed Slavery, Sparked the Civil War, and Seeded Civil Rights* (New York: Knopf, 2005), 53–54, 63–65, 96–97.

16. "Walker's Appeal. No. 1," *Liberator*, 8 January 1831.

17. "The Virginia Insurrection," *Liberator*, 20 October 1859.

18. "Our National Invitation. An Oration, by William Lloyd Garrison," *National Anti-Slavery Standard*, 13 September 1862.

19. Charles Sumner, *Emancipation! Its Policy and Necessity as a War Measure for the Suppression of the Rebellion* (Boston: s.n., 1862), 15–17; Edward Pierce, *Memoir and Letters of Charles Sumner*, vol. 4 (Boston: Roberts Brothers, 1893), 437.

20. "Horrors of St. Domingo," *Pine and Palm*, 19 June 1862.

21. Lydia Maria Child, *The Right Way the Safe Way, Proved by Emancipation in the British West Indies, and Elsewhere* (New York: 5 Beekman Street, 1862), 86–87.

22. "Historical Scarecrows," *New York Daily Tribune*, 13 January 1863.

23. "A Common Error," *Harper's Weekly*, 19 April 1862

24. "Editor's Easy Chair, *Harper's New Monthly Magazine* 24, 144 (May 1862):

846–47. The historians first mentioned are Robert Charles Dallas and John Ramsey McCulloch. The books referenced are respectively *The History of the Maroons, From Their Origin to the Establishment of Their Chief Tribe at Sierra Leone: Including the Expedition to Cuba for the Purpose of Procuring Spanish Chasseurs and the State of the Island of Jamaica for the Last Ten Years, With a Succinct History of the Island Previous to That Period*, 2 vols. (London: Strahan, 1803), and *A Catalogue of Books, the Property of a Political Economist* (London: s.n., 1862), 148. The Parisian-born abolitionist Victor Schoelcher traveled to Haiti and wrote multiple accounts of the Haitian Revolution. Alexis Beaubrun Ardouin was a Haitian politician and author best known for the mammoth tome *Études sur l'Histoire d'Haïti* (Paris: Dezobry et Magdeleine, 1853–60).

25. The two periodicals enjoyed wide circulation. "Circulation over 100,000," *Harper's Weekly*, 30 December 1865. Alice Fahs writes, "Harper's New Monthly Magazine . . . claimed an average circulation of 110,000 on the eve of the Civil War." *The Imagined Civil War: Popular Literature of the North & South, 1861–1865* (Chapel Hill: University of North Carolina Press, 2001), 42.

26. "Literary," *Harper's Weekly*, 19 December 1863.

27. "Emancipation. A Sermon Preached at Music Hall."

28. "Emancipation. No. 1. Hayti," *Boston Commonwealth*, 25 October 1862.

29. "Emancipation and its Fruits in Hayti," *National Anti-Slavery Standard*, 7 December 1861.

30. Abby Buchanan Longstreet, *Remy St. Remy, or The Boy in Blue* (New York: O'Kane, 1865), 76–77.

31. "The Holidays in Camp," *New York Herald*, 19 January 1864; "An Event in the History Of South Carolina," *Weekly Anglo-African*, 16 January 1854.

32. "Grand Anniversary," *Weekly Anglo-African*, 2 May 1863.

33. Samuel L. Horst, *Education for Manhood: The Education of Blacks in Virginia During the Civil War* (Lanham, Md.: University Press of America, 1987), 181.

34. "Market-Woman of San Domingo," *Weekly Anglo-African*, 2 January 1864.

35. Charlotte Forten, *The Journal of Charlotte Forten, With an Introduction and Notes by Ray Allen Billington* (New York: Dryden, 1953), 97, 150; Julie Winch, *A Gentleman of Color: The Life of James Forten* (Oxford: Oxford University Press, 2003), 347

36. Stanley, "TOUSSAINT L'OVERTURE."

37. Judith Weisenfeld, " 'Who is Sufficient for These Things': Sara G. Stanley and the American Missionary Association, 1864–1868," *Church History* 60, 4 (December 1991): 493–507.

38. Lydia Maria Child, *The Freedmen's Book* (Boston: Ticknor and Fields, 1865; reprint New York: Arno Press, 1968), 83, 269; Robert Charles Morris, ed., [*Freedman's Reader*] *Freedmen's Schools and Textbooks, an AM Reprint Series* (Boston: American Tract Society, 1865–66; reprint New York: AMS Press, 1980), 81, 83. Abolitionists distributed both among freedmen as part of their effort to increase literacy. The *Liberator* wished that "those who can read will read it aloud to" those who were unable to. "The Freedmen's Book," *Liberator*, 8 December 1863.

39. Child, *Freedmen's Book*, 46–48, 59–63.

40. *Freedmen's Third Reader*, 80–84.

41. Child, *Freedmen's Book*, 59–61; *Freedmen's Third Reader*, 81–86.

42. "The Coming Negro Nationality," *Liberator*, 12 June 1863.

43. "Address of Major General Nathaniel P. Banks," *Liberator*, 11 November 1864.

44. Eric Foner, *Reconstruction: America's Unfinished Revolution, 1863–1877* (New York: Harper & Row, 1988), 55–57.

45. "Miscellany," *Historical Magazine, and Notes and Queries Concerning the Antiquities* (April 1865): 136.

46. "An Authentic Portrait of Toussaint" *Weekly Anglo-African*, 29 October 1864.

47. Bigelow traveled to Haiti in December 1853 and left several accounts of his meeting with Emperor Soulouque. He also made a pilgrimage to Louverture's gravesite in France, and during the Civil War published an account of his experiences in a lengthy article that appeared in numerous abolitionist papers. *Liberator*, 7 September 1860; *Weekly Anglo-African*, 8 March 1862. See also Bigelow, *Jamaica in 1850. or, The Effects of Sixteen Years of Freedom on a Slave Colony* (New York: Putnam, 1851; reprint Westport, Conn.: Negro Universities Press, 1970), Appendix A; *Retrospections of an Active Life*, vol. 1 (New York: Baker & Taylor, 1909), 146–52. An article published more than a decade after the war indicates Bigelow's extraordinary respect for Haitian culture on its own terms. "The Wit and Wisdom of the Haytiens," *Harper's New Monthly Magazine* 51, 301–4 (June–September 1875): 130–36, 288–91, 438–41, 583–87.

48. "The Ladies Michigan State Fair," *Weekly Anglo-African*, 8 April 1865.

49. Fahs, *The Imagined Civil War*, 13, 164.

CHAPTER 6. "MANY A TOUISSANT L'OVERTURE AMONGST US": BLACK IDENTITY

1. Frederick Douglass, *My Bondage and My Freedom* (1855; New York: Dover, 1969), 241–46.

2. Stanley Harrold and John R. McKivigan's collection of essays highlights the militancy of abolitionists on the eve of the Civil War, in *Antislavery Violence: Sectional, Racial, and Cultural Conflict in Antebellum America* (Knoxville: University of Tennessee Press, 1999). For masculinity in the nineteenth century, see Bruce Dorsey, *Reforming Men and Women: Gender in the Antebellum City* (Ithaca, N.Y.: Cornell University Press, 2002); Amy S. Greenberg, *Manifest Manhood and the Antebellum American Empire* (Cambridge: Cambridge University Press, 2005); David Leverenz, *Manhood and the American Renaissance* (Ithaca, N.Y.: Cornell University Press, 274); E. Anthony Rotundo, *American Manhood: Transformations in Masculinity from the Revolution to the Modern Era* (New York: Basic Books, 1993). The best overview of black masculinity in early America is Darlene Clark Hine and Earnestine Jenkins, eds., *A Question of Manhood: A Reader in U.S. Black Men's History and Masculinity*, vol. 1 (Bloomington: Indiana University Press, 1999).

3. Following the Civil War, Douglass served as the first American Minister to Haiti. For one of Douglass's lengthiest treatments of Louverture, see "Toussaint L'Ouverture," *Frederick Douglass Papers*, Library of Congress, Container 31, Microfilm reel 19. David Turley describes British reactions to Douglass on a visit to England in 1846 and the subsequent comparisons to Louverture: "British Unitarians, Frederick Douglass and Race," in *Liberating Sojourn: Frederick Douglass and Transatlantic Reform*, ed. Martin Crawford and Alan Rice (Athens: University of Georgia Press, 1999), 12.

4. Frederick Douglass, "The Trials and Triumphs of Self-Made Men: An Address Delivered in Halifax, England, on 4 January 1860," in *The Frederick Douglass Papers, Series One, Speeches, Debates, and Interveiws*, ed. John Blassingame and John R. McKivigan, vol. 4 (New Haven, Conn.: Yale University Press, 1991), 291.

5. "A Trip to Hayti," *Douglass' Monthly*, May 1861.

6. "Men of Color, to Arms!" *Douglass' Monthly*, March 1863.

7. Douglass, like other abolitionists in the antebellum era, likely refrained from invoking the black republic before certain audiences to avoid conjuring images of race war and the failed experiment of black national independence contemporary Haiti provided. Yet he never shied from the opportunity in his own publications. For an example, see "Toussaint L'Overture," *Frederick Douglass' Paper*, 4 September 1851; Bruce Dain, "Haiti and Egypt in Early Black Racial Discourse in the United States," *Slavery and Abolition* 14, 3 (December 1993): 139–61; Mitch Kachun, *Festivals of Freedom: Memory and Meaning in African American Emancipation Celebrations, 1808–1915* (Amherst: University of Massachusetts Press, 2003), 57, 272n; Kachun, "Antebellum African Americans, Public Commemoration, and the Haitian Revolution: A Problem of Historical Mythmaking," *Journal of the Early Republic* 26, 2 (2006): 249–73.

8. Charles Wyllys Elliott, *Heroes Are Historic Men: St. Domingo, Its Revolution and Its Hero, Toussaint Louverture. An Historical Discourse Condensed for the New York Library Association, February 26, 1855* (New York: J.A. Dix, 1855), 14.

9. John Relly Beard, *The Life of Toussaint L'Ouverture, the Negro Patriot of Hayti: Comprising an Account of the Struggle for Liberty in the Island, and a Sketch of its History to the Present Period* (London: Ingram, Cooke, 1853), 107; James Redpath, *Toussaint L'Ouverture: Biography and Autobiography* (Boston: James Redpath, 1863), 99.

10. The Union army veteran and black historian George Washington Williams wrote, "black troops charged, singing, 'La Marseillaise,'" in *History of the Negro Troops in the War of the Rebellion, 1861–1865* (New York: Harper, 1888), 50; C. Peter Ripley, ed., *Black Abolitionist Papers*, vol. 5 (Chapel Hill: University of North Carolina Press, 1992), 51; "Flag Presentation in Baltimore," *Weekly Anglo-African*, 29 August 1863.

11. In "Toussaint Louverture" Lamartine repeats a black version of the Marseillaise slaves sang in revolutionary Haiti; Alphonse de Lamartine, *Oeuvres poétiques complètes de Lamartine* (1832; reprint, Paris: Gallimard, 1963), 1264–65, 1401.

12. "Aux armes!," *L'Union*, 2 June 1863.

13. W. E. B. Du Bois, *The Souls of Black Folk: Essays and Sketches* (Chicago: McClurg, 1903); John W. Blassingame, *The Slave Community: Plantation Life in the Antebellum South*,

rev., enl. ed. (New York: Oxford University Press, 1979); Charles Joyner, *Down by the River-side: A South Carolina Slave Community* (Urbana: University of Illinois Press, 1984).

14. Sterling Stuckey, *Slave Culture: Nationalist Theory and the Foundations of Black America* (New York: Oxford University Press, 1987), ix.

15. Patrick Rael, *Black Identity and Black Protest in the Antebellum North* (Chapel Hill: University of North Carolina Press, 2002), 8–11; "Free Black Activism in the Antebellum North," *History Teacher* 30, 2 (2006): 215–25.

16. Paul Gilroy, *The Black Atlantic: Modernity and Double Consciousness* (Cambridge, Mass.: Harvard University Press, 1993); Deborah Gray White, "Yes, There Is a Black Atlantic," *Itinerario* 23, 2 (1999): 127–40.

17. "The Colored Regiments of Massachusetts," *Weekly Anglo-African*, 19 December 1863.

18. "Letter from Washington," *Weekly Anglo-African*, 1 August 1863.

19. "Editor's Book Table, Toussaint L'Ouverture," *New York Independent*, 4 February 1864.

20. Martin J. Blatt, Thomas J. Brown, and Donald Yacove, eds., *Hope and Glory: Essays on the Legacy of the Fifty-Fourth Massachusetts Regiment* (Amherst: University of Massachusetts Press, 2001).

21. Edwin S. Redkey, "Brave Black Volunteers: A Profile of the Fifty-Fourth Massachusetts Regiment," in Blatt et al., *Hope and Glory*, 21–34.

22. "Morris Island," *Liberator*, 6 November 1863.

23. The *New Bedford Mercury* used "Toussaint Guards" when referencing the regiment throughout the spring of 1863. For example, see 23, 27 March, 20 April 1863. For examples in other papers see: "Letter to the Editor," *Christian Recorder*, 4 April 1863; "Reception of the Toussaint Guards," *Liberator*, 15 September 1865.

24. "The Morgan Guards," *New Bedford Mercury*, 4 March 1863.

25. "The 54th Regiment," *New Bedford Mercury*, 23 March 1863.

26. Ripley, *Black Abolitionist Papers*, vol. 5, 245.

27. Joseph T. Glatthaar, *Forged in Battle: The Civil War Alliance of Black Soldiers and White Officers* (New York: Free Press, 1990), 178.

28. Ripley, *Black Abolitionist Papers*, vol. 5, 243–45; *Frederick Douglass Papers*, vol. 4, 232.

29. Letter to the Editor, *Pine and Palm*, 20 June 1861.

30. "Volunteers for Hayti," *Pine and Palm*, 29 June 1861.

31. "Speaking of the San Domingo Spanish Imbroglio," *Weekly Anglo-African*, 4 May 1861. Douglas's story is remarkable. A light-skinned former slave from Virginia, he served in the early years of the war in the all-white 95th Illinois Regiment. In 1863 he relocated to Chicago where he recruited black soldiers. A year later, he enlisted as a captain of the black Kansas First Heavy Artillery. Soon after joining this black regiment, Douglas died due to illness. "Mournful News," *Weekly Anglo-African*, 16 November 1865; Robert L. Harris, Jr., "H. Ford Douglas: Afro-American Antislavery Emigrationist," *Journal of Negro History* 62, 3 (July 1977): 217–34.

32. Virginia Matzke Adams, *On the Altar of Freedom: A Black Soldier's Civil War Letters from the Front, Corporal James Henry Gooding* (Amherst: University of Massachusetts Press, 1991), xxx; Harry A. Ploski and James Williams, eds., *The Negro Almanac* (Detroit: Gale Research, 1989), 834.

33. "The Flag Presentation at Chelton Hills," *Weekly Anglo-African*, 12 September 1863.

34. George Washington Williams, *History of the Negro Race in America from 1619 to 1880*, vol. 1 (New York: Putnam's Sons, 1883), viii.

35. Williams, *Negro Troops in the War of the Rebellion*, 40, 45–46, 54; John Hope Franklin, "George Washington Williams, Historian," *Journal of Negro History* 31, 1 (January 1946): 60–90.

36. William Adams, *Historical Gazetteer and Biographical Memoir of Cattaraugus County* (Syracuse, N.Y.: Lyman, Horton, 1893), 989–90.

37. For colonists returned from Haiti and recruited for enlistment by Harriet Jacobs and her daughter, see, "Letter from Teachers of the Freedmen," *National Anti-Slavery Standard*, 16 April 1864. For reports of Africans fighting in the Union army, see "Native Africans Enlisting," *Douglass' Monthly*, April 1863; Joseph Glatthaar, *Forged in Battle: The Civil War Alliance of Black Soldiers and White Officers* (New York: Free Press, 1990), 41.

38. "The Colored Troops," *Newark North American*, 12 June 1863.

39. "The Siege of Vicksburgh," *New York Times*, 9 July 1863.

40. "Anniversary of the Association for the Relief of Contrabands in the District of Columbia," *Christian Recorder*, 22 August 1863.

41. Benjamin Quarles, *The Negro in the Civil War* (New York: Da Capo, 1981), 33; "The Schooner S. J. Waring," *Harper's Weekly*, 3 August 1861.

42. "A Black Hero," *Douglass' Monthly*, August 1861.

43. "Hon. Owen Lovejoy," *Weekly Anglo-African*, 25 January 1862.

44. "A Rival of Toussaint L'Ouverture," *New York Times*, 24 March 1862; "A New Toussaint L'Ouverture," *Chicago Tribune*, 27 March 1862.

45. "Visit to the Twenty-Ninth Regiment Connecticut Volunteers," *Weekly Anglo-African*, 13 February 1864.

46. Thomas Wentworth Higginson, *Army Life in A Black Regiment and Other Writings* (New York: Penguin, 1997), 44.

47. "A Sunday at Port Royal," *National Anti-Slavery Standard*, 26 July 1862.

48. John David Smith, *Black Soldiers in Blue: African American Troops in the Civil War Era* (Chapel Hill: University of North Carolina Press, 2002), 25.

49. Quarles, *The Negro in the Civil War*, 198–99.

50. "The Slaves of Maryland," *Chicago Tribune*, 18 September 1863.

51. "Conversation with Gen. Thomas," *New York Times*, 20 July 1863.

52. "Capacity of Blacks," *National Anti-Slavery Standard*, 20 September 1862.

53. "Toussaint L'Ouverture," *Boston Commonwealth*, 9 June 1866.

54. Benjamin Butler to General Richard Taylor, 10 September 1862. *O.R.*, ser. I, vol. 15, 566.

55. "Haytian Ideas Adopted in America," *Pine and Palm*, 5 June 1862.

56. Leon Litwack, *Been in the Storm so Long: The Aftermath of Slavery* (New York: Vintage, 1980), 86.

57. Frank A. Rollin, *Life and Public Services of Martin Delany: Sub-Assistant Commissioner Bureau of Refugees, Freedmen, and of Abandoned Lands, and Late Major 104th United States Colored Troops* (Boston: Lee & Shepard, 1883; reprint New York: Arno Press, 1969), 143.

58. "Haytian Ideas Adopted in America," *Pine and Palm*, 5 June 1862; "A Sermon Preached at Music Hall," *Weekly Anglo-African*, 20 April 1861.

59. Delany, who is often referred to as the father of black nationalism, came to appreciate Haiti during the Civil War more than previously. While in the 1850s thousands of African Americans preferred Haiti over alternative sites as a location for colonization, Delany steadfastly preferred West Africa. Nonetheless, he declared in 1854 that Haiti was "peopled by as brave and noble descendants of Africa as they who . . . constructed the everlasting pyramids and catacombs of Egypt—a people who freed themselves by the might of their own will, the force of their own right arms, and their unflinching determination to be free." Richard Newman, Patrick Rael, and Phillip Lapsansky, *Pamphlets of Protest: An Anthology of Early African-American Protest Literature, 1790–1860* (New York: Routledge, 2001), 233.

60. Robert S. Levine, *Martin Delany, Frederick Douglass, and the Politics of Representative Identity* (Chapel Hill: University of North Carolina Press, 1997), 222.

61. Rollin, *Life and Public Services of Martin Delany*, 169; Delany's positive response from Lincoln may be the result of selective memory. Nell Irvin Painter posits that leading African Americans, including Sojourner Truth and Frederick Douglass, reported being respectfully received by the president, for "When Lincoln patronized them, he violated Truth and Douglass's self-presentation as people commanding respect," in *Sojourner Truth: A Life, a Symbol* (New York: Norton, 1996), 207.

62. Up to this point, Delany had served in the 104th United States Colored Troops as a recruiter and medical officer. Thomas Holt, *Black over White: Negro Political Leadership in South Carolina During Reconstruction* (Urbana: University of Illinois Press, 1979), 74.

63. "Special Notices. Maj. Martin Delany, U.S.A.," *Weekly Anglo-African*, 19 August 1865.

64. Alice Fahs, *The Imagined Civil War: Popular Literature of the North and South, 1861–1865* (Chapel Hill: University of North Carolina Press, 2000); David Kaser, *Books and Libraries in Camp and Battle: The Civil War Experience* (Westport, Conn.: Greenwood Press, 1984).

65. Stephanie M. H. Camp, *Closer to Freedom: Enslaved Women & Everyday Resistance in the Plantation South* (Chapel Hill: University of North Carolina Press, 2004), 114–16.

66. "Letter from Reverend Daniel Forster," *Liberator*, 12 June 1863.

67. "The Freedmen. Education Among the Colored Soldiers," *Boston Commonwealth*, 5 November 1864.

68. "The South and the Negro," *National Anti-Slavery Standard*, 9 September 1865.

69. *Weekly Anglo-African*, 26 March 1864.

70. "The Army and the Negroes," *National Anti-Slavery Standard*, 8 November 1862.

71. W. Jeffrey Bolster, *Black Jacks: African American Seamen in the Age of Sail* (Cambridge, Mass.: Harvard University Press, 1997); Julius S. Scott, "The Common Wind: Currents of Afro-American Communication in the Era of the Haitian Revolution" (Ph.D. dissertation, Duke University, 1986); James Oliver Horton and Lois E. Horton, *In Hope of Liberty: Culture, Community, and Protest among Northern Free Blacks, 1700–1860* (New York: Oxford University Press, 1997).

72. Phillip Lapsansky, "Afro-Americana," *Annual Report of the Library Company of Philadelphia* (1989): 23–31.

73. "Will the Contrabands Fight," *Washington National Republican*, in *Weekly Anglo-African*, 15 February 1862.

74. "Colored People of the District of Colombia," *Weekly Anglo-African*, 19 April 1862.

75. "The Contrabands at Port Royal," *Liberator*, 20 December 1861.

76. "An Aged Negro," *National Anti-Slavery Standard*, 27 June 1863.

77. *Weekly Anglo-African*, 30 March 1861.

78. Irving H. Bartlett, *Wendell and Ann Phillips: The Community of Reform* (New York: Norton, 1979), 131–34 (emphasis original).

79. Civil War newspapers are filled with accounts of survivors of the American Revolution. For example, see "Nimium Ne Crede Colori," *Liberator*, 9 October 1863. For an example of a contraband claiming to remember George Washington, see "About Contrabands," *Weekly Anglo-African*, 24 January 1863. For a discussion of the tradition, see: Reiss, *Showman and the Slave*; Alfred Young, *The Shoemaker and the Tea Party: Memory and the American Revolution* (Boston: Beacon Press, 1999).

80. The best synthesis of Haitian refugees to America remains Alfred Hunt, *Haiti's Influence on Antebellum America: Slumbering Volcano in the Caribbean* (Baton Rouge: Louisiana State University Press, 1988), chap. 2. More recent accounts of Haitian refugees are Davis Patrick Geggus, *The Impact of the Haitian Revolution in the Atlantic World* (Columbia: University of South Carolina Press, 2001); Ashli White, "'A Flood of Impure Lava': Saint Domingue Refugees in the United States, 1791–1820" (Ph.D. dissertation, Columbia University, 2003); Nathalie Dessens, *From Saint-Domingue to New Orleans: Migration and Influences* (Gainesville: University of Florida Press, 2007).

81. "The Government and the Negroes," *New York Herald*, 6 January 1863.

82. Ira Berlin with Joseph P. Reidy and Leslie S. Rowland, eds., *The Black Military Experience* (New York: Cambridge University Press, 1982), 652, 683.

83. Ira Berlin in his seminal work on free black southerners states incorrectly that unlike the North, "No Southern city had . . . a 'Hayti.'" Ira Berlin, *Slaves Without Masters: The Free Negro in the Antebellum South* (New York: New Press, 1974), 257.

84. African Americans spelled Louverture's first and last name variously, as a cursory

glance at antebellum black newspapers reveals. "William Lambert," *Detroit Free Press*, 29 April 1890; Ulysses W. Boykin, *A Hand Book on the Detroit Negro* (Detroit: Minority Study Associates, 1943), 117.

85. Langston named his son, Arthur Dessalines Langston. *From the Virginia Plantation to the National Capital: or, The First and Only Negro Representative in Congress from the Old Dominion* (Hartford, Conn.: American Publishing, 1894; reprint New York: Kraus, 1969), 157.

86. James Harvey Anderson, *Biographical Souvenir Volume of the Twenty-Third Quadrennial Session of the General Conference of the African Methodist Episcopal Zion Church* (Philadelphia: Big Wesley AME Zion Church, 1908), 138–39.

87. Frank Lincoln Mather, *Who's Who of the Colored Race*, vol. 1 (Chicago: F.L. Mather, 1915), 150–51.

88. From Frederick Douglass (Bailey) and Sojourner Truth (Isabella) to Malcolm X (Little) and Martin (Michael) Luther King, Jr., the naming practices of African Americans signify an important transition. Blassingame, *Slave Community*, 181–83; Sterling Stuckey, *Slave Culture: Nationalist Theory and the Foundations of Black America*, 194–98.

89. A. J. H. Duganne, *Camps and Prisons: Twenty Months in the Department of the Gulf* (New York: Robens, 1865), 92–93.

90. Duganne, *Camps and Prisons*, 93–95.

91. Stephen G. Bulfinch, *Honor; or, The Slave-Dealer's Daughter* (Boston: William Spence, 1864), 122–24, 131–34, 204–29.

92. Edmund Kirke [James R. Gilmore], *Among the Pines: or South in Secession Time* (New York: J.R. Gilmore, 1862), 19–21. In summer 1863, Americans bought more than 30,000 copies of *Among the Pines*, which first appeared as a serial in *Continental Monthly*. Writing under the pen name Edmund Kirke, James Gilmore assured readers of the veracity of his work, promising only a "record of facts." He continued, "the characters I have introduced are real. They are not drawn with the pencil of fancy, nor, I trust, colored with the tints of prejudice. The scenes I have described are true," 33. Northern critics hailed *Among the Pines* as "one of the most readable books of Southern life we have ever seen," and "a striking and truthful portraiture of slave society." Kirke [Gilmore], *My Southern Friends* (New York: Carleton, 1863), advertisement.

93. "Among the Pines: or South in Secession Time," *North American Review* 95, 197 (October 1862): 534–45.

94. Fahs, *Imagined Civil War*, 160.

95. "Among the Pines," 534.

96. James R. Gilmore, *Personal Recollections of Abraham Lincoln and the Civil War* (Boston: Page and Co., 1898); James M. McPherson, *Battle Cry of Freedom: The Civil War Era* (New York: Oxford University Press, 1988), 767-68; Carl Sandburg, *Abraham Lincoln: The Prairie Years and the War Years*, 1-volume ed. (New York: Harcourt, Brace, 1954), 419, 423–24, 431, 535.

97. "An Intelligent Contraband," *Boston Commonwealth*, 8 November 1862; "Views of an Intelligent Negro," *Douglass' Monthly*, January 1863.

CHAPTER 7. "A REPETITION OF SAN DOMINGO?": SOUTHERN WHITE
IDENTITY

1. "Campaign on the Combahee," *Boston Commonwealth*, 10 July 1863; Catherine Clinton, *Harriet Tubman: The Road to Freedom* (New York: Little, Brown, 2004), 164–71, 173–74.

2. "The Raid on the Combahee," *Charleston Mercury*, 19 June 1863.

3. Benedict Anderson, *Imagined Communities: Reflections on the Origin and Spread of Nationalism*, rev. ed. (London: Verso, 1991).

4. Emory M. Thomas, *The Confederate Nation: 1861–65* (New York: Harper and Row, 1979); Richard E. Beringer, Herman Hattaway, Archer Jones, and William N. Still, Jr., *Why the South Lost the Civil War* (Athens: University of Georgia Press, 1986); David M. Potter, *The Impending Crisis: 1848–1861* (New York: Harper and Row, 1976), 471–75.

5. Gary Gallagher, *The Confederate War: How Popular Will, Nationalism, and Military Strategy Could Not Stave Off Defeat* (Cambridge, Mass.: Harvard University Press, 1997), 7.

6. Anne Sarah Rubin, *A Shattered Nation: The Rise and Fall of the Confederacy, 1861–1868* (Chapel Hill: University of North Carolina Press, 2005),

7. Drew Gilpin Faust, *The Creation of Confederate Nationalism: Ideology and Identity in the Civil War South* (Baton Rouge: Louisiana State University Press, 1988), 61.

8. The classic "cornerstone" reference is from Alexander Stephens, vice president of the Confederacy: "Our new government is founded upon exactly the opposite idea; its foundations are laid, its corner-stone rests upon the great truth that the negro is not equal to the white man. That slavery—subordination to the superior race—is his natural and moral condition." William Lloyd Garrison, Garrett Davis, and Alexander Stephens, *Three Unlike Speeches, by William Lloyd Garrison, of Massachusetts, Garrett Davis, of Kentucky, Alexander H. Stephens, of Georgia. The Abolitionists, and Their Relations to the War. The War Not for Emancipation. African Slavery, the Corner-stone of the Southern Confederacy* (New York: E.D. Barker, 1862), 70.

9. Though the women of the Confederacy frequently defied gendered boundaries, violence was the exclusive domain of white men. Rubin, *A Shattered Nation*, 54–55; Catherine Clinton and Nina Silber, eds., *Divided Houses: Gender and the Civil War* (New York: Oxford University Press, 1992).

10. "Crittenden Rangers," *Memphis Appeal*, 17 April 1861.

11. "FEARS OF INSURRECTION," *National Anti-Slavery Standard*, 8 July 1861.

12. "All Yankees in Georgia After the First Day of January to be Hung," *Richmond Whig*, in *Boston Herald*, 5 December 1862.

13. Edwin Anderson Alderman and Armistead Churchill Gordon, *J. L. M. Curry: A Biography* (New York: Macmillan, 1911), 173–74.

14. J. L. M. Curry, *Address of Congress to the People of the Confederate States. Joint Resolution in Relation to the War: Conf. States of America*, 22 January 1864, O.R., ser. 4, vol. 3: 126–37.

15. Curry, *Address of Congress to the People of the Confederate States*, 126–37.

16. Alderman and Gordon, *J. L. M. Curry: A Biography*, 173–74.

17. Faust, *The Creation of Confederate Nationalism*, 60.

18. Thomas Verner Moore, *God Our Refuge and Strength in This War. A Discourse Before the Congregations of the First and Second Presbyterian Churches, on the Day of Humiliation, Fasting and Prayer, Appointed by President Davis, Friday, Nov. 15, 1861* (Richmond: W. Hargrave White, 1861), 3, 12, 19.

19. Moore, *God Our Refuge and Strength in This War*, 13, 21–24.

20. James M. McPherson, *Battle Cry of Freedom: The Civil War Era* (New York: Oxford University Press, 1988), 563.

21. "The War of Cavalry and Negroes," *Chattanooga Rebel*, 3 June 1863, in *National Anti-Slavery Standard*, 4 July 1863.

22. "The Horrors of St. Domingo Repeated," *New York News*, in *Macon Daily Telegraph*, 30 August 1864.

23. "The First South Carolina Regiment," *Liberator*, 10 April 1863.

24. Joseph P. Reidy, "Armed Slaves and the Struggle for Republican Liberty in the U.S. Civil War," in *Arming Slaves: From Classical Times to the Modern Age*, ed. Christopher Leslie Brown and Philip D. Morgan (New Haven, Conn.: Yale University Press, 2006), 276.

25. *O.R.*, ser. 1, vol. 52, Part 2: 589–91.

26. Bruce C. Levine, *Confederate Emancipation: Southern Plans to Free and Arm Slaves During the Civil War* (New York: Oxford University Press, 2005), 95; Robert Durden, *The Gray and the Black: The Confederate Debate on Emancipation* (Baton Rouge: Louisiana State University Press, 1972), 95.

27. Mark L. Bradley, "'The Monstrous Proposition': North Carolina and the Confederate Debate on Arming the Slaves," *North Carolina Historical Review* 80, 2 (April 2003): 171.

28. Durden, *The Gray and the Black*, 141.

29. The speech was widely reprinted in northern and southern newspapers and in pamphlet form.

30. "The Question of Arming Negroes, Speech by Hon. H. C. Chambers, of Mississippi," *Richmond Whig*, in *New York Times*, 19 November 1864.

31. *A Particular Account of the Insurrection of the Negroes of St. Domingo, Begun in August, 1791: Translated From the French*, 4th ed. (London: s.n., 1792), 3.

32. Bryan Edwards, *An Historical Survey of the French Colony in the Island of St. Domingo* (Philadelphia: James Humphreys, 1806), 75.

33. Archibald Alison, *History of Europe: From the Commencement of the French Revolution in 1789, to the Restoration of the Bourbons in 1815*, vol. 2 (New York: Harper, 1850–52), 241–42.

34. Laurent Dubois points out that two other first-hand accounts of the sacking of the Gallifet plantations make no mention of such an occurrence. Dubois writes of infant impalement, "This detail was not mentioned in the descriptions of the attack on Gallifet

by Pierre Mossut or Antoine Dalma, neither of whom would have been likely to suppress so memorable an image had they been aware of it." Dubois. *Avengers of the New World: The Story of the Haitian Revolution* (Cambridge, Mass.: Belknap Press of Harvard University Press, 2004), 111.

35. T. W. MacMahon, *Cause and Contrast*, 90; see also Faust, *The Creation of Confederate Nationalism*, 62; "The Great Essay, Cause and Contrast," *Richmond Examiner*, 26 January 1863.

36. "General Butler's Address to the People of New Orleans," *Richmond Examiner*, 19 January 1863.

37. Eric H. Walther, *William Lowndes Yancey and the Coming of the Civil War* (Chapel Hill: University of North Carolina Press, 2006), 75.

38. "Speech of Mr. Yancey, of Alabama," *Appendix to the Cong. Globe*, 28th Cong. 2nd Sess. (1845), 90. The speech created a stir in the national media, and for many Americans provided an introduction to the fiery Alabama statesman. Walther, *William Lowndes Yancey and the Coming of the Civil War*, 74–77; Walther, *The Fire-Eaters* (Baton Rouge: Louisiana State University Press, 1992), chap. 2; William Garrott Brown, *The Lower South in American History* (New York: Haskell House, 1968), 115.

39. "The Rebellion: How Can Slavery be Turned Against the Rebellion," *New York Times*, 5 December 1861.

40 Kate Stone, *Brokenburn: The Journal of Kate Stone 1861–1868*, ed. John Q. Anderson (Baton Rouge: Louisiana State University Press, 1995), 313–14.

41. Eric Foner, *Reconstruction: America's Unfinished Revolution, 1863–1877* (New York: Harper and Row, 1988), xxv.

42. George Frederick Holmes, "Aspects of the Hour," *De Bow's Review* III, 4, 5 (April and May 1867): 337, 344, 352; George Fitzhugh, "Exodus from the South," *De Bow's Review* III, 4, 5 (April and May 1867): 352.

CHAPTER 8. "DO WE WANT ANOTHER SAN DOMINGO TO BE REPEATED IN THE SOUTH?" NORTHERN WHITE IDENTITY

1. *The Union and the Constitution. Public Meeting in Faneuil Hall, Boston, Dec. 8, 1859. Speeches of Hon. Levi Lincoln, Hon. Edward Everett, Hon. Caleb Cushing, and letter of Ex-President Pierce* (Boston: s.n., 1859), 2–3.

2. "The Conservative Movement," *New York Herald*, 9 December 1859.

3. Ronald F. Reid, *Edward Everett: Unionist Orator* (New York: Greenwood Press, 1990), 88.

4. For a southern paper applauding Everett's speech and in particular his invocation of the Haitian Revolution, see "Union Speeches," *Richmond Daily Dispatch*, 13 December 1859.

5. Alexander Saxton, *The Rise and Fall of the White Republic: Class Politics and Mass Culture in Nineteenth-Century America* (London: Verso, 2003); Noel Ignatiev, *How the*

Irish Became White (New York: Routledge, 1996); Matthew Frye Jacobson, *Whiteness of a Different Color: European Immigrants and the Alchemy of Race* (Cambridge, Mass.: Harvard University Press, 1998); Reginald Horsman, *Race and Manifest Destiny: The Origins of American Racial Anglo-Saxons* (Cambridge, Mass.: Harvard University Press, 1981).

6. Edward J. Blum, *Reforging the White Republic: Race, Religion, and American Nationalism, 1865–1898* (Baton Rouge: Louisiana State University Press, 2005), 4, 6.

7. Eric Foner, *Reconstruction: America's Unfinished Revolution, 1863–1877* (New York: Harper & Row, 1988); Blum, *Reforging the White Republic.*

8. For a discussion of the concept of a white Atlantic see David Armitage and Michael J. Braddick, eds., *The British Atlantic World, 1500–1800* (New York: Palgrave Macmillan, 2002), 12–17; Seymour Drescher, "White Atlantic? The Choice for African Slave Labor in the Plantation Americas," in *Slavery in the Development of the Americas*, ed. David Eltis, Frank D. Lewis, and Kenneth L. Sokoloff (New York: Cambridge University Press. 2004), 31–69 .

9. Jennifer L. Weber, *Copperheads: The Rise and Fall of Lincoln's Opponents in the North* (New York: Oxford University Press, 2006), 6.

10. Louis Schade, *A Book for the "Impending Crisis"! Appeal to the Common Sense and Patriotism of the People of the United States. "Helperism" Annihilated! The "Irrepressible Conflict" and its Consequences!* (Washington, D.C.: Little, Morris, 1860), 6–7, 29–30, 33, 58, 60.

11. "The New Abolition Developments in Congress—Their Danger to the North," *New York Herald*, 29 March 1860.

12. "The National Crisis. Further Illustrations of Popular Sentiment," *New York Times*, 26 January 1860.

13. "The Syracuse Convention," *New York Times*, 8 February 1860.

14. "History of Negro Insurrections," *New York Herald*, 6 January 1860.

15. "More Successes—Expected Fall of Fort Donelson—Defeat of the Rebels in Missouri," *New York Herald*, 17 February 1862.

16. "The Blacks at Port Royal—The Dangers of Bloodthirsty Fanaticism," *New York Herald*, 2 April 1862.

17. Larry E. Tise, *Proslavery: A History of the Defense of Slavery in America, 1701–1840* (Athens: University of Georgia Press, 1990), 254–60.

18. *Emancipation and its Results—Is Ohio to be Africanized? Speech of Hon. S.S. Cox, of Ohio, Delivered in the House of Representatives, June 6, 1862* (Washington, D.C.: 1862), 5, 8.

19. Formed in response to the Emancipation Proclamation and led by Samuel Morse, the radical and well-funded group published a series of essays, which "stressed defenses of slavery and condemnation of abolitionism." Tise, *Proslavery*, 256–57; *Papers from the Society for the Diffusion of Political Knowledge. Emancipation and Its Results*, no. 6 (New York: s.n., 1863), 3, 6–7.

20. Charles Frederick Blake, "Prerogative Rights and Public Law," *Monthly Law*

Reporter 25, 3 (January 1863): 145–50; For information on Blake, see "Death in a Very Sad Way," *New York Times,* 22 February 1881.

21. *Copperhead Minstrel: A Choice Collection of Democratic Poems and Songs, for the Use of Political Clubs and the Social Circle* (New York: Feeks & Bancker, 1863), 31–32.

22. "Massacre, the Natural Result of the 'Proclamation'," *Boston Pilot,* in *Liberator,* 3 April 1863.

23. *Address of the Democratic State Central Committee. Together with the Proceedings of the Democratic State Convention, Held at Harrisburg, July 4, 1862, and the Proceedings of the Democratic State Central Committee, Held at Philadelphia. July 29, 1862* (Philadelphia: F.W. Hughes, 1862), 13.

24. *The True Conditions of American Loyalty: a Speech Delivered by George Ticknor Curtis, Before the Democratic Union Association, March 28th, 1863* (New York: The Society, 1863), 13.

25. *The Alliance With the Negro: Speech of Hon Charles J. Biddle, of PA, Delivered in the House of Representatives of the United States, March 6, 1862* (Washington, D.C.: Towers, 1862), 2, 4, 8.

26. "Confiscation of Rebel Property. Speech of Hon. John Law, of Indiana, In the House of Representatives, May 26, 1862," *Congressional Globe,* House of Representatives, 37th Cong., 2nd Sess. (1862): 271.

27. Webber, *Copperheads,* 160.

28. James M. McPherson, *Battle Cry of Freedom: The Civil War Era* (New York: Oxford University Press, 1988), 788–90; Weber, *Copperheads,* 159–62.

29. [David Goodman, Croly, E .C. Howell, and George Wakeman], *Miscegenation: The Theory of the Blending of the Races, Applied to the American White Man and Negro* (New York: Dexter, Hamilton, 1864), 56–57; Sidney Kaplan, "The Miscegenation Issue in the Election of 1864," *Journal of Negro History* 34, 3 (July 1949): 274–343.

30. John H. Van Evrie, *Abolition and Secession; or, Cause and Effect, Together with the Remedy for Our Sectional Troubles. By a Unionist.* Anti-Abolition Tracts 1 (New York: Van Evrie, Horton, 1862), 12, 23–24.

31. *The Democratic Almanac* (New York: Van Evrie, Horton, 1868), 19, 35.

32. John H. Van Evrie, *Abolition Is National Death; or, the Attempt to Equalize Races the Destruction of Society.* Anti-Abolition Tracts 1 (New York: Van Evrie, Horton, 1866), 25–29.

33. Alice Fahs, *The Imagined Civil War: Popular Literature of the North and South, 1861–1865* (Chapel Hill: University of North Carolina Press, 2001), 4.

CONCLUSION

1. Hubert Howe Bancroft, *The Book of the Fair: An Historical and Descriptive Presentation of the World's Science, Art, and Industry, as Viewed Through the Columbia Exposition at Chicago in 1893* (Chicago: Bancroft, 1893), 957, 964.

2. Frederick Douglass, *Lecture on Haiti* (Washington, D.C.: Violet Agents Supply Co., 1893), 23, 34. The fair included a Haitian pavilion, which displayed relics of the revolution, including a portrait of Louverture along with one of his rapiers. *Book of the Fair*, 918.

3. Robert C. O. Benjamin, *Life of Toussaint L'Ouverture, Warrior and Statesman, with an Historical Survey of the Island of San Domingo from the Discovery of the Island by Christopher Columbus, in 1492, to the Death of Toussaint, in 1803* (Los Angeles: Evening Express Print, 1888); Charles W. Mossell, *Toussaint L'Ouverture, the Hero of Saint Domingo, Soldier, Statesman, Martyr: or, Hayti's Struggle, Triumph, Independence, and Achievements* (Lockport, N.Y.: Ward & Cobb, 1896); Theophilus Gould Steward, *The Haitian Revolution, 1791 to 1804: Or, Side Lights on the French Revolution*, 2nd ed. (New York: Crowell, 1914); David Augustus Straker, *Reflections on the Life and Times of Toussaint L'Ouverture, the Negro Haytien, Commander-in-Chief of the Army, Ruler Under the Dominion of France, and Author of the Independence of Hayti* (Columbia, S.C.: Charles A. Calvo, Jr., 1886); William Wells Brown, *The Rising Son; or, the Antecedents and Advancement of the Colored Race* (Boston: A.G. Brown), 1874.

4. W. E. B. Du Bois, *The Suppression of the African Slave Trade to the United States of America 1638-1870* (New York: Longmans, Green, 1896; reprint Baton Rouge: Louisiana State University Press, 1969), 70.

5. Benjamin Griffith Brawley, *The Negro Genius; a New Appraisal of the Achievement of the American Negro in Literature and the Fine Arts* (New York: Dodd Mead, 1937); John Edward Bruce, *Short Biographical Sketches of Eminent Negro Men and Women in Europe and the United States with Brief Extracts from Their Writings and Public Utterances* (Yonkers, N.Y.: Gazette Press, 1910); Charles C. Dawson, *ABC's of Great Negroes* (Chicago: Dawson, 1933); William Henry Ferris, *The African Abroad, or, His Evolution in Western Civilization Tracing His Development Under Caucasian Milieu* (New Haven, Conn.: Tuttle, Morehouse & Taylor, 1913); William Henry Quick, *Negro Stars in All Ages of the World* (Henderson, N.C.: D.E. Aycock, 1890); William J. Simmons, *Men of Mark: Eminent, Progressive and Rising* (Cleveland: G.M. Rewell, 1887).

6. Straker, *Life and Times of Toussaint L'Ouverture*, Preface.

7. James Theodore Holly, "Thoughts on Hayti," *Anglo-African Magazine* 1, 6 (June 1859): 186.

8. It is a tradition that continues. Today, Phillips's "Toussaint L'Ouverture" is readily available in literary anthologies as well in any number of digital collections available on-line. Wendell Phillips, *Speeches, Lectures, and Letters* (Boston: Lee and Shepard, 1884), 468-94; *Toussaint L'Ouverture: An Address by Wendell Phillips, Delivered at New York, March 11, 1863. Revised by Carrie Chapman Catt.* (Cleveland: G.M. Rewell, 1891).

9. Rossiter Johnson, Charles F. Horne, and John Rudd, eds., *The Great Events by Famous Historians: A Comprehensive and Readable Account of the World's History*, vol. 17 (New York: National Alumni, 1905), 236-51.

10. Henry Adams, *The Education of Henry Adams* (New York: Modern Library, 1931), 25.

11. Henry Adams, *History of the United States of American During the First Administration of Thomas Jefferson*, vol. 1 (New York: Charles Scribner's Sons, 1889), 378.

12. David Blight, *Race and Reunion: The Civil War in American Memory* (Cambridge, Mass.: Belknap Press of Harvard University Press, 2001), 389.

INDEX

ACKNOWLEDGMENTS

WHAT A PLEASURE it is finally, to thank those who assisted in the completion of this endeavor. My greatest debt is to Karin Wulf, Alan Kraut, and Andrew Lewis for their continued guidance as scholars and mentors. This project began at American University, and without their assistance it would not exist. Nor would it appear in its current form without the support of those who offered comments and criticism on numerous papers, articles, and chapters, especially Ira Berlin, Douglas Egerton, Alison Games, Amy Greenberg, Joshua Greenberg, Stewart King, Jane Landers, Andrew McMichael, and Sarah Purcell. At the University of West Florida, a summer travel grant and a commitment to scholarship by both the Dean of the College of Arts and Sciences Jane Halonen and Chair of the History Department Jay Clune have allowed me to bring this project to completion sooner than expected.

Numerous organizations, libraries, and archives across the United States provided critical assistance. The generous support I received from the Andrew W. Mellon Foundation, American Antiquarian Society, Cosmos Club of Washington, D.C., Gilder Lehrman Institute of American History, Library Company of Philadelphia, Historical Society of Pennsylvania, Massachusetts Historical Society, Schomburg Center for Research in Black Culture, and the Virginia Historical Society enabled me to imagine, research, and write this book. I am truly thankful for the assistance provided by each of these wonderful institutions.

At the University of Pennsylvania Press, Bob Lockhart demonstrated great enthusiasm for my project, Alison Anderson provided essential editorial support, and Edward Blum and Douglas Egerton gave the entire manuscript a close reading and offered invaluable suggestions. I am indebted to each of them. I am also grateful to the editors of academic journals who allowed me to reprint portions of articles that appeared in their publications: "A Second Haitian Revolution: John Brown, Toussaint Louverture, and the Making of the American Civil War," *Civil War History* 54, 2 (June 2008): 117–45; and "American Toussaints: Symbol, Subversion, and the Black Atlantic Tradition in the American Civil War," *Slavery and Abolition: A Journal of Slave and Post-Slave Studies* 28, 1 (April 2007): 87–113.

Finally, I thank Gladys, Maddie, Joey, and Joshie for providing me with a never-ending supply of love, laughter, and affection. I dedicate this book to them.